The Long Ref

PROBLEMS IN EUROPEAN CIVILIZATION SERIES

General Editor
Merry E. Wiesner

The Long Reformation

Edited with an introduction by

Jeffrey R. Watt
University of Mississippi

Houghton Mifflin Company   Boston   New York

Publisher: Charles Hartford
Senior Sponsoring Editor: Nancy Blaine
Development Editor: Julie Swasey
Editorial Associate: Annette Fantasia
Project Editor: Reba Libby
Editorial Assistant: Deborah Berkman
Senior Manufacturing Coordinator: Marie Barnes
Senior Art and Design Coordinator: Jill Haber Atkins
Senior Composition Buyer: Sarah Ambrose
Senior Marketing Manager: Sandra McGuire
Marketing Assistant: Molly Parke

Cover image: Emmanuel De Witte, *Interior of the Oude Kerk, Delft*, 1651.
Credit: Reproduced by the kind permission of the trustees of The Wallace
Collection, London.

Printed in the U.S.A.

Library of Congress Control Number: 2005924056

ISBN: 0-618-43577-8

123456789-CS-09 08 07 06 05

Contents

v

Preface

Early modern Europe witnessed a series of religious movements whose social, intellectual, and cultural effects were so profound that they collectively have given a name to an entire epoch: the Reformation. The very term, *Reformation,* tends to evoke images of intense, even violent religious conflicts: Martin Luther's defiant refusal to recant his views before the Emperor Charles V, the burning in Geneva of Michael Servetus for his unorthodox ideas on the Trinity, Protestants' iconoclastic attacks on Catholic churches, and the massacre of Huguenots in Paris on Saint Bartholomew's Day, 1572. In light of these bitter religious conflicts, scholars long depicted the Protestant and Catholic Reformations as utterly opposed to each other, stressing the differences in theology and church structure between Protestants and Catholics and among competing Protestant camps. While those differences were very real, they must not blind us to the many parallels in religious reform among Catholics, Lutherans, Calvinists, and Anglicans.

This volume bears witness to some important changes in emphasis in recent scholarship on the Reformation. While Catholic and Protestant groups vied with each other for the souls of Europeans, numerous scholars have seen similarities in the methods they employed, even though their respective religious doctrines differed in very important ways. In the past quarter century or so, many historians have concentrated less on theology per se than on various practical effects of the reform movements: changes in worship services, the imposition of moral discipline, the control of popular religious practices, and transformations in the status of women. This volume takes its title from another theme common to much recent scholarship—many of the Reformation's social and cultural changes were fully realized only after a very lengthy period, extending in some cases through the late seventeenth century and beyond.

Part I of this volume concentrates on the theory of "confessionalization," a paradigm that has generated considerable debate since the

1970s and stresses the similarities between the Protestant and Catholic Reformations. As the selected readings show, this theory was originally conceived by scholars of the German Reformation but has since stimulated thoughtful historical research in both Protestant and Catholic settings throughout Europe. It takes its name from the different confessions of faith that were written in the sixteenth century for the Lutheran, Catholic, and Calvinist Reformations. For all these religious groups, proponents of confessionalization stress the important coercive role of the state in ensuring that the beliefs and practices of the population conformed to the official confession. Critics argue that the confessionalization paradigm exaggerates the degree of religious uniformity that was achieved and overemphasizes the role of the state, asserting that many ordinary lay people sought a disciplined, Godly society.

Parts II and III deal respectively with popular religion and the reformation of rituals, both of which are closely related to the theory of confessionalization. Some historians have observed a real disparity in beliefs and practices between the "official" religion promoted by religious and political leaders and the piety of common folk. It has been argued, for example, that most Europeans were not truly Christian prior to the Protestant and Catholic Reformations, as religion for most peasants was basically a mixture of paganism and magic, adorned with just a thin veneer of Christianity. The aggressive actions of political and religious leaders in the sixteenth and seventeenth centuries eventually succeeded in eradicating the popular beliefs and practices deemed unacceptable. Various other historians either deny the dichotomy between elite and popular religion or stress continuity over change in religious life in late medieval and early modern Europe. Rituals were a vitally important part of the religious experience in Reformation Europe, and Protestant and, to a lesser extent, Catholic leaders attacked a number of religious ceremonies and practices as semi-pagan or superstitious. The essays in the third section show a wide range of changes in liturgy and other forms of rituals, varying considerably in different geographical, social, and confessional contexts.

The selections in Part IV, "The Reformation and Gender," demonstrate the growing importance of gender analysis in historical research. They reveal very different interpretations concerning the Reformations' impact on female religious expression and on women's position in the home and community. The fifth part, which deals with the "success" of the various Reformations, aptly ties together the previous sections of this volume. Some historians have challenged the long-held assumption that the Reformations were successful in effecting revolutionary change in the lives of Europeans, insisting that prevailing popular piety never came close to meeting the goals of the reformers. While conceding that Protestant and Catholic reformers were not satisfied with the results, other scholars argue nonetheless that important lasting changes eventually took hold in the religious behavior and beliefs of millions of Europeans. The common theme that unites all the subjects treated in this volume is the conjunction between religion and society. Research on social discipline, popular religious practices, and the position of women all reflect the interest in the impact of religious developments on European society.

I have incurred a number of debts over the past few years while working on this volume. I am above all grateful to Merry E. Wiesner, the series editor and an expert on the Reformation, who kindly invited me to write a proposal for this series. I developed the concept of this volume in close collaboration with her, and I deeply appreciate her many astute suggestions. The scholarship on the Reformation in its various forms is vast, and narrowing down the themes of debate to a manageable length was quite a challenge. Several other Reformation historians generously shared their ideas with me about what issues should and should not be included in this collection. For their valuable advice, many thanks to Amy Nelson Burnett, Joel F. Harrington, Mack P. Holt, Robert M. Kingdon, Raymond A. Mentzer, H. C. Erik Midelfort, Thomas Max Safley, and Anne Jacobson Schutte. I also owe a special debt to the volume's reviewers: Gayle K. Brunelle, California State University, Fullerton; David R. Carr, University of South Florida; William J. Connell, Seton Hall University; Anna Marie Roos, University of Minnesota, Duluth; and Silvia C. Shannon, Saint Anselm College. Their discerning criticisms and suggestions improved this work considerably, giving it much better focus. Finally, I warmly thank Julie Swasey, Annette Fantasia, and Nancy Blaine of Houghton Mifflin, whose encouragement, support, and guidance have made working on this volume a real pleasure.

Jeffrey R. Watt
University of Mississippi

Editor's Preface to Instructors

There are many ways to date ourselves as teachers and scholars of history: the questions that we regard as essential to ask about any historical development, the theorists whose words we quote and whose names appear in our footnotes, the price of the books that we purchased for courses and that are on our shelves. Looking over my own shelves, it struck me that another way we could be dated was by the color of the oldest books we owned in this series, which used to be published by D. C. Heath. I first used a "Heath series" book—green and white, as I recall—when I was a freshman in college and taking a modern European history course. That book, by Dwight E. Lee on the Munich crisis, has long since disappeared, but several Heath books that I acquired later as an undergraduate are still on my shelves. Those that I used in graduate school, including ones on the Renaissance and Reformation, are also there, as are several I assigned my students when I first started teaching or have used in the years since. As with any system of historical periodization, of course, this method of dating a historian is flawed and open to misinterpretation. When a colleague retired, he gave me some of his even older Heath series books, in red and black, which had actually appeared when I was still in elementary and junior high school, so that a glance at my shelves might make me seem ready for retirement.

The longevity of this series, despite its changing cover design and its transition from D. C. Heath to Houghton Mifflin, could serve as an indication of several things. One might be that historians are conservative, unwilling to change the way they approach the past or teach about it. The rest of the books on my shelves suggest that this conservatism is not the case, however, for many of the books discuss topics that were unheard of as subjects of historical investigation when I took that course as a freshman thirty years ago: memory, masculinity, visual culture, sexuality.

Another way to account for the longevity of this series is that several generations of teachers have found it a useful way for their students to approach historical subjects. As teachers, one of the first issues we confront in any course is what materials we will assign our students to read. (This decision is often, in fact, paramount, for we have to order books months before the class begins.) We may include a textbook to provide an overview of the subject matter covered in the course and often have several from which to choose. We may use a reader of original sources, or several sources in their entirety, because we feel that it is important for our students to hear the voices of people of the past directly. We may add a novel from the period, for fictional works often give one details and insights that do not emerge from other types of sources. We may direct our students to visual materials, either in books or on the Web, for artifacts, objects, and art can give one access to aspects of life never mentioned in written sources.

Along with these types of assignments, we may also choose to assign books such as those in this series, which present the ideas and opinions of scholars on a particular topic. Textbooks are, of course, written by scholars with definite opinions, but they are designed to present material in a relatively bland manner. They may suggest areas about which there is historical debate (often couched in phrases such as "scholars disagree about . . .") but do not participate in those debates themselves. By contrast, the books in this series highlight points of dispute, and cover topics and developments about which historians often disagree vehemently. Students who are used to the textbook approach to history may be surprised at the range of opinions on certain matters, but we hope that the selections in each of these volumes will allow readers to understand why there is such a diversity. Each volume covers several issues of interpretive debate and highlights newer research directions.

Variety of interpretation in history is sometimes portrayed as a recent development, but the age of this series in its many cover styles indicates that this account is not accurate. Historians have long recognized that historical sources are produced by particular individuals with particular interests and biases that consciously and unconsciously shape their content. They have also long—one is tempted to say "always"—recognized that different people approach the past differently, making choices about which topics to study, which sources to use, which developments and individuals to highlight. This diversity in both sources and methodologies is part of what makes history exciting for those of us who study it, for new materials and new approaches allow us to see things that have never been seen before, in the same way that astronomers find new stars with better tools and new ways of looking.

The variety and innovation that is an essential part of good historical scholarship allow this series both to continue and to change. Some of the volumes now being prepared have the same titles as those I read as an undergraduate, but the scholarship on these topics has changed so much in the last several decades that they had to be completely redone, not simply revised. Some of the volumes now in print examine topics that were rarely covered in undergraduate courses when the series began publication, and a few former volumes are no longer in print because the topics they investigated now show up more rarely. We endeavor to keep the series up-to-date and welcome suggestions about volumes that would prove helpful for teaching undergraduate and graduate courses. You can contact us at http://college.hmco.com.

Merry E. Wiesner

Editor's Preface
to Students

History is often presented as facts marching along a timeline, and historical research is often viewed as the unearthing of information so that more facts can be placed on the timeline. Like geologists in caves or physicists using elaborate microscopes, historians discover new bits of data, which allow them to recover more of the past.

To some degree, this model is accurate. Like laboratory scientists, historians do conduct primary research, using materials in archives, libraries, and many other places to discover new things about the past. Over the last thirty years, for example, the timeline of history has changed from a story that was largely political and military to one that includes the experiences of women, peasants, slaves, children, and workers. Even the political and military story has changed and now includes the experiences of ordinary soldiers and minority groups rather than simply those of generals, rulers, and political elites. This expansion of the timeline has come in part through intensive research in original sources, which has vastly increased what we know about people of the past.

Original research is only part of what historians do, however, in the same way that laboratory or field research is only part of science. Historical and scientific information is useless until someone tries to make sense of what is happening, tries to explain why and how things developed the way they did. In making these analyses and conclusions, however, both historians and scientists often come to disagree vehemently about the underlying reasons for what they have observed or discovered, and sometimes about the observations themselves. Certain elements of those observations are irrefutable—a substance either caught fire or it did not, a person lived and died or he or she did not—but many more of them are open to debate: Was the event (whether historical or scientific) significant? Why and how did it happen? Under what circumstances might it not have happened? What factors influenced the way that it happened? What larger consequences did it have?

The books in this series focus on just those types of questions. They take one particular event or development in European history and present you with the analyses of several historians and other authors regarding this issue. In some cases the authors may disagree about what actually happened—in the same way that eyewitnesses of a traffic accident or crime may all see different things—but more often they disagree about the interpretation. Was the Renaissance a continuation of earlier ideas, or did it represent a new way of looking at the world? Was nineteenth-century European imperialism primarily political and economic in its origins and impact, or were cultural and intellectual factors more significant? Was ancient Athens a democracy worthy of emulation, an expansionary state seeking to swallow its neighbors, or both? Within each volume are often more specific points of debate, which add complexity to the main question and introduce you to further points of disagreement.

Each of the volumes begins with an introduction by the editor, which you should read carefully before you turn to the selections themselves. This introduction sets out the *historical* context of the issue, adding depth to what you may have learned in a textbook account or other reading, and also explains the *historiographical* context—that is, how historians (including those excerpted in the volume) have viewed the issue over time. Many volumes also include a timeline of events and several reference maps that situate the issue chronologically and geographically. These may be more detailed than the timelines and maps in your textbook, and consulting them as you read will help deepen your understanding of the selections.

Some of the volumes in the series include historical analyses that are more than a century old, and all include writings stretching over several decades. The editors include this chronological range not only to allow you to see that interpretations change, but also to see how lines of argument and analysis develop. Every historian approaching an issue depends not only on his or her own original research, but also on the secondary analyses of those who have gone before, which he or she then accepts, rejects, modifies, or adapts. Thus, within the book as a whole or within each section, the selections are generally arranged in chronological order; reading them in the order they are presented will allow you to get a better sense of the historiographical development and to make comparisons among the selections more easily and appropriately.

The description of the scholarly process noted above is somewhat misleading, for in both science and history, research and analysis are not sequential but simultaneous. Historians do not wander around archives looking for interesting bits of information but turn to their sources with specific questions in mind, questions that have often been developed by reading earlier historians. These questions shape where they will look, what they will pay attention to, and therefore what conclusions they will make. Thus, the fact that we now know so much more about women, peasants, or workers than we did several decades ago did not result primarily from sources on these people suddenly appearing where there had been none, but from historians, with new questions in mind, going back to the same archives and libraries that had yielded information on kings and generals. The same is true in science, of course; scientists examining an issue begin with a hypothesis and then test it through the accumulation of information, reaching a conclusion that leads to further hypotheses.

In both history and science, one's hypotheses can sometimes be so powerful that one simply cannot see what the sources or experiments show, which is one reason there is always opportunity for more research or a reanalysis of data. A scholar's analysis may also be shaped by many other factors, and in this volume the editor may have provided you with information about individual authors, such as their national origin, intellectual background, or philosophical perspective, if these factors are judged important to your understanding of their writings or points of view. You might be tempted to view certain of these factors as creating "bias" on the part of an author and thus to reduce the value of his or her analysis. It is important to recognize, however, that every historian or commentator has a particular point of view and writes at a particular historical moment; very often what scholars view as complete objectivity on their own part is seen as subjective bias by those who disagree. The central aim of this series over its forty-plus years of publication has been to help you and other students understand how and why the analyses and judgments of historians have differed and changed over time, to see that scholarly controversy is at the heart of the historical enterprise.

The instructor in your course may have provided you with detailed directions for using this book, but here are some basic questions that you can ask yourself as you read the selections:

- What is the author's central argument?
- What evidence does the author put forward to support this argument?
- What is the significance of the author's argument?
- What other interpretation might there be of the evidence that the author presents?
- How does each author's argument intersect with the others in the part? In the rest of the book?
- How convincing do you find the author's interpretation?

These questions are exactly the same as those that professional historians ask themselves, and in analyzing and comparing the selections in this book, you, too, are engaged in the business of historical interpretation.

Merry E. Wiesner

Chronology

1542   Pope Paul III establishes the Roman Inquisition.

1545   Council of Trent convenes.

1547   "Chambre ardente" is created in France to combat heresy.

1548   Publication of Loyola's *Spiritual Exercises*

1549   Publication of the first English Book of Common Prayer

1553   Mary Tudor ascends the throne in England, reintroducing Catholicism. Michael Servetus is executed in Geneva.

1555   Religious Peace of Augsburg. Burning of Protestants starts in England. Calvin consolidates power in Geneva by defeating the "Perrinists."

1559   The Geneva Academy is founded. Pope Paul IV issues Index of Prohibited Books.

1560   Church of Scotland is founded.

1562   Massacre of Huguenots occurs at Vassy; outbreak of French Wars of Religion.

1563   Council of Trent closes.

1564   Carlo Borromeo, Tridentine reformer, is named Archbishop of Milan.

1566   Beginning of Dutch rebellion against Spain

1572   St. Bartholomew's Day Massacre in Paris

1576   Formation of Holy Catholic League in France

1579   Union of Utrecht and Union of Arras divide the Low Countries in two.

1580   Publication of Lutheran *Book of Concord*

1582   Jesuit missionaries arrive in China.

1587   Start of intense witch-hunting in Trier

1588   Pope Sixtus V reorganizes Roman Curia.

1589   Assassination of Henry III; accession of Henry of Navarre, marking the beginning of the Bourbon dynasty in France

1598   Edict of Nantes grants toleration and liberties to Huguenots.

1603   Death of Elizabeth I; accession of James I, marking the beginning of the Stuart dynasty in England

1611   Publication of King James Bible

1618   Synod of Dort opens. Defenestration of Prague; outbreak of the Thirty Years' War

1629   Edict of Restitution

1642   Outbreak of English Civil War

1645   Execution of Archbishop William Laud, opponent of Puritanism

1648   Thirty Years' War ends with Peace of Westphalia.

1649   Execution of Charles I

1685   Louis XIV revokes Edict of Nantes.

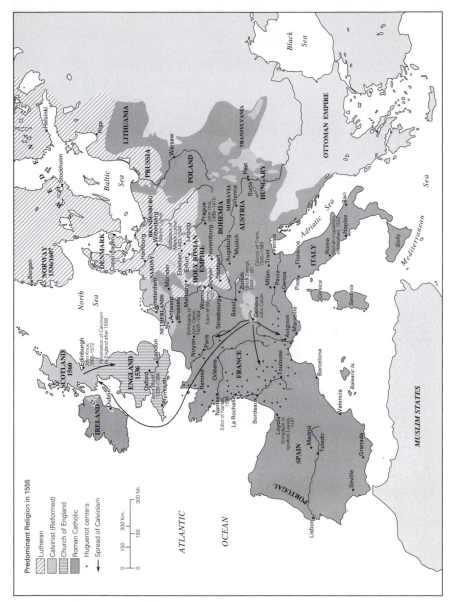

Protestants and Catholics in 1555

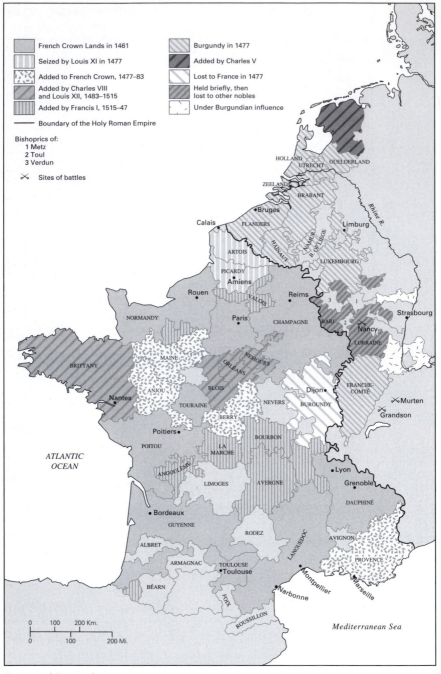

France and Burgundy

Legend:

French Crown Lands in 1461
Seized by Louis XI in 1477
Added to French Crown, 1477–83
Added by Charles VIII and Louis XII, 1483–1515
Added by Francis I, 1515–47
Burgundy in 1477
Added by Charles V
Lost to France in 1477
Held briefly, then lost to other nobles
Under Burgundian influence

—— Boundary of the Holy Roman Empire

Bishoprics of:
1 Metz
2 Toul
3 Verdun

✕ Sites of battles

HOLLAND
UTRECHT
GUELDERLAND
ZEELAND
BRABANT
Bruges
Calais
FLANDERS
Limburg
Rhine R.
ARTOIS
HAINAUT
NAMUR
B. OF LIÈGE
LUXEMBOURG
PICARDY
Amiens
Rouen
VALOIS
Reims
3   1
NORMANDY
Paris
CHAMPAGNE
BARI
2
Nancy
Strasbourg
BRITTANY
MAINE
ORLÉANS
NEMOURS
LORRAINE
Nantes
ANJOU
BLOIS
NEVERS
Dijon
FRANCHE-COMTÉ
TOURAINE
BERRY
BURGUNDY
Murten
Poitiers
BOURBON
Grandson
POITOU
LA MARCHE
ANGOULÊME
LIMOGES
AUVERGNE
Lyon
Grenoble
ATLANTIC OCEAN
Bordeaux
GUYENNE
RODEZ
DAUPHINÉ
AVIGNON
ALBRET
LANGUEDOC
PROVENCE
ARMAGNAC
TOULOUSE
Toulouse
Marseille
BÉARN
FOIX
Narbonne
Montpellier
ROUSSILLON
Mediterranean Sea

0   100   200 Km.
0   100   200 Mi.

Reform in Germany

Italy in the time of the Medici

Introduction

This volume is intended to introduce students to some of the principal historiographical debates on the Reformation, a series of religious movements that had a profound impact on European society and culture, affecting to varying degrees virtually all regions and social groups. For centuries, historians who studied the Reformation concentrated heavily on theological issues. After all, the historical figure most commonly associated with the Reformation is probably Martin Luther (1483–1546), the Augustinian monk and theology professor who became upset over the sale of indulgences in his native Saxony. Complaining that many of his parishioners complacently believed that purchasing indulgences assured them of salvation, Luther posted his Ninety-Five Theses in Wittenberg on October 31, 1517, the date that traditionally marks the beginning of the Protestant Reformation, which resulted in the definitive disintegration of religious unity in Western Christendom. Historians have accordingly analyzed in minute detail the writings of Luther, John Calvin (1509–1564), Huldrych Zwingli (1484–1531), Ignatius Loyola (1491–1556), and other religious leaders, evaluating their ideas on salvation, the sacraments, liturgy, and church structure.

While there is still plenty of interest in the theological side of the Protestant and Catholic Reformations, some of the most exciting work in recent years has concentrated less on the history of ideas per se than on the relationship between religious movements and political developments, society, and popular culture. This volume bears witness to this interest in the connections between religion, on the one hand, and early modern society and culture in general, on the other.

Over the past two or three decades, historians of the Reformation have written a vast number of brilliant scholarly works, and selecting the themes to be treated and the specific publications to be reproduced in this volume has been a daunting task. Potential topics had to pass three criteria to be chosen as subjects for this volume's five parts. One is that the issues under debate must pertain in some way to religion. The *Reformation* has often been used as simply a term to identify an epoch of European history lasting from, say, 1517 to 1648. In this volume, however, the term refers to efforts to promote religious change, be they initiated by Protestants or Catholics, from the fifteenth century into the early eighteenth century. Thus, while the growth of absolutism is a very important theme for sixteenth- and seventeenth-century Europe, it would not be an appropriate topic for this collection since religious change was not central to the growth in royal power. The broad chronological framework used here reflects a common theme in the scholarship of the past three decades: The Reformation's effects took a long time to be played out, often extending into the eighteenth century. This contrasts with research of decades past, which was particularly intense on the years that immediately preceded and followed the birth of Protestantism, an emphasis that was aptly seen in the earlier volume in this series on the Reformation (Lewis W. Spitz, ed., *The Reformation: Basic Interpretations* [Lexington, Mass. and Toronto, 1972]).

Another criterion for the selection of themes is that the current scholarship addressing the issues must show real differences of opinion. There has been an impressive body of scholarship dedicated to the impact of printing on the Reformation, and the invention of movable type in the fifteenth century produced a veritable revolution in communication by dramatically increasing the availability of books. But while interpretations may vary concerning the quantity and the types of religious literature that were published, historians all agree that the invention of the printing press was a necessary prerequisite for the expansion of the religious movements initiated by Luther and others. Similarly, much fascinating research has been done on poor relief and charity, as new attitudes toward and treatment of the poor appeared during the sixteenth and seventeenth centuries. Although there have been some noteworthy variations in their findings, historians have generally found a trend toward greater centralization in the administration of poor relief among both Protestants and Catholics. By contrast, Max Weber's thesis that Calvinism nurtured the spirit of capitalism formerly provoked very intense debate, clearly seen in an earlier volume in this Problems in European History Series (Robert W. Green, ed., *Protestantism, Capitalism, and Social Science: The Weber Thesis Controversy*, 2nd ed. [Lexington, Mass., 1973]). That thesis, however, has pretty much run its course and is no longer the subject of much historical research.

The third principal criterion is that the issues debated must cross both national and confessional boundaries. Consequently, although there has been a very impressive body of literature pertaining to religious violence and the causes of conflict in the French Wars of Religion, these issues do not lend themselves to comparisons with other countries as readily as the five topics outlined below. Recent scholarship reveals very significant changes in our understanding of the relationship between the Protestant and Catholic (or Counter-)Reformations. In light of the striking differences in theology, the Protestant and Catholic Reformations until fairly recently have been treated as diametrically opposed to one another. Moreover, scholars' interpretations of the major figures and events of the Reformation were often strongly influenced by their own religious convictions. Though not denying that important theological differences existed among Christian groups in Reformation Europe, historians of the past couple decades have concentrated more on the many parallels among the Lutheran, Calvinist, and Catholic Reformations, and the partisan element that characterized some earlier scholarship has largely disappeared.

Part I, "The Theory of Confessionalization," is an excellent example of a thesis that has been applied to both Protestant and Catholic movements in many different contexts. Conceived by German scholars and first applied to the German Reformation, the "confessionalization" paradigm has served since the 1970s as a useful framework for very fruitful historical research on the Protestant and Catholic Reformations throughout Europe. The theory gets its name from the different "confessions," detailed and rigid statements about proper Christian beliefs and practices, that were written for the Lutheran, Catholic, and Reformed (or Calvinist) faiths in the sixteenth century. The term *confessionalism* is commonly used to refer to the division of Christians into these three competing well-defined groups, while the theory of confessionalization stresses the role of the state in effecting social and religious change, be they in Lutheran, Calvinist, or Catholic regions. The first selection is a piece by Wolfgang Reinhard, one of the most important and articulate exponents of the confessionalization theory. While theological differences were significant, Reinhard stresses the parallels among Lutherans, Calvinists, and Catholics, who all aggressively sought to enforce popular adherence to their respective confessions, especially after 1550. Into the eighteenth century, the three groups employed similar methods, including mandatory schooling and catechism lessons, to inculcate appropriate Christian beliefs and practices among common folk, and the state assumed the central role in bringing about confessional uniformity within its borders, imposing strict social discipline through close scrutiny of religious and moral behavior by "morals courts" or consistories.

The theory of confessionalization has elicited a variety of reactions from historians, including some who believe that it needs to be modified when applied to areas outside the Holy Roman Empire. Benjamin Kaplan, for example, finds that, to a degree, the paradigm of confessionalization can be usefully applied to the Calvinists in the Netherlands. Unlike Reinhard, however, Kaplan claims that the desire to impose strict discipline and order based on Calvinist morality did not simply come from the top down, as many ordinary laypeople were among those fervently in favor of the close supervision of behavior. James Farr finds that the theory of confessionalization, along with the concept of social discipline, has informed—sometimes explicitly but often tacitly—much recent research on the religious history of sixteenth- and seventeenth-century France. The body of evidence suggests that from the 1530s through the late seventeenth century, a period that both predates and follows the most decisive decades of confessionalization in Germany, the crown pursued, as far as politically possible, the "catholicization" of France and increasing numbers of both Catholics and Protestants conformed to the norms of behavior espoused by religious and political elites. Some scholars insist that in Germany, confessionalization did not occur as tidily as has been suggested. Marc Forster, for example, criticizes the theory for not taking into account a wide range of differences in religious experiences among Catholics in early modern Germany and claims that the church and state's efforts to effect uniformity were less successful than the proponents of "confessionalization" would have us believe.

Closely tied to the issue of confessionalization is "Popular Religion," the subject of Part II. Many historians have observed a gap between the "official" Christian beliefs and practices promoted by religious and political leaders and the piety of common parishioners. Basing his research on Catholic France, Jean Delumeau published a very provocative thesis in 1971, asserting that Europeans were not actually Christian until the Protestant and Catholic Reformations. Until then, popular religion had essentially remained a mixture of paganism and magic with only a superficial Christian façade superimposed upon it. Only the aggressive actions of Christian leaders and institutions—the same actions analyzed in the confessionalization theory—eventually weaned European common folk from their semipagan beliefs and practices to make them truly Christians, a process that was not completed until the eighteenth century. In his work on Germany, Robert Scribner found that Protestant clergymen, like their Catholic counterparts, complained that common folk regularly resorted to magic, continuing to cast spells even if, in accordance with Protestant sensibilities, they had ceased to include in them references to the saints and Virgin Mary. These findings run contrary to the view, developed by the great sociologist Max Weber, that Protestantism removed magic from religion, ultimately leading to a more secular mentality. By contrast, in his work on England, Eamon Duffy rejects the dichotomy of the official religion of the elite, on the one hand, and that of the people, on the other. Denying that the religion of common folk in fifteenth-century England was superstitious, magic, or semipagan, Duffy asserts that late medieval English Catholicism was a very strong, vibrant faith that enjoyed widespread popularity and that the conversion to Protestantism amounted to the "stripping of the altars," which was strongly resented by many parishioners. An expert on Counter-Reformation Spain, Sara Nalle also rejects the dichotomy of popular versus elite religion but she does see, in response to the guidance of religious leaders, significant changes in the religious practices of people of all classes during the course of the sixteenth and seventeenth centuries. In her examination of cheap printed material in England, Tessa Watt claims that the piety expressed in pamphlets, ballads, and broadsides did not amount to the replacement of Catholic values by Protestant mores but rather a continuation of traditional piety into which Protestant precepts were unobtrusively inserted.

As several of the above selections indicate, rituals were a fundamental part of popular religious experiences in this era, and Part III, "The Reformation of Rituals," concentrates on the impact of the Protestant and Catholic Reformations on various religious ceremonies. Protestants attacked a wide range of ceremonies and practices that they deemed unbiblical, semipagan, or superstitious; and Catholic theologians also objected to certain rituals that were popularly used in the sixteenth and seventeenth centuries. The essays in this section show that the impact of the Reformation on religious rituals varied enormously, depending on the geographical, social, and confessional context. In the first selection, Robert Kingdon looks at popular religious practices through the registers of the Consistory of Geneva, a quasi-tribunal that was created under Calvin's guidance with the goal of enforcing Reformed morality. These records indicate that there was a revolution in worship with the conversion to Protestantism, as the church service was no longer centered around the mass—primarily a visual experience, but rather around the sermon, an auditory experience focused on the word. David Cressy has written an intriguing article, reproduced here, on the practice of the "churching" of women in Reformation England. In late medieval Europe, a woman who had just given birth went through this ritual before she could be readmitted to church services. Although most Protestant critics dismissed this ceremony as a holdover of the Jewish belief that women are ritually unclean after childbirth, churching continued to be celebrated long after the conversion to Protestantism in England. Susan Karant-Nunn looks at some important changes related to the Eucharist in Lutheran Germany. Although Martin Luther believed that one is saved by faith alone and that the believer can do nothing to influence God in matters of salvation, Karant-Nunn points out that Lutherans—especially through their belief that communicants ate Christ's flesh and drank His blood—nonetheless nurtured the notions that God was approachable and that humans could even "act in ways to obtain His benefit." In a synthesis on the impact of the Counter-Reformation on rituals, Edward Muir observes that in the wake of the Council of Trent, Roman Catholic leaders sought uniformity in church liturgy and retained in their services many things that some Protestants aggressively attacked: clerical vestments, images of saints, holy water, polyphonic music. According to Muir, in the late sixteenth and seventeenth centuries, bishops who pursued the uniformity of religious practices among the laity enjoyed greatest success when they were able to co-opt the laity by redirecting existing practices, particularly those they were able to change from semiprivate cults into forms of collective worship that enhanced community spirit.

Part IV, "The Reformation and Gender," bears witness to the growing use of gender analysis, surely one of the most important developments in historical writing in recent years. At one level, this has simply meant that much greater attention is being paid to the history of women. More important, scholars have analyzed how social and economic developments and cultural movements had different effects on women and men; and they have studied the ways in which the concept of gender has changed over the centuries—ideas about what it means to be a man or a woman can vary dramatically from century to century and culture to culture. One of the principal leaders in the gender analysis of the Reformation has been Merry Wiesner-Hanks. In the work reproduced here, Wiesner-Hanks looks briefly both at how male leaders tried to control female behavior and, even more, at how some women actively took part in the Protestant and Catholic Reformations. Obstacles notwithstanding, various Protestant and Catholic women succeeded in finding a spiritual niche for themselves. Lyndal Roper examines the place of women in the notion of "community," a concept that purportedly played a key role in the conversion of many German cities to Protestantism. Although "community" meant different things to different people, Roper finds that women were consistently prevented from representing the community and from serving as political actors—the concept of community in German cities considered the political domain as purely male. In the next essay, Gabriella Zarri maintains, on the one hand, that the Catholic Reformation definitely enhanced educational opportunities for women

in Italy. On the other hand, she finds that while female reformers of religious orders were highly esteemed, in other respects the opportunities
for women as spiritual leaders declined in the sixteenth and seventeenth
centuries. By the post-Tridentine era, the Catholic Church downplayed
prophecy and mysticism, traits that were traditionally common among
female saints. Looking at the other end of the social spectrum, Sherrill
Cohen finds that the Catholic Reformation brought progressive change
for some women. Cohen examines new asylums that were established
in many Italian cities, some of which aimed at reforming prostitutes. A
stay in such an asylum could amount to an act of purification, allowing
a woman to be reintegrated into society with her honor restored.

The history of the family was among the first areas of research in
which gender analysis played an important role, not very surprising
insofar as early modern women were generally identified above all as
wives and mothers. Some historians have argued that the Protestant
Reformation enhanced patriarchal power, making women more subordinate to their husbands. Other scholars insist that Protestantism promoted domestic equality in marriage, an important expression of which
was the introduction of the possibility of divorce and remarriage. In his
discussion of marriage and the control of matrimony, Jeffrey Watt sees
little change for women among both Protestants and Catholics; divorce,
for example, remained extremely rare into the eighteenth century and
was possible only on very restricted grounds.

Part V, "The 'Success' of the Reformation," effectively ties together
the previous parts of this volume. Until the past couple of decades, the
Reformation was traditionally assumed to have been a catalyst for dramatic change, amounting to a revolution in religious practices that affected the lives of people in all social classes. In a provocative essay that
is abridged here, Gerald Strauss challenges this assumption. Strauss
studied visitation reports, annual statements made by officials who were
sent out by ecclesiastical and political authorities to examine the state
of affairs in rural Lutheran parishes. Finding ignorance of and hostility
toward the Lutheran faith among peasants, whose piety—like the subjects
of Delumeau's study in France—was thoroughly imbued with magic,
Strauss concludes that the Reformation was a failure.

Strauss's essay has stimulated much debate, as evidenced by the
other selections reproduced here. In his work on Reformation Germany,
C. Scott Dixon finds much evidence that lends support to Strauss's thesis
of failure but nonetheless sees some significant changes taking place
in peasant mentality. While their church attendance and knowledge of

doctrines were, in the minds of the Lutheran clergy, less than satisfactory, peasants eventually assimilated some key ideas first expressed by the clerical elite, such as associating witchcraft with the worship of the devil. In his broad synthetic study on the success of the Reformations, Geoffrey Parker examines the Protestant and Catholic movements throughout Europe. He finds that Catholic reformers were perhaps more likely to reach their goals than Protestants, in part because they made a greater effort to adapt, with some alterations, existing religious practices rather than simply trying to eliminate them. Most generally, Parker finds that by 1650, the Reformations had indeed enjoyed some success in effecting changes in the religious behavior and beliefs of millions of Europeans. The changes had been slow to take hold, however, and fell well short of what both Catholic and Protestant reformers had sought. In a superb synthesis of the history of the Reformed faith, Philip Benedict is more sanguine in discussing the success of Calvinism. Though conceding that the results among the populations at large did not measure up to the objectives of Calvin and other reformers, Benedict still sees important changes in behavior taking hold relatively quickly in regions that firmly embraced the Reformed faith. Rituals considered "idolatrous" soon fell into disuse, and violence and illicit sexuality tended to decline, indicating a certain success in nurturing new moral sensibilities.

The common thread that runs through all the themes treated in this volume is the intersection between religion and society. The works reproduced here reveal historians' strong interest in uncovering the links between theological and ecclesiastical changes and social developments — connections that can be found in various forms in the Holy Roman Empire and Britain; in the kingdom of France and Italian city-states; and in Calvinist Geneva, Catholic Spain, and the pluralistic Low Countries. Social discipline, popular religious practices, and the position of women are all part of inquiries concerning the impact of religious change on European society.

It is important to note that space limitations preclude addressing a host of topics on which much fascinating scholarship has been written. The Radical Reformation, for example, will not be addressed in any of the following pieces. The myriad historical Protestant figures who are lumped together under the rubric of "radicals" were an intriguing lot. The German Thomas Müntzer (ca. 1490–1525), the charismatic leader of rebellious peasants in Thuringia; the Dutchman Menno Simons (1496–1561), a founder of the pacifist form of Dutch Anabaptism; and the Savoyard

Sebastian Castellio (1515–1563), the defender of religious toleration who coined the term "liberty of conscience," all played important roles in Reformation Europe. But the Radical Reformation, itself a very amorphous group of competing movements, affected only a very small percentage of Europe's population. While some of the ideas introduced by the Protestant radicals, such as toleration and religious freedom, later became axiomatic among Western thinkers, in the Reformation era itself they were very much outside of mainstream thought. Moreover, there were far fewer parallels between the radical movements, on the one hand, and Lutheranism, Calvinism, Anglicanism, and Catholicism, on the other.

Although several essays in this collection discuss the relationship between religion and magic in this era, regrettably, limitations of space do not allow a detailed examination of the subject of witchcraft, a topic of great historiographical interest. The period 1560–1640 witnessed the most intense witch-hunting in European history, and changes wrought by the Reformation contributed in an important way to these hunts. Studies have shown, for example, that the most severe hunting occurred in places such as Scotland, Switzerland, and above all Germany, areas where people of different religious confessions lived in close proximity to each other. By contrast, the religiously homogeneous populations of Catholic Spain and Italy had very low execution rates for witchcraft and magic. Women comprised the large majority of those tried and convicted of witchcraft, and a case could be made that the section on gender should include some entries dealing with witches. The literature on witchcraft, however, is so vast that we cannot possibly do justice to the subject in this volume, particularly if we try to address the issues of both gender and religious change. Finally, studying witchcraft trials tells us much about early modern mentality, but the vast majority of Europeans of the Reformation era lived their lives utterly unaffected by witch-hunting. The most recent estimates indicate that from the late fifteenth through the end of the seventeenth century, probably about 40,000 people, mostly women, were executed for witchcraft. The number of women tried or executed for witchcraft, however, was insignificant when compared with the numbers of female religious, of laywomen active in Protestant and Catholic movements, or, most obviously, of the number of women who got married and were therefore subject to changing doctrines and laws pertaining to matrimony. Simply put, the Protestant and Catholic Reformations had an immediate impact on women in so many ways, but the hunting of witches directly affected only a tiny percentage of European females.

Titian, "The Council of Trent." (© *Bridgeman Art Library/Lauros/Giraudon*)
Convening at Trent between 1545 and 1563, Catholic delegates pursued reform and
devised responses to Protestantism, playing a decisive role in the formation of Roman
Catholicism's "confession."

The Theory of Confessionalization

Many scholars have contributed to the theory of confessionalization, but two German historians—Wolfgang Reinhard and Heinz Schilling—have been most instrumental in its development. They both see important parallel movements among Lutherans, Calvinists, and Catholics, particularly after 1550, in their quest for social and religious order. While acknowledging the important theological differences among these groups, Reinhard and Schilling stress their structural similarities. Following the formulation in the sixteenth century of confessions of faith, whereby each group defined what it meant to be a Christian, magistrates and church leaders embarked on an ambitious mission—lasting into the early eighteenth century—of enforcing these confessions, an endeavor that included imposing social discipline. Becoming a branch of the state, the church was assuming unprecedented power over society, while the state was appearing more "sacral" than ever before, as enforcement of religious behavior was becoming an increasingly important function of the state. Because the state was acquiring increased centralized authority replete with ever more intrusive police powers, confessionalization reputedly represented an important phase in the development of the modern state. Although the evidence for confessionalization was strongest in the Holy Roman Empire, Reinhard and Schilling see parallel developments throughout western and central Europe in both Catholic and Protestant areas. The piece by Reinhard that is reproduced here, first published in German in 1977, is the best introduction to the provocative theory of confessionalization, aptly showing the alleged conjunction among religious reform, social discipline, and state-building.

Benjamin Kaplan examines the Netherlands, the most religiously pluralistic region of Europe, a land where Calvinists, Lutherans, Catholics, Mennonites, Jews, and others all lived and worshiped. Although the Dutch demonstrated more religious toleration than any other people in Reformation Europe, a significant number of Calvinists sought to suppress all other forms of worship and impose strict Reformed discipline. Concentrating on the city of Utrecht for the years 1578–1620, Kaplan studies the conflicts between Calvinists and so-called "Libertines," the latter a pejorative term given to them by Calvinists. Espousing religious liberty, the Libertines professed to be members of the Reformed faith, the state's "official" church, even though they rejected some important characteristics of Calvinism, most notably church discipline. Kaplan insists that these conflicts were not unique to the Netherlands; many other Europeans, like the Dutch Libertines, sincerely adhered to individualistic forms of Christian piety and resisted efforts to impose rigid confessions of faith. For Kaplan, events in the Netherlands deviated in some important ways from the confessionalization model. While Reinhard and Schilling envision a process whereby social discipline and order were imposed from above on an often-unwilling populace, Kaplan finds that among Dutch Reformed Protestants, many ordinary laypeople, even of modest means, desired the introduction of strict discipline based on Calvinist morality. Wielding political power did prove decisive, however—Calvinists tried to impose strict social control in the 1580s, but when they lost control of Utrecht's government, their confessional aims collapsed with them. In the Netherlands, the Calvinists' goals of *confessionalism* succeeded in the Dutch Reformed Church—the institution of the church developed a very well-defined confessional identity that was rigidly Calvinistic, aptly seen in its emphatic rejection in the second decade of the seventeenth century of the Remonstrants, a group of Dutch Protestants who espoused free will. On the other hand, Calvinists' hopes for *confessionalization,* entailing a complete reordering of Dutch society based on discipline and strict Reformed morality, would never be realized in the Netherlands, where people could continue to practice in private a wide range of forms of worship.

In his review of recent literature, James Farr observes that the religious history of sixteenth- and seventeenth-century France does not appear, at first glance, to fit the confessionalization paradigm very well. In 1598, when confessionalization was supposedly in full force in Germany, Henry IV issued the Edict of Nantes, granting Huguenots (French Protestants) full civil rights and the right to public worship in many parts of France; this action might suggest the state was not promoting religious uniformity, a key part of confessionalization. Be that as it may, during the era of the religious wars (1562–1598), ultra-Catholics, including many laypeople, viewed Protestant "heresy" as a type of spiritual cancer that threatened the collective salvation of France and must therefore be extirpated. Moreover, the degree of toleration that the royal government showed Protestants was a matter of political expediency; ultimately, the crown consistently remained committed to the concept of "One King, One Law, One Faith." In the seventeenth century, there is evidence, on the one hand, that the different faiths coexisted peacefully and that some people subordinated their religious allegiance to considerations of social rank, apparent signs of weakening confessional ties; on the other hand, in some regions Catholics and Protestants restricted their closest social ties more and more to their co-religionists, an indication of strengthening confessional identity in both religious communities. In any event, both the coexistence of the two faiths and the subsequent enforcement of religious uniformity in the late 1600s depended on and enhanced the power of the state. Many scholars of early modern French religion have drawn considerable inspiration from John Bossy, who does not use the term *confessionalization* but claims that Christianity, with its new emphasis on interior discipline, contributed in the early modern period to the civilizing process through which Europeans sought to curb violence and promote peace—developments that dovetail easily with the theory of confessionalization. All told, Farr finds that a modified version of confessionalization, especially when combined with the concept of social discipline, can be usefully applied to the religious history of early modern France.

In his article on Germany, Marc Forster claims that uniformity of belief and practices was not achieved within the Catholic "confession." In spite of the efforts of magistrates and church leaders, German Catholics continued to adhere to a variety of practices. Forster argues that, contrary to what is commonly believed, the Council of Trent—the church council that was called to devise the Roman Catholic response to the Protestant challenge, meeting off and on from 1545 to 1563—did not deserve all or even most of the credit for shaping Catholicism into a clearly defined confessional group in Germany. Forster notes that political authorities and church leaders did work together closely in certain regions, such as Bavaria, which probably came closest to experiencing confessionalization in the manner described by Reinhard and Schilling. Be that as it may, while he finds a very strong Catholic identity in different German regions, this was not something imposed from above on an unwilling population; to a considerable extent, Catholic identity had its roots in popular religious mores.

Wolfgang Reinhard

Pressures Towards Confessionalization? Prolegomena to a Theory of the Confessional Age

There is no particular need for me to justify this attempt to use the findings of two previous studies in ecclesiastical history to cast further light on the development of the early modern political system. On the contrary: if I did not do so I would incur criticism for having paid too little

Wolfgang Reinhard, "Pressures Towards Confessionalization? Prolegomena to a Theory of the Confessional Age," in *The German Reformation*, ed. C. Scott Dixon (Oxford: Blackwell, 1999), 172–192. Copyright © 1999 by Blackwell Publishing. Reprinted with permission of Blackwell Publishing.

attention to the political aspect in those studies, for in Europe of the six-teenth and seventeenth centuries, our subject here, ecclesiastical and political action still coincided if not entirely then to a considerable extent. Consequently, in answering the questions, "When, how and why were large social groups in the form of the new churches created by 'confessionalization'?", it becomes immediately obvious that political ambition at the time had little option but to take part in the process. The popular notion that the supra-confessional neutrality of the state power was a necessary or even sufficient condition for the further growth of that power will prove anachronistic: a retrospective projection of circumstances that prevailed at a later date. Instead, "confessionalization" turns out to be an early phase of modern European state formation, a phase found with remarkable regularity.

This fact means that our general subject—"Political opportunities in the Holy Roman Empire"—will not be directly addressed here, although it will appear all the more effective approached indirectly. I am not discussing the Empire itself, but the territories within it and the other "states" of Europe. However, the "confessionalization" of German territories sometimes does seem to differ from that of those other European "states"; despite uniformity of substance, the particular circumstance of being part of the Empire makes itself incidentally felt. In this way, then, I am in fact taking our main subject into account: the general "confessionalization" of these territories was not only fundamental to *politics in the Empire*, it also determined the sphere of action of *Imperial policy*. . . .

A prerequisite for my theses here is the revision of traditional scholarly ideas which have long ceased to pass unchallenged, and of their traditional division of history into periods, which has moulded society's awareness of history in general and is thus prejudicial to research.

Thesis I: Parallels Between the "Reformation" and the "Counter-Reformation"

The idea that the Reformation and the Counter-Reformation were irreconcilable opposites and consecutive historical phases can no longer be supported. It now seems more accurate to distinguish between a relatively short-lived "evangelical movement" which does, however, represent the culmination of two centuries of efforts to introduce reform, and a process of "confessionalization" lasting around another two centuries, beginning as early as the 1520s and coming to an end in the early eighteenth century.

The important point is that the process occurred to a great and to some extent chronologically parallel degree in all three confessional areas: Calvinism, Catholicism and Lutheranism.

Both parts of that dialectical pair of opposites, the "middle-class and progressive Reformation" and the "feudal and reactionary Counter-Reformation," need correction. The "modernity" of the "Reformation," once so readily cited, has long been in doubt, or at least the concept has been considerably restricted by precise statements of what it actually means. Recently it has also been discovered that in many ways the "Counter-Reformation" was more "modern" than was previously thought (and often still is). Not only do the forward-looking features of both Reformation and Counter-Reformation often correspond, they were also linked by a common past in the shape of two hundred years of attempts to reform the church. As a Catholic, Hubert Jedin may have felt some partisan satisfaction in establishing that reforms in the old church preceded the Protestant Reformation, but there is no reason to suppose that Pierre Chaunu, a Protestant, felt the same in simply classifying the "Reformation" and the "Counter-Reformation" as the second and third in a series of *réformes.*

The pressure of population in the "crowded world," followed by the economic crises and catastrophic plagues of the fourteenth century, the growing importance of towns with the consequent rise of the money economy and education of the laity, to sum up the elements involved: increasing social division of labour and the complexity of differentiated lifestyles now that large numbers of people were living together, severe crises in the political and ecclesiastical system, in particular schisms and the extensive failure of the reforming councils to which they gave rise, and finally new trends in intellectual life that were at least partially connected with these other phenomena, even if we do not know exactly how—all this led to more and more attempts between the thirteenth and sixteenth centuries to reform the church and the secular world.

From today's viewpoint, then, the supposedly irreconcilable opposites of the "Reformation" and the "Counter-Reformation" seem closer than ever in origin and character. None the less, the early "evangelical movement" does occupy a special position in this context, entailing as it did unusually energetic innovation and modernizing tendencies. However, that was not the end of it. Once the princes took a hand in the 1520s and the "Reformation" began to be organized by secular authorities, then for all the innovations one cannot help detecting conservativism in the measures adopted, and an approach to the behaviour of the opposite side. The *Confessio Augustana* itself, marking the start of evangelical confessionalization, was careful to dissociate itself from "the left," the radical currents in the evangelical movement, and made a deliberate approach to the forces of the old church. And anyone hoping to trace the principle of progress found in radical Calvinism in more conservative Lutheranism will discover that the Reformed church too was overwhelmingly introduced into the Empire under princely authority, with the consequences one might expect. Although Calvinism, on the other hand, developed autonomously and in the context of political opposition in western Europe, it was as the result of historical contingency, not an expression of its alleged "nature": Calvin's political doctrines and correspondence leave no room for doubt on that point.

In fact studying the history of political ideas to find the origins of the sovereignty of the people and the right to resist will show how little such developments depend on the supposed qualities of any particular confession, and on the other hand how important the political circumstances involved always were. The justification of resistance derived from a crisis in the usually rather conservative Lutheran confession; Calvinistic monarch-making was followed by the Catholic variety when the cause of the old church seemed to be endangered by the monarchy, until both confessions went over to supporting absolutism as soon as it became a guarantee of their confessional rights. Consequently we find both supporters of "the sovereignty of the people" and absolutist theoreticians among the Jesuits, and neither friends nor foes of the order lack evidence to cite in support of their own interests.

The Jesuit order, still rightly regarded as one of the most important exponents of the new Catholicism, is a particularly good example of modernity in the supposedly "reactionary Counter-Reformation." Compared to the traditional monastic orders, the Society of Jesus was positively revolutionary; not for nothing were their opponents such conservative churchmen as Carafa, later Pope Paul IV. And it was no coincidence that attempts to found a parallel order of Jesuit nuns failed; it would have been intolerable to see the ecclesiastical emancipation of women added to the innovations introduced by the male Jesuits. The founding of a *new* order in the shape of the Jesuits was startling in itself; previously there had been, at the most, reforms of the old orders. The elitist recruitment policy of the Jesuits was new, and so was the extremely careful training they gave, in which spiritual exercises occupied a central position. Although the content of those exercises may have been anything but "modern," the institution itself was one of fascinating modernity in three ways. First, the internalization of the group's central values was planned and organized with considerable psychological acuity. Second, the process concentrated on individuals in an entirely new way. Third, individual internalization made it possible to dispense with traditional forms of monastic community life such as choral prayer and seclusion, and allowed the Jesuits unrestricted activity in the world. It is not surprising that such an order was particularly famous for its schools, and significantly enough there are parallels here with evangelical achievements, which have led to accusations of "plagiarism."

If we add to all this the sometimes disquietingly modern economic organization of the Jesuits, we come to an area—the economy—where the reactionary character of early modern Catholicism also seemed to be established beyond doubt. In the matter of credit Reformation doctrine may have been more honest, but despite occasional attacks of rigour the casuistry of the old faith could deal just as well with financial transactions; perhaps even better, since Catholicism was more elastic. The papacy itself had been the major financial power in the Middle Ages and remained one of the most important borrowers, with a financial system superior to any western European and German parallels. . . .

The undisputed theological oppositions, then, were by no means expressed in practical life in the form of consistent structural divergencies between the large religious communities. On the contrary: one might venture to say that irreconcilable theological positions actually led to the development of largely similar answers to problems, particularly the fundamental problem of ensuring confessional identity, on the basis of a common tradition and the actual situation. Thus closely related processes of discrimination and discipline among the adherents of the various religious tendencies led to the formation of confessions: large, new, self-contained groups. Confessionalization began with the evangelical visitations of the 1520s and various inadequate measures taken at the same time by Catholicism, and ended with the forcible establishment of confessional homogeneity in France in 1685, the guaranteeing of the Protestant character of the English monarchy between 1688 and 1707, and the expulsion of the Salzburg Protestants in 1731. It has long been recognized that confessionalization in the Empire by no means ended in 1648.

Thesis 2: The Methodical Establishment of Large New Groups

The self-contained nature of the large new group called a "confession" was achieved in Calvinism, Catholicism and Lutheranism by the following methods:

1. *A return to clear theoretical ideas;*
2. *The dissemination and establishment of new standards;*
3. *Propaganda, and the taking of measures against counter-propaganda;*
4. *Internalization of the new order through education and training;*
5. *The disciplining of adherents (in the narrower sense);*
6. *The practice of ritual;*
7. *The influencing of language.*

I shall try to give a brief account of these different methods and the variations on them.

1. The clarity of firm convictions and the stern pleasure of taking practical decisions could be acquired as basics only if a desire for pacification and compromise were regarded as an obstacle to be overcome. This was achieved theoretically with the construction of firm confessions of faith; hence the key function of the *confessio* at this time. In addition, the meaning of the term "confession" was extended in the process of "confessionalization": from denoting a personal act of confession, it became a term for the organization consisting of those who confessed to the faith. However, the positive achievement of establishing confessions of faith did not mean all was won, particularly in the religious confusion prevalent in the Empire; a negative achievement, the eradication of confessional obscurities, was also required. A typical example is the lay chalice, the receiving of communion in both forms, an issue not of theology but of church discipline. In view of the apparently small theological risk involved, it had been permitted in Jülich-Cleve and Bavaria, but soon turned out to be a vehicle of the new faith, and so although the practice had only just been authorized in Bavaria, it was immediately suppressed again.

2. The clarification of religious positions was less of a deciding factor than the subsequent dissemination and institutional establishment of the new norms. People in positions of authority—theologians, pastors, teachers, doctors and midwives, and sometimes the secular authorities—were examined and bound to maintain the new standards; with increasing

frequency they had to take an actual oath. As for the institutions, the hierarchical apparatus of the old church proved less of a help than a hindrance because of its unwieldy nature and initially unsuitable personnel. After the Council of Trent, however, spiritual and institutional innovations were introduced, and in the longer term ensured the survival of the old church, now regenerated as a confession. The decisions of the Council and the Popes were put into practice by nuncios working together, not always harmoniously, with new orders of the stamp of the Jesuits. Provincial and diocesan synods to be held regularly served the promulgation and specification of new norms; the Milan of Carlo Borromeo was the most successful example. Missions spread the new spirit among the people. As well as the nuncios, another method of control was the regular visits paid by bishops to Rome to make their reports. The churches of the Reformation themselves developed no similarly rigid organization; consequently the new standards here—and not only here—were frequently carried out with the aid of the political apparatus of a city or a principality.

3.   Propaganda and censorship went hand in hand, and were based on the deliberate extension of book printing. The theology of controversy was suited to the needs of the confessional struggle. Group norms were to be reinforced and the errors of adversaries denounced by constant repetition. In addition there were forms of indoctrination more suited to ordinary people; catechisms, sermons and sacred music, and in Catholicism plays as well as such cult forms as processions, pilgrimages, and the veneration of relics and the saints. Censors made sure that no incorrect ideas were allowed in. The Roman and Spanish indexes of prohibited books are the best known examples of censorship, but it was also expressly encouraged by the Lutheran Formula of Concord and was practised in Calvinism.

4.   All the measures mentioned, however, were only preliminaries to the internalization of the new norms in the process of socialization: ultimately, that was the deciding factor. Every confession expanded and controlled its educational facilities so as to convey "correct" ideas to younger generations in the group. The many school regulations published place religious education and religious exercises, with the control of moral and religious conduct, at the centre of their concern. Most striking of all, however, is the founding of many new educational institutions at this period. The rapid spread of Jesuit colleges in Europe helped to maintain Catholic elites. Even more important, however, was the training of reliable teachers to spread doctrine; for this purpose Catholic priests' seminaries were founded, as well as additional central training institutes in

Rome such as the Collegium Germanicum. In the evangelical churches, Wittenberg had almost spontaneously become the centre of education, but was then superseded by Geneva, where the training of future generations of preachers to cover the whole of Europe was systematically organized. Subsequently many universities were founded, to prevent members of the local group from going abroad to be educated and to attract outstanding minds in conformity with the system. In the Empire and the Netherlands in the confessional age, twelve Catholic, twelve Lutheran and eight Reformed universities were founded, and five more Reformed universities in Switzerland alone.

5.   Besides educational policy, however, there were other disciplinary procedures available to create a confessionally homogeneous group. First of all, minorities were expelled, from the Italian Protestants of the sixteenth century to the Salzburg Protestants of the eighteenth century. Then the outside contacts of the group were cut off, and it was limited to internal contacts, a process that reinforced and went hand in hand with the deliberate fostering of hostility to "others." The central instrument of discipline, however, was the visitation, when individual communities and institutions were subjected to rigorous examination; in contrast to earlier times, precise records of the visitations were kept. Where there was no superior authority, as in the autonomous Reformed communities, the presbytery or consistory of pastors and elders acted as a functional equivalent, and had indeed been founded expressly for purposes of religious and moral supervision. In fact social control by the local community itself may have been more effective than control by the Spanish Inquisition or the Bavarian "police."

6.   In view of their importance for the coherence of the group, rituals also had to be subject to discipline, initially exercised through checks on participation. Lists of communicants were kept, and registers of baptisms, marriages and funerals, not for statistical purposes but to control life in the confession. Furthermore, rites that might serve as the distinguishing marks of a confession were deliberately encouraged or suppressed. In the Catholic church the lay chalice was regarded as heretical, while the cult of the sacraments, the saints and holy pictures was seen as the quintessence of Catholicism. In the evangelical churches the removal of holy pictures, with rejection of the remnants of the old liturgy of the mass and exorcism in the baptism service were salient features of the transition from Lutheranism to Calvinism. . . .

7.   Finally, the desire for confessional identity extended to language and its regulation in conformity with the group—a subject into which little

research has yet been done. In Geneva people's first names were subject to confessional regulations. The traditional predominance of New Testament names was maintained, but certain names of saints and other typically Catholic first names were forbidden, and the well-known increase in the use of Old Testament names came in. Among Catholics, however, the old custom of choosing saints' names was established by law in 1566.

Regardless of theological opposition and the different instruments employed by different confessions, the process of confessionalization went ahead with remarkable uniformity and simultaneity. It is also noticeable that it involved a good deal of participation by the secular authorities, and indeed many of the most effective measures could never have been introduced without authoritative secular cooperation. Confessionalization was by no means in state hands only in Lutheran areas; it was the same in Calvinistic areas, although such an idea theoretically ran counter to the autonomous constitutions of the churches, and in the Catholic area, where in theory there was no lack of ecclesiastical organization to justify state intervention. . . . [T]he efforts toward confessionalization already made by noble elites had a political dimension, even if they were carried out in conflict with the "power of the state"—or perhaps for that very reason. If we turn to the confessional policies of urban oligarchies, for instance in Switzerland, there is an unmistakable similarity to measures undertaken by princely authorities. There were times when a tolerant religious policy was in the interests of leading civic groups, as with the council of the imperial city of Augsburg or the "Regents" of the Netherlands. However, tolerant communities were politically weak in the sixteenth and seventeenth centuries; the emergent modern state required confessional intolerance as a prerequisite for the development of its power.

Thesis 3: Confessionalization in the Service of Political Growth

If the emergent "modern style" clearly encouraged confessionalization, the reason lay in three crucial advantages it thereby gained for its further development:

1. *Reinforcement of its national or territorial identity, both at home and abroad;*
2. *Control over the church as a powerful rival of the new state power, and not least over church property as an important means of power;*

3. *Discipline and homogenization of its subjects, for "confessionaliza-tion" was the first phase of what Gerhard Oestreich has called the absolutist "imposition of social discipline." It was therefore necessary for the politically ambitious to pursue a policy of confessionalization.*

1. After the general late medieval process of differentiation described above, both the European "Corpus Christianum" and the Empire disin-tegrated into a multiplicity of churches, states and territories. However, the mere fact of their multiplicity brought these new structures under the pressure of competition, not least in justifying their existence. The process of differentiation did not initially reflect the present state of affairs, where autonomous sub-systems of "politics," "religion," "the economy" and so forth are found side by side and it is usual for an individual to be affiliated to more than one of them; instead, the new sub-systems maintained the claim to totality of the old, all-embracing system, and membership of one excluded membership of any other. In other words, the religious concept of the time extended to politics, and conversely the political concept ex-tended to the church and religion. The early modern state could thus not develop entirely independently of the confessional issue, but only on the basis of "a fundamental consensus on religion, the church and culture embracing the authority and its subjects alike."

   Consequently Catholicism in Portugal, Spain and after some hesi-tation also in France became as much a constituent part of national political identity as Protestantism in England, a country that today still sometimes promotes its image as a "Protestant nation." Significantly, confessional uncertainty was not settled in Sweden until national iden-tity seemed threatened by the succession to the throne of the Polish Sigismund Vasa. Only then, in 1593, did the Swedes accept the *Con-fessio Augustana*; in 1595 the Catholic national shrine of Vadstena was closed and Catholics were forbidden in the country.

   Recourse to confessionalism was almost more important to the ter-ritories of the Empire, for they had no national legitimate basis for polit-ical independence. The confession as a means of political demarcation is a particularly interesting phenomenon where even the dynastic factor was absent, in rival lines of the same house in Saxony and Hesse, and in the case of the Wittelsbachs of Bavaria and the Palatinate. Can it be historical coincidence that confessional conflicts regularly took place in these very areas, between different branches of the same dynasties? Even territories of the same confession used to discriminate between their national churches in terms of organization, worship and sometimes doctrine. Catholic princes had few such opportunities, but they tried to do the same by setting up "national bishoprics."

Early confessional demarcation in Switzerland, reaching a temporary conclusion as early as the Kappel Peace of 1531, is also extremely typical. Thereafter, confessionalization was almost established. Obviously early territorialization made early confessionalization possible, just as confessionalization, conversely, reinforced the drawing of territorial boundaries.

The exclusion of hostile influences was the negative basis of new political and religious identity. Besides the notorious restrictions on mobility and the marriages of subjects, fears of loyalty to foreign powers loomed large. John Locke still saw Catholicism as a danger because Catholics owed obedience to a foreign prince, the Pope. The concept of the papacy as a state among other states, encountered here as elsewhere, is extremely typical of the ideas of the time. In the Empire, the equivalent was the efforts of Brandenburg "territorialism" to keep the archbishop of Cologne, who bore responsibility for Cleves, away from the city at all costs.

However, political identity was not created merely negatively, by demarcation from opponents, but also positively through consistent internal confessionalization. The process by no means primarily involved using the faith as an instrument to political ends. Even the political religion of a Machiavelli or a Rousseau should not be confused with cynical modern strategies for manipulating voters. In the preface to the *Bavaria sancta* published for Duke Maximilian in 1615–28, the Jesuit Matthäus Rader writes:

> Cities, boroughs, markets, districts, villages, fields, woods, mountains, and valleys live and breathe the old Catholic religion in Bavaria . . . for the whole area is nothing but religion, and appears to be a single community church of the people.

"Tota regio nil nisi religio" is more than a wordplay on the phrase "cuius regio eius religio": it describes a programme largely realized by Maximilian's "ecclesiastical police government" and in the long term led to considerable internalization.

2.   "Your princely Grace shall be our Pope and Emperor," wrote the peasants of Balhorn to Philip of Hesse as early as 1523. The new sacralization of politics, going hand in hand with confessionalization, meant a functional increase for the emergent modern state power. Theoretically and practically, the church became an integral part of the state, and in practice that was the case for the Catholic almost as much as for the

evangelical church. Although the Duke of Bavaria, unlike the Elector of Saxony, had no say on doctrinal matters, the "Spiritual Council" in Munich remained structurally and functionally related to the Saxon Upper Consistory and the Palatinate Church Council. When Thomas Hobbes says that ecclesiastical eminences are part of the power of the state, and every prince is both ruler and teacher of his subjects, but the power of the Pope remains confined to his own principality, the church state, he is not aggressively anticipating a theory but giving a plain description of political facts. In line with these ideas, the electorate of Saxony ensured that the installation of evangelical bishops foreseen in the *Confessio Augustana* was not carried out.

In Catholic areas the church retained its autonomous institutions and elites. Conflicts between "church" and "state" therefore accompanied the expansion of state power. Significantly, this was true even of the ecclesiastical state, where the "state" hierarchy, in fact consisting of clerics, stood up to the "ecclesiastical" authority just as much as in other territories, even as the reforming principles on the autonomy of bishops proposed by the Council of Trent and energetically pursued elsewhere fell by the wayside. Moreover, Ferdinand of Wittelsbach, in his capacity as prince-bishop of Münster, carried the day for the ecclesiastical authority over the subordinate foundation belonging to the diocese of Osnabrück by virtue of his princely *cura religionis*. Only attempts to ensure control over local territorial churches by eradicating the imperial church and setting up local bishoprics were usually thwarted by Rome, even in Bavaria. The imperial church system with its ecclesiastical principalities proved an obstacle to the expansion of territorial states, as comparison with western and southern Europe shows, for the kings of France and Spain, like most of the Italian princes and republics, had ensured extensive control over their provincial churches and in some cases had even introduced a new organization, particularly in the Spanish Netherlands.

Princely rule of the church did not have to be as ecclesiastically dysfunctional as it proved in France. The "Catholic kings" introduced ecclesiastical reform to Spain just as the dukes did later in Bavaria. From the political viewpoint, there was no difference between this process and the introduction of the "Reformation" by evangelical princes, particularly as long as there was a general feeling that it was not a case of founding a new "church" but of purging the old one. However, even purely religious initiatives in policies of confessionalization had a political dimension. The Wettins, the ruling house of Saxony, used church visitations to make their political claims to power, and in Bavaria even

Catholic worship could be put to the service of the mediatization of the many monastic intermediate powers. . . .

To be safe from competition, the churches had to pay a high price to their princely rulers, not only through the loss of their autonomous rights but also literally, by transferring estates and revenues. It had been possible to alienate church property even before the Reformation. Extensive partial expropriations in the Catholic regions matched the many instances of Protestant secularization. The French crown had financed the Huguenot Wars by the sale of church property, and churchmen were exempt from taxation only in canonical theory. In practice the sovereign taxed the ecclesiastical state, and the duke of Bavaria taxed Bavarian clerics, just as the Spanish crown and the French crown did.

3.   State rule of the church in general and abolition of the privileges of the clergy in particular were important steps towards evening out the status of all subjects. In this the Reformation did give considerable stimulus to the growth of the modern state. However, Catholics could already be seen employing their own means of closing the gap, up to and including the prince-abbot of Fulda who established absolutism in his territory at the end of the seventeenth century, basing his actions on the authority ascribed to him by the rule of St Benedict.

It is in this context that the modernization of church administration by the Reformation should be seen. The Council of Trent did the same for the old church. The evangelical "superintendent" might appear to derive his title from a translation of the Catholic term "episkopos" (= overseer), but none the less, like the later French "Intendant," he was a modern official of the "commissar" type, and no longer held any benefice. According to Elton, the early stages of the English "Reformation" under Henry VIII could be seen simply as part of an administrative reform—so long as we do not apply modern ideas to the process. The Catholic church overcame the pre-modern society of privilege by concentrating the discipline of the faithful in the priest and the bishop, and filling any gaps with the new marriage law and the keeping of registers. All confessions made written administrative records and laid down an abundance of detailed regulations. Bureaucracy was on its way. The apparatus of church and state worked together to discipline their subjects. . . .

The early modern secular authorities could thus expect that it would pay off politically to regulate the religious and moral lives of their subjects in every intimate detail, controlling them through officials, informers and spies; it would pay off not just in terms of political stability, but through political gains. For while purely political expansion of the princely power must in the nature of things encounter vigorous resistance from those who formerly held power and their subjects, in some circumstances it was easier to make gains with the approval of their subjects, through ecclesiastical innovations given legitimate status by religion. The participation of the estates in the introduction of the Reformation into Sweden, England and German territories represented the most striking triumph of this strategy, which in a more subtle form also constituted the basis of the actual confessional disciplinary process. Resistance to measures which were justified by their importance to the eternal salvation of the subject concerned not only meant resistance to authority and the public order of things: the longer it went on the less it could be reconciled with a man's own conscience. Incidentally, this state of affairs provides an answer to the latent contradiction set out in Gerhard Oestreich's well-known study: how is absolute "social disciplining" possible when the "state" disposes of the requisite administrative apparatus only to an inadequate degree, and local autonomies make it harder for subjects to be directly influenced through central offices? It is still not clear how far Prussia was actually affected by the many measures its "soldier king" introduced. In my view the church filled the gap. It provided its own apparatus and made the consensus of those affected possible. In this way, then, "confessionalization" became the first phase of "social discipline."

As mentioned above, in assessing the confessional policies of the emergent modern state the modern historian must be careful to avoid the mistake of simply viewing the entire process as an instrument. As early as 1600 Traiano Boccalini wrote that the Reformation was nothing but a skilful device of German princes to assert their own power against the Emperor, and to this end they had allowed the ambitious professor Martin Luther to appeal to the lower instincts of the populace, thereafter using the movement thus created for their own purposes. However, this was certainly only a half-truth. Even a witness as unsuspecting of blind idealism as Thomas Hobbes bases princely rule of the church not on the sovereign's interests but on his conscience. More historically interesting is the *manner* in which the "Christian king" contrived to serve his own interest *while* following the dictates of his conscience.

For politics in the confessional period in general, and the sphere of action of politics in the Empire in particular, significant consequences do emerge from this appeal to the conscience of leading political figures, and it is to be taken seriously. Not only did confession become the nucleus of political crystallization, so that the confessional link was a constituent part of the estates of the Empire, not only did the formation of political fronts in the Empire almost automatically correspond to connections with the various European confessions, but most important of all, confessionalization drastically impaired the ability to make political compromises, and it could be won back only in the course of a painful learning process.

Benjamin J. Kaplan

Calvinists and Libertines: Confession and Community in Utrecht 1578–1620

. . . [T]he points at issue between Calvinists and Libertines were not relevant only to Reformed Protestantism. In the late sixteenth and early seventeenth centuries, not a single Christian denomination was exempt from a fundamental tension between two tendencies. The dominant tendency was a quest for organizational strength, definition, discipline, and order; the other wavered between a yearning for unmediated, personal contact with the divine and a common-sense equation of virtue with piety. As the most powerful representatives in the Netherlands of this second tendency, Libertine reformers spoke for a multitude of old-fashioned Catholics, Waterlander Mennonites, and Lutherans whose piety did not fall neatly into exclusive, confessional categories. If tolerance succeeded in the Netherlands, it was not because pragmatic concerns for political and social order (which were real enough) simply overrode all religious considerations. It was in part due to the strength of this a-confessional religious culture and the power and number of those people who subscribed to it. . . .

Dutch toleration, then, was neither wholly innovative nor wholly conservative, but a constructive mix of the two. Unlike modern religious

Benjamin J. Kaplan, "Unity in a Multiconfessional Society," *Calvinists and Libertines: Confessions and Community in Utrecht 1578–1620* (Oxford: Clarendon Press, 1995). Copyright © 1995 Oxford University Press. By permission of Oxford University Press.

toleration, it did not have the unqualified support of official ideology, nor did it express itself through the complete separation of Church and State. The Dutch were of a split mind. They clung to the medieval belief that religious unity was necessary for the health of State and society. For a brief period in the late 1570s, some among them, like William of Orange, hoped to relegate this belief to the past and give the different confessions equal freedom and status under law. Political pressure and war hysteria soon ended this bold experiment. Over the course of the sixteenth century, though, the Dutch came to adopt equally passionately a new principle, freedom of conscience. With massive popular support, this principle drew strength both from the spiritualist tradition of the Middle Ages and from the Protestant call for Christian freedom. Rejected by the most confessionally committed Calvinists, this principle triumphed nevertheless in Dutch society as a whole. Ironically, though, such Calvinists helped in their own way to foster religious pluralism. The peculiar heritage of Dutch Calvinism—what one historian has called its "sectarian tendencies"—made reformers positively reluctant to accept for their church the social role of an established church. The same people who were eager to make the Netherlands a godly, thoroughly Calvinist nation accepted with surprising ease the limits placed on their ability to promote their own faith at the expense of others'.

The Dutch did not find in the early modern period a way to resolve the tension between these two principles, religious unity and freedom of conscience. They did, though, discover an effective way to regulate it, through a new distinction between public and private, a distinction that many people now consider one of the hallmarks of modernity. Yet conservatism, too, contributed greatly to Dutch toleration. The "conservative" intermingling of civic and sacral, for example, worked both ways: if it made the Dutch reluctant officially to concede religious division, out of fear of civic dissension, it also meant that every unit of community whose members included people of different confessions fostered religious as well as civic ties. Forms of social organization that long predated the Reformation, like the neighbourhood, proved highly resistant to that divisive innovation, confessional division. Their form, moreover, did not lack substance. In such matters as charity, death, and morality, Netherlanders of different confessions shared a common mental ground, one that lacked sharp boundaries between the sacred and the profane. Those Netherlanders who rejected the spirit of Trent and Geneva cherished this a-confessional yet still Christian culture. They found in the common Christianity of Dutch society the most important justification for religious toleration. . . .

While Calvinists yearned for "holy uniformity," Libertines valued the autonomy that would enable churches to vary by province, city, and even parish in accord with the needs of local communities. What they wanted was not a national church, but a *Gemeindekirche*, a communal church. Calvinists and Libertines differed also in their views of clerical authority. Calvinists saw clerics as God's mouthpiece in religious affairs, vested with an authority not superior to magistrates' but co-ordinate with it. Libertines, by contrast, were deeply suspicious of all claims to religious authority; they aimed to make sure that Reformed ministers functioned as servants of the laity and not its masters. They failed to appreciate the fraternal quality of ecclesiastic discipline or the charitable, caring im- pulses that Calvinists saw behind its enforcement. Thirdly, Libertines resented the new moral rigour championed by Calvinists. The very label "Libertine" they deemed an insult—as if they were immoral! Whereas Calvinists sought to bring existing moral standards in line with a biblical norm, Libertines found a bona fide Christian morality already embedded in their civic culture. This was a morality set by custom and secular ordi- nance as well as church teaching; it is exemplified by the neighbourhood statutes that allowed gambling but limited the stakes. Claims that such traditional morality was no morality at all Libertines regarded as sheer sanctimony. Finally, Libertines clashed with Calvinists on the degree to which religious considerations should inform ostensibly secular affairs. Calvinist reformers found in Scripture a comprehensive plan for life on earth, a divine order to be realized within the political and social as well as religious sphere. Libertines found no such plan in Scripture, only some general guidelines and a Holy Spirit that they hoped might per- vade all their attitudes and actions. In their view, some matters, like the basic political structure of the Republic, simply lay outside the purview of the church. In all these respects, Calvinists and Libertines championed fundamentally different models of religious community.

Brandt's presentation of Calvinist–Libertine conflict as chiefly be- tween ministers and magistrates has had a limiting effect as well. It has encouraged a tendency to see the conflict as pitting "Church" against "State," the fallacy being that the latter was scarcely a unified entity at all in the Netherlands. It has thus made it more difficult to appreciate the dimension of the conflict pitting uniformity against particularism. Brandt's presentation also does scant justice to the social composition of the two parties. In Utrecht, the majority of Libertines were not patricians, never mind magistrates (though obviously those who were had the greatest clout). Utrecht's Jacobskerk drew at most a third of its following from the local élite, the rest most likely coming from some of the poorer segments of Utrecht burgherdom. The core of Utrecht's Calvinist congregation, by contrast, consisted of immigrants and of independent master craftsmen. No impoverished rabble, as sometimes portrayed, these were the proud guildsmen who had shared in local government until the coming of the Habsburgs. In the late sixteenth century they became the driving force behind the most confrontational policies of Utrecht's Calvinist congregation. To be sure, the firebrand minister Modetus egged them on, but he was extreme even among Calvinist ministers, and would have had little power without a lay following that snapped up his exhortations.

Of all the findings presented in this book, those on the social composition of the two parties are probably the least generalizable from Utrecht to other Dutch cities. Historians agree on the distinctiveness of Utrecht's social structure, with its sharp polarization between guildsmen and a gentry-dominated patriciate. The few facts known about Dordrecht suggest a picture quite different from Utrecht's: there Calvinist ministers counted many members of the patriciate among their most enthusiastic supporters; when the Libertine minister Herbert Herbertsz came into conflict with them, the deacons of the civic militia spoke out on his behalf. Similar anecdotal evidence suggests that in a majority of Dutch cities the social configuration of Calvinist–Libertine conflict was unlike that in either Utrecht or Dordrecht. Unfortunately, social analyses comparable to the one presented here have not yet been attempted for other Dutch cities. What one can say with certainty at this point is that "discipline and order" were not simply imposed "from above" on Calvinist congregations in the Netherlands, any more than they were on the separatist Puritan congregations of England. These qualities were opposed by Libertine ministers in whose interest their enforcement purportedly operated; they were rejected by a large number of regents; and they were supported by many ordinary lay people who were their chief objects.

The ambitious attempt made in the mid-1580s to impose Calvinist "discipline and order" on Utrecht society as a whole did not come solely from above, either. Guildsmen and immigrants did not merely support the rise of confessionalism within the Dutch Reformed Church; they wanted to see "confessionalization," with all the sweeping changes—social, political, and cultural, as well as religious—that such a policy entailed. For the sake of such changes they waged a fierce political war against Utrecht's regents. As long as Libertines dominated local government, though, Utrecht's Calvinists were stymied. Without Leicester, their policies would not have triumphed even briefly, and when he left, they collapsed. One thing the course of events in Utrecht reveals clearly is how crucial the support of a strong central authority was for confessionalization to succeed. Ultimately, the lack of such a strong central authority, of which the stadholders were a pale imitation, doomed to failure the ambitions of Calvinist reformers to make a "New Israel" of the Republic. This perspective suggests that Calvinists faced an impossible challenge from the beginning. Having fought against Spain and the Catholic church for their local "privileges and freedoms," most of the Dutch were not about to cede these cherished possessions to any new theocratic centralizers, even if the latter were Protestant.

Of course, things would have been different if a much larger number of the Dutch had shared the Calvinists' beliefs and world-view. Then no degree of particularism might have sufficed to thwart the process of confessionalization. In this sense, it was the religious and cultural sensibilities of the Dutch majority that proved decisive. Those whom the Calvinists called "Libertines" formed a vast group, the largest in Dutch society. Yet this group had little in common besides their rejection of ecclesiastic discipline and the confessional mode of piety that went with it. It is no wonder that more specific descriptions of it inevitably seem partial and inadequate. To the extent that one can generalize from the sermons of Hubert Duifhuis and the writings of other outspoken Libertines, it appears that spiritualism and a distinctly Protestant brand of anticlericalism formed the chief strains of Libertine piety, not only in Utrecht but throughout the Netherlands. At least some Libertines burned with a genuine ardour for Christian freedom and spiritual union with God. Just because their piety did not impel them to demand sweeping institutional changes does not make it shallow or insincere.

Humanism was a significant influence on Dutch Libertines as well, but not as significant as has often been claimed. Here, too, historians' misconceptions have a long genealogy. It was the Remonstrants themselves who, interpreting the Calvinist–Libertine conflict in the light of their own struggle, highlighted the importance of Erasmian humanism. In their search for an illustrious predecessor, the Remonstrants fixed quite naturally on the famed scholar from Rotterdam. Their identification with Erasmus, so strong and personal in the case of some, like Hugo Grotius, was an artefacted one; it gave their movement a respectable age and an-cestry, and a ready rebuttal to the Contra-Remonstrants' accusations of doctrinal innovation. Looking back, Remonstrants saw Erasmus as equally important for the Libertines as for themselves, and the competing doc-trines of predestination and free will as taking as central a place in the earlier conflict as it did in their own. This was not so, and to the extent that humanism did figure as a component of Libertine piety, it took the form chiefly of a commonsensical equation of piety with morality. Such an equation existed quite independently of the coherent educational and scholarly programme championed by Erasmus.

Both Calvinist and Libertine piety, though, had broad ramifications for life outside the strictly religious sphere. Calvinist piety expressed itself in a particular model of religious community and a desire to remake society as a whole in accordance with that model. Libertine piety did the same. Whereas the one, however, encouraged centralization and local di-visions, the other encouraged particularism and communalism. In these two respects the Libertine model of community proved far more compat-ible with the existing structure of Dutch society than the Calvinists'. In an age when Calvinist, Lutheran, and Tridentine reforms were disrupting and remoulding Europe's secular realm, Libertines fashioned a church whose shape largely mirrored the traditional shape of Dutch society, thus reinforcing it. In this sense, the Libertine programme of religious reform was a conservative one; its conservatism was a crucial part of its appeal. This is not to say that Libertine reform lacked all secular dynamism: in the early phases of the Dutch Revolt, the future shape of all institutions was uncertain, and local élites struggled not only to preserve but to in-crease their autonomy and power. It served their interests very well to have a Libertine church susceptible to their control. Libertinism thus reflected and encouraged the oligarchic tendency in Dutch society. Like-wise, it greatly accelerated the trend begun in the fifteenth century for the laity to assert control over the clergy. When faced with a choice, though, between Calvinist and Libertine reform programmes, Utrechters, at least, had no doubt which promised more radical change.

Eventually, Utrecht's Libertines had to admit the failure of their original programme. Not that Calvinists had defeated them in an open struggle for power: on the contrary, the seizure of power by Utrecht's Calvinist radicals in 1586 had ultimately had the opposite of the in-tended effect, fortifying Libertines' control of the city and making them doubly resistant to Calvinist demands. What actually occurred is both more puzzling and more revealing: by 1605 Utrecht's Libertines came themselves to acknowledge that their original desire, to turn the Dutch Reformed Church into a congeries of *Gemeindekirchen*, was impractical. Two considerations in particular dictated against its fulfilment. One was the determined, persistent opposition of Dutch Calvinists, whose confidence, clarity of purpose, and organizational genius gave them extraordinary power, even in times of suppression. Without their support any Reformed church was, in the long run, utterly untenable. The other consideration reflected a shift in the sensibilities of Libertines themselves. Spurred on by the outrageous behaviour of Johannes Bergerus, Utrecht's Libertines came to recognize that such a loose form of church governance offered no check against serious abuse; eventually they saw certain advantages to a moderately applied ecclesiastic discipline. As it did elsewhere in Europe, so in Utrecht time brought a natural progression in the course of Protestant reform: when the excesses and abuses of "Christian freedom" became painfully apparent, calls for such freedom gave way to institutional consolidation.

From the beginning, though, Libertine regents had a fallback strategy. If they could not shape the Dutch Reformed Church as they pleased, they could at least shape the relations between that church and the rest of Dutch society. In the 1570s Utrecht's regents experimented with different ways of giving multiple churches equal status and freedom. After these early experiments failed, they quickly settled upon another, highly successful approach: while acknowledging Calvinist religious predominance, they severely limited its scope. They made sure that the Reformed church could not coerce people who were not its members; drawing a distinction between public and private realms, they demarcated the latter as a space where all could worship as they pleased; finally, they protected forms of social organization, like Utrecht's neighbourhood and parish corporations, that brought together people of different beliefs. In these ways, Utrecht's regents, like those elsewhere in the Republic, engineered a system of religious toleration.

This does not mean that the regents bore sole responsibility for the system. On the contrary, the regents' policy of toleration would not have succeeded had it not had broad popular support among both the a-confessional and the members of non-Reformed churches. Unlike Poland, whose government also contrived a system of toleration, the Republic did not see interconfessional riots and attacks swelling up from below. To say that the regent "engineered" a system of toleration does not mean either that they constructed something wholly new. In fact, the system that so flourished in the Dutch Republic bears little resemblance to any modern one, and its intent was deeply conservative: to prevent the rise of confessionalism from disrupting the extant structure of Dutch society. In contemporary context, it was confessionalization and the intolerance that came with it that represented the cutting edge of innovation and "modernization." Outside the strictly religious realm, where it was truly original, toleration preserved the status quo. It is in this sense that the regents found it beneficial for "peace and order."

Thus the final result of the Dutch Reformation was that peculiar combination of severe Calvinism and religious freedom that characterized the Dutch Republic. Within the Dutch Reformed Church, confessionalism triumphed; in Dutch society as a whole, confessionalization failed. Indeed, one can speak of a trade-off between the two. The more confessional the church became, the less compatible it was with the broader social vision of Dutch regents. Ironically, had Dutch Calvinists been more willing to dilute their confessionalism, they might eventually have come closer to realizing their Dutch New Israel. For in so doing they would certainly have gained more support than they did, both from the regents and from the majority of ordinary lay folk.

In this respect, the case of Utrecht probably represents an extreme. Old social tensions made relations between Calvinists and Libertines particularly bitter in Utrecht, and as a result both parties showed a greater intransigence there than they did elsewhere. In Zeeland, for example, local government had more influence over Calvinist congregations than did Utrecht's and were more supportive of them. Haarlem's consistory likewise made major tactical concessions: until 1618, it left magistrates tacitly outside the purview of its discipline and, on occasion, fought against the regional classis for local autonomy. Utrecht's Calvinists refused to make such concessions. In other respects, though, they were no more intransigent than their colleagues elsewhere. Throughout the Netherlands, the Dutch Reformed Church attacked venerable civic customs, restricted access to communion, sought uniformity of worship, and refused to bend to the needs of the "weak in faith." As a result, Calvinist–Libertine conflict was one of the most pervasive and characteristic phenomena of the Dutch Reformation. Significant for the stamp it gave to religious life in the Republic, such conflict also serves as a highly dramatic example of the resistance provoked in many parts of Europe by the rise of confessionalism.

James R. Farr

Confessionalization and Social Discipline in France, 1530–1685

The historiography of religious conflict and state-building in France has rarely invoked the concept of "confessionalization," somewhat more frequently that of "social discipline." A review of some recent literature on French religious history between 1530 and 1685 reveals, however, that both concepts inform those works, sometimes tacitly, sometimes explicitly. When brought together, furthermore, they help us to understand better both the singularity of the French experience and its place in broader, shared historical developments of European scope. . . .

When [Heinz] Schilling and [Wolfgang] Reinhard first formulated the theory of confessionalization, France did not seem to fit it particularly well. After all, when confessionalization was in full swing (1560–1650), according to the model, France was first torn by a series of religious civil wars (1562–1598) and then of political necessity officially tolerating two faiths within its borders (1598–1685). Ironically, the state was anything but the promoter of confessional unity among its subjects during the time of confessionalization, and by the time the French crown began to serve this role, the age of confessionalization was supposedly over. When the chronological lens is widened, however, France comes more sharply into focus. Some historians have pushed the starting point back to the 1530s, while others take it beyond 1650.

Marc Venard clearly believes that the confessionalization thesis has applicability to France. By 1530, doctrinal schism had been launched in France, and for thirty years thereafter the repression of heresy and the isolation and dispersal of Calvinists was the order of the day. 1560 to 1600, in contrast, was marked by the formation of confessional identity and the organization of Calvinist churches in the crucible of religious conflict.

James R. Farr, "Confessionalization and Social Discipline in France, 1530–1685." *Archiv für Reformationsgeschichte* 94 (2003): 276–293. Copyright © 2003. Reprinted with permission of James R. Farr.

Indeed, in 1559 at a clandestine synod in Paris, the Calvinists hammered out the French Confession of Faith (one of many confessions or "disciplines" drawn up and sworn to by Protestants across Europe in the sixteenth century). Consistories charged with enforcing moral discipline at the local level among the faithful and provincial and national synods gathering regularly to define and refine orthodoxy, the main guardians of the incipient confession, assured that Calvinism would survive these "times of troubles," as the French of the age called them. The first forty years of the next century feature the "Catholic Reconquest," the apogee of aggressive catholicity spearheaded by devout lay men and women. Inspired by the spiritual message of François De Sales [—a bishop of the early seventeenth century who urged believers to pursue spiritual perfection and made aggressive efforts to convert Calvinists to Catholicism—] or the organizational and educational efforts of the Jesuits, new sermons, catechisms, more frequent confessions, examinations and directors of conscience, spectacular ceremonies—sometimes rolled together in interior missions to the rural hinterlands of France—became the stuff of a revitalized and anti-Protestant catholicity.

Anti-Protestantism was nothing new to Catholic French men and women, and if we view the sixteenth and seventeenth centuries as a whole, we can see it as a consistent motif, if not always in state policy then certainly in the attitudes of millions of French people. Indeed, even in state policy the "toleration" of the Calvinist faith in the kingdom of France was born of the political necessity of pacification, and when no longer deemed necessary, it was abolished. In fact, from 1530 to 1560, and then again from 1656 to 1685, the agents of the state (if not always the king himself) actively and sometimes aggressively sought the extirpation of Calvinism.

William Monter is inclined to push the dates of confessionalization back as well. His prime subjects are the judges of the parlements of the realm rather than its king, and his focus is on heresy prosecution in these courts before the outbreak of the Wars of Religion in 1562. Monter's account is consciously situated in the historiography of confessionalization, and he shows through painstaking research in trial records of heresy cases heard by Parlements throughout the realm how the edges between the confessions hardened and confessional identity coalesced in the cauldron of heated persecution.

Interestingly, it was the Catholic side that came together first, beginning in 1540 with the Edict of Fontainebleau. This royal decree by Francis I, signaling a full-blown campaign against heresy, transferred jurisdiction over heresy cases from ecclesiastical courts to the Parlements. This launched "the Great Heresy Hunt," which raged for nearly a decade. The result was a surge in heresy trials on the dockets of Parlements — in 1544 at the Parlement of Paris mounting to one in four of all criminal cases heard!

By the end of the decade, however, it was becoming apparent that the judicial system — in Monter's estimation "the best-run . . . court system in Europe" — was buckling under the increased caseload and was facing virtual breakdown. In 1549 Henry II transferred heresy cases back to the ecclesiastical courts, and then in 1551 created the secular presidial courts to share this jurisdiction with them. Ironically, . . . the beginning of Henry II's reign is not the high point of French heresy prosecution as once believed, but rather the beginning of a steep decline. True, in 1551 Henry issued the Edict of Chateaubriand, the most comprehensive body of anti-heresy legislation to date, but, as Monter discovered by counting individual cases, it had almost no effect on the number of trials heard or executions carried out. In fact, none of the royal anti-heresy decrees of that presumed bloodthirsty decade (the Edict of Compiègne in 1557 or the Edict of Ecouen in 1559) had much effect on arresting the trend of diminishing prosecution.

That this was a time when French Protestant confessionalization was taking firm hold is no accident. Huguenot confessionalization, in contrast to the German model, may have taken place "in defiance of state authority rather than under its patronage," but it was greatly enabled by a court system that simply was no longer willing to expend resources it did not have on a heresy it could no longer contain. Monter concludes that political (and fiscal) necessity drove the engine of toleration. The Edicts of Amboise and Romorantin (March and May 1560) capped this development by decriminalizing "the newly confessionalized Reformed churches of France."

As Monter emphasizes, the judicial elite of France was instrumental in confessionalization taking hold on both sides of the religious divide. Many parlementaires, and not just the ultra-Catholic ones, were committed to the religious unity of Gallican Catholicism and believed that a sacralization of society was an integral part of the new moral vision of a recorded world that must emerge from the one shattered by the Wars of Religion. This vision was authoritarian: many a magistrate believed that the path to the new moral order must follow the road of self-discipline and social control (piety wed to civility). . . .

As early as 1563, a judge at a provincial parlement had challenged the royal edict of 1563, which officially tolerated Protestantism in the realm by boldly asserting that good polity must have only one law, one king, and one faith, and plurality in any of these destroys the others. This position . . . was embraced by the ultra-Catholic Holy League formed in 1585. As Ann Ramsey writes, this League, which lasted until 1594, was populated by clerics as well as "zealous laypeople," many of them judges in royal courts. These militants, she argues, could never accept toleration, for that violated the core of their faith: the belief that the sacred inhered in this world, and specifically in the civic community. Because the sacred was known to be unified and inviolable, the penetration of a foreign body (heresy) into the sacral commune would imperil the salvation of all. . . . The problem with Protestantism for Leaguers, asserts Ramsey, was its belief in religious transcendence. The sacred here no longer inheres in the world (or in the Eucharist), but "is displaced to the heavens and shorn of human kinship." . . .

To many Frenchmen . . . the Catholic Reformation was a religious process with profound political and social stakes, and its moralistic writings cut a broad swath through the literature of early modern France. In these works the lexicon of discipline, propriety, and hierarchy found prominent expression, . . . concepts [which] suggests a concern for boundary marking and boundary transgression. The fashioning of an orderly system by ritualized relations of separation that purify and punish are suggestive because they seem to apply directly to the process of confessionalization being examined here. . . .

[T]he authoritarian moral vision of the Catholic Reform contained two interrelated premises: an internal discipline of the individual and an external control of social behavior. The new ideas on civility as well as the teachings of the Catholic Reformation converged to reinforce these premises, which in turn informed assumptions about proper thought, belief, and behavior. François De Sales and Pierre de Bérulle [, a cardinal who energized the clergy and promoted missionary work in France,] were enormously influential in the spiritual surge of the early seventeenth century, the former emphasizing systematic interior monitoring by the individual and the latter a program of hierarchical reformism aimed at the world. Where De Sales guided his followers down a path on which self-discipline directed the soul to the love of God and through that to the purified (and asexual) love of fellow man and woman, Bérullian hierarchical reformism was explicitly suited for the social control that was so important to the Gallican Church and the early modern French state. Hierarchical reformism, like the secular political and social hierarchies of the day, had a prescribed place for women, which was beneath and obedient to men. Salesian spirituality (and De Sales himself), however, left the door open for female initiative in the spiritual life, the subject of Elizabeth Rapley's path-breaking book. In De Sales' *Introduction to the Devout Life* (1608), the "Doctor of Love" had seemingly endorsed hierarchy when he wrote that "it was incumbent on every Christian to accept his allotted state," but he added that every rank "possessed its own particular virtues, the practice of which could lead to holiness." De Sales actively cultivated a large female audience; many women were fired with spiritual passion by his teachings and quickly "invad[ed] not just the Church's prayer life, but also its active life." In tune with the self-disciplinary drift of their age, these female counterparts to the *dévots* confessed frequently, read and meditated upon devotional works as they examined their consciences, and developed the practice of methodical prayer. But these women also rapidly organized themselves into uncloistered religious orders (the Ursulines and the Filles de La Charité led the way) bent on educating (mostly girls) through catechism and dispensing charity to the poor and sick. As catechizers, "they became full participants in the war of words that was raging against the reformed religion." The first uncloistered wave of feminine spiritual energy, however, was neither expected nor wanted by the institutional church. The response to it was increased episcopal (and male) surveillance and ultimately, by the mid-seventeenth century, clausura.

The wave of religious enthusiasm that swept across the elite population of France in the early seventeenth century can be seen as part of a century-long process of catholicization dating to at least 1530 which sought the extirpation of French Protestantism. After the Edict of Nantes, many fervent Catholics felt that a hot war had simply been replaced with a cold one. Tolerance in the modern sense was foreign to both faiths; and both sought to achieve their ultimate ambition, the triumph of the "true religion," theirs. Given that in 1600 only about 6 per cent of the population of France considered themselves Protestants, they faced a distinctly uphill battle. Catholics, for their part, may have been legally obliged to suffer what they disparagingly called the *réligion prétendue reformée* in their midst, but they mounted catholicizing efforts nonetheless, ranging from the formation of secret devout societies like the Compagnie du Saint-Sacrement to female organizations bent on educating

the faithful in the true religion to missionary activity in the rural hinterlands of France. . . .

Much of the scholarship on early modern French religious history
under review here sees the era from the appearance of Protestantism in
the late 1520s to the Revocation of the Edict of Nantes in 1685 as unified
by a logic of catholicization. The decriminalization of Protestantism in
the 1560s and the "toleration" legalized by the Edict of Nantes, in this
perspective, were interruptions demanded by political necessity rather
than harbingers of modern notions of toleration. Elizabeth Labrousse
reminds us that the Edict of Nantes not only legitimized a second faith
in France, but just as importantly, restored Catholicism everywhere in
the kingdom. It even returned property to the church that had been
confiscated by the Protestants during the Wars of Religion. For the first
sixty years that the Edict of Nantes was on the books, it is true, the state
was not the primary agent of catholicization. During Louis XIV's reign
that changed. In 1656, in patent violation of the Edict, Mazarin suppressed the national synods of the Huguenots, the key in the vault of
reformed organization, delivering a crippling blow to its ability to coor-
dinate itself nationally. In 1662 the king sent forth royal commissioners
into the provinces to verify that Protestant churches were operating in
strict accord with the Edict of Nantes. Those found in violation were
closed down. Then, as parlementaires began increasingly to describe
Huguenots as "schismatics," in 1665 Louis XIV issued a declaration that
forbade conversion to Protestantism by any Catholic clergy, a prohibition
that was extended to all French men and women in 1680. Between 1669
and 1679 the Chambres de l'édit, the judicial courts created by the Edict
to adjudicate disputes between Huguenots and Catholics, were dissolved.
By the 1680s the objective of royal policy clearly was the elimination of
Protestantism in France. In 1680 intermarriage between faiths was forbidden. In August 1684 all property of Calvinist consistories was transferred
to Catholic hospitals, and two weeks later Protestants were forbidden to
give charitable assistance to any poor or sick fellow Huguenots. The coup
de grâce of the long process of catholicization came on 17 October 1685,
when the Edict of Fontainebleau revoked the Edict of Nantes. Far from
being an impetuous or sudden action by the king, Labrousse suggests, it
was the capstone of a cultural movement of broader scope than religion,
that of "normalization" and "conformism" that had been gathering
steam for nearly 200 years. As Labrousse concludes, the religiosity of the
elites was the vehicle for accomplishing a "civilizing mission" by which

all French men and women would embrace the values of decorum, discipline, docility, and deference.

Labrousse is certainly not alone in embracing a disciplinary model of catholicization, and most historians agree that it is accurate, as far as it goes. However, it offers only one perspective on a story that recent research is showing to be much more complex. One historical topic that lays bare such complexity and takes the confessionalization thesis head on is mixed confessionalism. Gregory Hanlon asks two simple but penetrating questions. Was religious tolerance widespread in France during the period during which the Edict of Nantes was on the books? And why was the Protestant minority absorbed despite the absence in many locales of overt persecution? Behind these questions lurks an important historiographical observation: the confessionalization debate has focused scholarly attention on interconfessional *conflict* rather than harmony, and thus has displaced from historical scrutiny instances of peaceful coexistence between Protestants and Catholics. Hanlon makes the many daily interactions between Protestants and Catholics the subject of his book. Along the way he finds that we would do well to place religiosity on a spectrum, with zealous cells of the rival faiths pushing for confessionalization at each end. In between, however, was a zone of confessional ambiguity and indifference. Intolerance characterized the zealous, who found indifference unacceptable, but for the rest "tolerance was the outgrowth of a piety in which few people were highly sensitive to theological distinctions or else were reluctant to emphasize their importance."

An important part of Hanlon's case rests on the evidence that local elites were literally wedded to interconfessional cooperation because many families were begun in mixed marriages. Between 1598 and 1700 in Layrac, for example, Hanlon finds 279 mixed marriages. Coupled with other evidence of mixed confessionalism, or at least indifference (Protestants witnessed Catholic marriages and vice versa, and Catholic and Protestant master artisans seemed unconcerned about whether their apprentices confessed), Hanlon must account for the disappearance of Protestantism by 1700. He agrees with Bossy and Labrousse that confessionalization merged with the civilizing process, as order, hierarchy, social conformity, and good manners became part of Christian duty. Moreover, he argues that local Protestant notables increasingly identified with the "royal establishment," because its values—hierarchy, paternalism, propriety—squared with theirs and served their social and familial interest. When the Catholic religion internalized these values as well, a return to that faith was made all the more easy. Moreover, Hanlon points out, state-sponsored confessionalization under Louis XIV stripped the Protestant churches of their institutional structure. In the confessionalizing cold war between the zealous of the two faiths, now "rudderless churches without ministers or bibles" decidedly tipped the balance toward the Catholics. All of this played out demographically, for Protestants by century's end had lost the capacity "to reproduce themselves around a set of beliefs and practices." There simply were not enough of them to propagate the faith.

Few historians in the last decade or so have scrutinized the Huguenot communities in France as thoroughly as Philip Benedict. Steadfast in a methodological commitment to quantification and demography, Benedict demonstrates that the number of Protestants in France declined steadily during the seventeenth century, so that by the time of the revocation in 1685 there were 25 per cent fewer than there had been in 1600. Despite this drop-off, however, Benedict sees evidence for the continuation of a "well-structured community" held together by a widespread "commitment to Protestant tenets." In his view, Protestantism was still cohesive and coherent enough during the century of aggressive catholicization to constitute a viable "confession." This is far from the rudderless ship that drifted toward extinction as mixed confessionalism blurred the distinctions between Protestants and Catholics. Benedict asserts that for all "the evidence of frequent, cordial interaction between members of the two faiths," we must recognize "that a continuing sense of difference set them apart—differences that could, in certain situations, spark violence or panic."

Benedict is troubled by historians who seem "content to underscore the fact of Catholic-Protestant cooperation, rather than trying to measure its precise frequency." His own recent research in Montpellier shows that "a powerful cultural dynamic . . . worked to heighten awareness of confessional differences." His findings are as yet admittedly provisional, but he notes trends across the seventeenth century toward reduced incidence of mixed marriages, declining occurrences of godparents of one faith standing at the baptismal font for a child of parents of the other, and an increased tendency of members of one faith to do business with notaries of the same faith. This leads him to conclude that the two confessions seem to have become *more* distinct from one another rather than less—largely due to pronounced confessional endogamy, communities as self-enclosed as they had been at the beginning of the century. Thus, when the Edict of Nantes was revoked in 1685, Huguenots preferred to emigrate, or if among the Nouveaux Catholiques who had been forced to abjure their former faith, to abstain from worship and gather clandestinely in the "desert." . . .

Recent scholarship concurs on the fact that catholicization was royal policy from the 1530s on and that even during the Wars of Religion, as well as after the Edict of Nantes became law, royal policy strove to unite the kingdom under one faith, the Catholic one. Toleration was only a temporary necessity dictated by the desire for pacification. As Benedict writes, "Successive rulers whittled away at the various rights and privileges granted the Reformed, until at last they were entirely revoked." Such a policy would seem to encourage violence and persecution, and at times it did, but we must still come to grips with findings like Hanlon's of peaceful religious co-existence. Keith Luria explores peaceful relations between members of the two faiths, focusing on evidence of cemetery sharing and even ceremonial similarities. Local funeral customs, for example, merged Protestant and Catholic practices and, in any case, were more concerned to announce social status than strict theological adherence. This seems to challenge Benedict's argument that the two faiths were increasingly separated and distinct. So what are we to make of these paradoxical findings that point compellingly to simultaneous religious discrimination *and* coexistence?

Luria offers a useful model that may help guide future research. He suggests that there were three types of confessional boundaries that could even overlap or exist simultaneously. The first type blurred religious distinctions as people differentiated themselves by other social or cultural markers like rank, privilege, or occupation. The second type acknowledged confessional difference but, as reflected in the Edict of Nantes, protected by law the right to difference "without necessarily implying rejection or exclusion." Here the state's role was essential, although not as an agent of confessionalization. Rather, it promoted a carefully constructed coexistence that served the aims of state-builders just as much as confessionalization would under Louis XIV. The Edict of Nantes pacified the kingdom. It also made the monarch the arbiter of confessional disputes and hence the guarantor of religious peace and civil order. The third type of confessional boundaries, more well-known historiographically by the name confessionalization, gathered steam in the seventeenth century and culminated in the revocation of the Edict of Nantes and the persecution of Protestants that would follow. . . .

When Schilling and Reinhard advanced and refined their confessionalization thesis over a decade ago, most French historians initially assumed that it had little applicability to religious history in France. . . . Research on French religious history undertaken in the last ten years or so, however, prompts us to reconsider the applicability of the thesis to France and to refine the thesis itself. First, the Huguenot experience in France forces us to explain how confessional organization and confessional identity can emerge and develop in the absence, and even when facing the hostility, of the state or its agents. Indeed, one could frame the *dévot* movement in much the same way, for the drive for a unified Catholic France passed to devout lay men and women—often independent of the church and state—in the early seventeenth century, precisely when the state was pursuing a policy of toleration of a second, minority faith. Second, if we broaden our focus chronologically from the dates announced by the confessionalization thesis (1560–1650) to dates better adapted to French history (1530–1685), then we can see that there *was* a relatively consistent state policy of catholicization. The continued institutionalized existence of two formal faiths in the kingdom during the Wars of Religion and then under the Edict of Nantes was a result of practical and political necessity more than of any modern spirit of toleration. When the state was strong enough to resume pursuing its policy of religious unity, it did so, culminating in the revocation of the Edict of Nantes.

The experience of France allows the confessionalization model to be modified in substantive ways as well. . . . John Bossy has brilliantly applied insights . . . to religious history. Whatever we may think of Bossy's construct of "traditional Christianity," by focusing on discipline, civility, and the maintenance of peace, he has brought together powerful currents that profoundly shaped not just religion but the entire culture. Indeed, he shows how social values, political power, and religious ideas and practices overlapped and intertwined. The meaning and practice of discipline and civility were fundamentally transformed at a time when the "holy"— primarily in the garb of sacred peace mediated by royal justice—was migrating from the church to the state. Nowhere does Bossy invoke the term "confessionalization," but his vision broadly coincides with that of Schilling, Reinhard, and the others who fashioned the model based on primarily German developments. With the guidance of Bossy and the numerous works on French religious history that have appeared in the last ten years or so, we can now see better how France fits into a European movement that, as all agree, was fundamentally transformative.

Marc R. Forster

With and Without Confessionalization: Varieties of Early Modern German Catholicism

... The dominant "confessionalization" thesis asserts that confessionalism originated in the policies of church officials and state bureaucrats intent on imposing order, discipline, and religious uniformity on the population from above. This thesis provides at best an explanation of the creation of Catholic unity and identity in several of the larger Catholic principalities of the Empire, particularly Bavaria. It is less successful in explaining the nature and development of Catholic culture in the majority of Catholic territories where states were weak. Furthermore, even if we emphasize the role of the state, confessionalization does not account for the important creative role of the population in Catholicism. Catholic *confessionalism*, that is a broad popular loyalty to and identification with Catholicism, did not arise exclusively, or even primarily, from a policy of *confessionalization* pursued by government officials. Instead, its origins were diverse, as was its character. . . .

I will use the term confessionalism in a broader way. Confessionalism describes the distinct confessional cultures which developed after the Protestant Reformation. Competing religious theologies and institutions, different education systems, and diverging ties to the rest of Europe led to the creation of three cultural spheres (Catholic, Lutheran, Reformed), a process that was well under way by 1600, and clearly apparent by the late seventeenth century. Confessionalism further designates the strong sense of group identity that was so apparent to foreign visitors to Germany, which always included the identification of enemies and excluded groups. For the common people, especially in Catholic Germany, confessionalism also meant an active popular piety and a strong *Kirchlichkeit*,

Marc R. Forster, "With and Without Confessionalization: Varieties of Early Modern German Catholicism," *Journal of Early Modern History* 1 (1998): 315–343. Copyright © 1998 by BRILL. Reprinted with permission.

or churchliness. *Kirchlichkeit* meant, of course, loyalty to the Roman Catholic Church and active participation in its rites. Recent research has shown that the wider population did not internalize a sense of confessional identity until after the Thirty Years' War, and in many places not until after 1700. . . .

The many fine regional studies produced in recent years lead to several conclusions about Catholic Germany. The first is that all of Catholic Germany was affected by Tridentine reforms. But institutions like cathedral chapters and monasteries, fearing episcopal centralization and an increase in papal power, frequently hindered Tridentine reform. Furthermore, Catholic reform in Germany stalled and then collapsed during the Thirty Years' War; in short, Tridentine reform was just an episode in the history of German Catholicism and cannot serve as an organizing category for the whole early modern period.

Historians of confessionalization, like those of church reform, tend to overemphasize the uniformity of developments in Catholic Germany. The confessionalization thesis emphasizes the close cooperation between church and state, yet within Catholic Germany one finds a whole spectrum of church/state relations. If Bavaria provides a classic example of cooperation between secular and ecclesiastical officials in the imposition of religious uniformity, vast regions (the Southwest, the Rhineland, Catholic Switzerland) developed confessionalism in the absence of active states. Confessionalization as state policy did play a role in Catholic Germany, but it is not the whole story.

Widespread Catholic confessionalism developed after the Thirty Years' War. Traditional Catholicism, Tridentine reform, and confessionalization all contributed to the "baroque Catholicism" of this period, but Catholic culture continued to evolve. Many central aspects of German Catholicism developed out of the interplay between elite initiatives and popular religion. Studies of pilgrimages, the cult of saints, and eucharistic piety show not only how these traditional Catholic practices changed their character during the early modern period, but also how vital a role the population played in their development. These popular roots of Catholic confessionalism also contributed to its diversity. Religious practice was central to popular Catholicism, and differences in practice helped to create regional varieties of German Catholicism. . . .

What then did German Catholics have in common by the eighteenth century? Most obviously, they shared a sense of confessional identity and a strong loyalty to the Catholic Church. Because there were a number of paths to confessional identity and *Kirchlichkeit*, there were several varieties of Catholicism in early modern Germany. Catholicism, despite its institutional identity, was no more uniform than Protestantism in this period.

I. The Counter-Reformation Episode, 1570–1620

. . . Tridentine reform affected all of Catholic Germany to some extent and some German bishops embraced it wholeheartedly. On the other hand, church reform cannot be credited alone, or even primarily, with the creation of Catholic confessionalism. Indeed, I would argue that Tridentine reform constituted only one episode in the history of early modern Catholicism, and does not encompass developments throughout the 300 years from 1500 to 1800. . . .

Research on conditions within Catholic regions in the mid-sixteenth century shows, however, that the rural population had not abandoned Catholic practice. Peasants in the bishopric of Speyer protested the poor training of their priests and resented paying tithes for the upkeep of monasteries and collegiate chapters, but they faithfully attended church and partook of the sacraments. Concubinage, which was widespread in western and southern Germany, caught the attention of Catholic reformers and Protestant polemicists, but did not provoke widespread popular protest. In general, by the 1560s the Catholic Church had experienced a weakening of church structures, which was especially pronounced in those regions where the dominant states had gone over to Protestantism, but there was no collapse of popular Catholicism.

The Council of Trent did reinvigorate the Catholic Church. Bishops and church officials were well aware of the provisions of the Council. Tridentine decrees were published and disseminated in various forms throughout Germany, although not before the 1590s in many places. Most German bishops paid at least lip service to the reform program of the Council and attempted to institute the reform measures. The Tridentine program certainly appealed to activist bishops, for it greatly strengthened episcopal authority, but it had an impact at all levels of the church. Self-consciously Tridentine reformers sometimes even took control of smaller ecclesiastical institutions. . . .

Most bishops [, however,] had neither the resources nor the inclination to embark on a vigorous reform. The Jesuits provided the first unambiguous support for reform measures. Although the early Jesuits focused their efforts on pastoral work, the order became active in church reform by the 1560s. This was particularly the case in Germany, which attracted the interest of Ignatius quite early. Jesuit activities in Germany centered on preaching and teaching, with the interrelated goals of reinvigorating Catholic religious life, converting Protestants, and reforming the church. . . .

Although known best for their confrontations with Protestants, the Jesuits were most successful as teachers. As they did throughout Catholic Europe, they administered many secondary schools in German cities, and gradually colonized the most important Catholic universities as well. Jesuit *Gymnasien* were such a great success that they even attracted Protestant students in cities like Speyer. . . .

Yet one should not overestimate the influence of the Jesuits . . . and the papacy. The Jesuits could not be everywhere. Their presence outside the larger cities was limited, and there were large areas of Catholic Germany where the black-robed fathers only appeared sporadically. . . . Papal activity and interest in Germany was very sporadic, as was the ability of nuncios to influence church reform. . . .

[P]olitical and institutional factors caused the church hierarchy to refuse to support an ambitious reform program. German bishops, abbots, and abbesses did not want to lose their secular authority or their political role within the Empire, roles considered suspect by Trent. Furthermore, the pastoral focus of Tridentine reform threatened to destroy the traditional role of the church as a career for younger sons of the nobility. . . . These institutional restraints did not necessarily prevent reform; more often they brought a measure of moderation and a sense of practical limitations to the endeavors of reformers. . . .

Tridentine reform did bring about several important changes in German Catholicism. The most obvious was the enforcement of clerical celibacy. Open concubinage disappeared in Catholic cities in the late sixteenth century and in the countryside by the first decades of the seventeenth century. Church authorities not only did not tolerate concubinage, but moved aggressively to punish transgressors. Furthermore, there is some evidence that the people were also converted to clerical celibacy and gradually came to see it as a distinguishing mark of the Catholic clergy. Most other successful reforms also involved the clergy. Educational standards for priests did rise, at least in most regions, and the number of Catholic *Gymnasien* and universities grew. By 1620, churchmen were beginning to accept the centrality of pastoral work, although there was no real shift of resources from monasteries and ecclesiastical chapters to the parishes before the late eighteenth century. Other aims of Tridentine reform, especially the programs to "sanitize" and regulate popular religion had barely gotten off the ground before the Thirty Years' War. It is important to credit the reformers for what they did do, rather than criticize them for failing to realize a very ambitious program, but one also has to avoid overemphasizing the impact of Tridentine reform on both the Catholic clergy and the lay population.

II. Confessionalization

Tridentine reform in Germany, as elsewhere in Europe, was rarely a purely church affair. Indeed, the most effective efforts to reform the church occurred where Catholic reformers and state officials worked closely together. The cooperation of church and state in several important states has led German historians to develop the confessionalization thesis. Wolfgang Reinhard and Heinz Schilling present confessionalization as an "ideal-type" of political, social, and religious development in both Protestant and Catholic regions in the period 1550–1650. . . .

Bavaria provides an example of confessionalization that comes close to the ideal described by Reinhard. Already in the 1550s, Bavarian officials began to enforce religious conformity, especially by moving against Protestant (and Protestant-leaning) nobles and burghers. . . .

Confessionalization reached its peak in the 1620s and 1630s, as Bavaria led the Catholic League to military victories over the Protestants. The successful conversion of the Upper Palatinate (*Oberpfalz*) to Catholicism, achieved with a generous application of military force, seemed to epitomize the close cooperation of a resurgent Catholic Church and the confessionalized state. Yet the destruction of the later years of the Thirty Years' War undermined all state activities, including religious reform. In the late seventeenth century, Bavarian officials continued to supervise religious life, but now the lay population and the orders took the religious initiative. The Jesuits, Capuchins, and Franciscans led what has been called "a second wave of Catholic reform," focusing their efforts on encouraging popular piety. Perhaps because Bavarian rulers were less concerned than they had been in the immediate aftermath of the Protestant Reformation with the loyalty of the population to Catholicism, there was more room for popular initiatives in the baroque church. Although Bavaria remained a *Konfessionsstaat*, confessionalization, in the sense of close church-state cooperation in the policing of religious behavior, ended after 1650.

Confessionalization could and did occur outside the large secular principalities of the Empire. The prince-bishopric of Würzburg is the classic example of confessionalization in an ecclesiastical territory. . . . The unity of church and state in the prince-bishoprics of the Empire made such an aggressive policy possible [but] . . . confessionalization in the ecclesiastical territories depended on the character, abilities, and longevity of individual bishops. . . .

Confessionalization and Tridentine reform usefully designate a cluster of policies, most of which were implemented in Catholic Germany in the period 1570–1620. The two processes proceeded at different paces and with varied emphases in the diverse regions of Catholic Germany. Despite the Tridentine goal of centralizing church administration and bringing more uniformity to religious practice, reforms may have actually increased the diversity of German Catholicism. By increasing the role of the state in Catholic life and creating (in some places) "confessional states," confessionalization also added to the variety of forms of Catholicism.

There is no question that confessionalization (Catholic and Protestant) contributed directly to the political and constitutional conflicts that led to the Thirty Years' War. Catholic reform and especially the educational endeavors of the Jesuits also played a major role in the creation of distinct Catholic and Protestant spheres within German elite culture. Yet before 1620 or even before 1650, the Catholic lay population did not share the confessional identity of the clergy and the educated. . . .

III. Catholic Confessionalism, 1650–1750

Although imperial (and European) politics no longer revolved around religion in the century after the Thirty Years' War, this period was truly the heyday of confessionalism. Confessional divisions hardened in German cities and towns, even where Protestants and Catholics had lived together peacefully for a century or more. Tensions also rose in those regions where Catholic peasants came into direct contact with Protestant neighbors. In all Catholic regions the population participated in church rites, especially pilgrimages, processions, and the cult of the Virgin Mary. This ongoing outburst of popular piety was accompanied by a growing popular loyalty to and dependence on the clergy (a kind of clericalism) and a commitment to the church more generally.

Clericalism and *Kirchlichkeit* did not lead to unquestioned obedience to the church or its representatives. In fact, another central aspect of Catholic confessionalism in the baroque era was its popular character.

Religious change, which between 1580 and 1650 had mostly originated with the Catholic elite, now came as often as not from the wider population. Peasants founded and patronized new shrines, processions, and pilgrimages. Rural communes and town councils administered parish property, supervised the clergy, and promoted new devotions. The active role of the population, of local officials, and of parish priests, who played a constant intermediary role in the villages and towns, tended to bring further variety and diversity to German Catholicism. . . .

The increasingly central role of the parish clergy in popular Catholicism was, at least in part, one of the successes of church reform. Catholics considered priests essential, of course, for the sacraments, especially baptism, the mass, and death-bed confession. Peasants and townspeople also treated parish priests as servants of the community, an attitude that did not change substantially throughout the early modern period. As the number of pilgrimages and processions grew, village communities found it necessary to pressure parish priests to participate, or to spend money to hire a priest for the purpose. A number of new devotions, particularly the rosary, required clerical participation as well.

Clericalism developed in part because the parish clergy consciously accepted the role of intermediary between the church and the population. This was a natural consequence of living in the villages and among the population. . . . The outcomes of ecclesiastical investigations of new miracles and shrines are instructive. Although trained to be skeptical of popular "superstition," episcopal officials and parish priests were almost always convinced by the testimony of the common people, even in the mid-eighteenth century. . . . Those priests who chose to correct the religious, moral, or social life of their parishioners were readily denounced as arrogant and unacceptable. Unlike much of the Protestant clergy in this period, Catholic priests found it difficult to become agents of the church or the state.

The religious orders filled a number of important roles in baroque Catholicism. In doing so they contributed to the clericalization of popular Catholicism and to the diversity of popular practice. Almost all the religious orders experienced a revival in the period after 1650. A striking feature of the period was the shift in the fortunes of two of the most important "reformed" orders, the Capuchins and the Jesuits. As the Society of Jesus struggled in the seventeenth century to retain the influence they had exerted in the late sixteenth century and during the Thirty Years' War, the Capuchins expanded rapidly. . . . The popularity of the Capuchins, especially in the countryside, came from their flexibility, their populist preaching style, and their willingness to serve as parish priests. The Jesuits, in contrast, were considered rigid and elitist in many places. . . .

Strikingly, it was village and town leaders, not the official church, who favored increasing the number of priests. . . . [M]ost villagers knew exactly how much tithe went to pay the local clergyman, and how much was siphoned off to support monasteries and other more distant institutions. In the eighteenth century, the popular view that the tithe should pay primarily for pastoral work dovetailed neatly with the program of "enlightened" reformers in the Habsburg lands, which did lead to the creation of a considerable number of new parishes.

The communalism of German Catholicism has not been well studied, especially outside the cities. It is clear that city governments in Catholic cities, as in Protestant cities, participated actively in the administration of parish finances and often controlled clerical appointments. . . . Ultimately, the ability of a village commune to participate in the administration of the local parish, or even control it, depended on communal traditions and on the effectiveness of state institutions. . . .

Clericalism and communalism were two important attributes of seventeenth- and eighteenth-century Catholicism, and both tended to reinforce the local character of religious life. Popular religious practice, which was central to confessional identity, reinforced this localism, despite the long effort of church reformers to bring more uniformity. As with all aspects of German Catholicism, popular practice remained diverse and local, even when one can identify some broad trends. . . .

Because popular Catholicism, with its emphasis on the sacraments, especially the eucharist, and its preoccupation with the Virgin Mary, was practiced during processions, on pilgrimage, and in confraternities, it retained a strong local character. Processions were by nature local. The villagers of Ettenkirch in Upper Swabia, for example, went on eleven major processions during the year, to destinations up to two hours away. In addition, once a month, as well as on Palm Sunday and on All Souls Day, there was a procession around the church. . . . Processions around and through the parish reinforced local religion, but other processions drew people out of their villages. Longer processions, to neighboring parishes or local shrines, created ties with neighboring Catholic communities and created a sense of regional Catholicism.

Pilgrimages, like processions, served the dual purpose of reinforcing regional loyalties and underpinning local Catholicism. Catholics in southern Germany increasingly favored local shrines. . . . For every great regional shrine, like Walldürn in Franconia, Altötting in Bavaria,

Kevelaer on the lower Rhine, or Einsiedeln in Catholic Switzerland, there were hundreds of local shrines. Pilgrims also used shrines in a flexible way. The many new shrines founded in the seventeenth and eighteenth centuries generally supplemented existing shrines, rather than replacing them. . . . The population used shrines, then, in an inclusive way that linked local, regional, and international Catholicism.

Even the increasing dominance of the cult of the Virgin brought only a modicum of unity to Catholic practice and piety. Mary became more popular than many saints, some of whom were linked to the original Christianization of western and southern Germany, but the cult of Mary remained almost as local as those earlier cults. Marian shrines, as in Italy and Spain, were linked to their village or even geographical settings. . . . [A]ll of Catholic Germany experienced the interaction of church and popular promotion of pilgrimage. The relative weight of popular and official interest . . . varied, further contributing to the diversity of Catholic life.

Confraternities were also found across Catholic Germany. Their character and importance, needless to say, varied considerably. In the sixteenth century, traditional confraternities disappeared in the villages, yet by the eighteenth century much of religious life in the parishes was organized by confraternities. This process began in the late sixteenth century when the Jesuits organized Marian sodalities for men, with the aim of creating and strengthening a new Catholic elite. These urban, middle class confraternities were concentrated in western and southern Germany and were strongest in towns that were neither episcopal or political centers. Marian sodalities declined in the late eighteenth century, but other kinds of confraternities became important institutions in Catholic life. Rural confraternities of the rosary, with male *and* female members, were as typical in southwest Germany in the eighteenth century as were the urban sodalities in the late sixteenth century. In the Rhineland, confraternities slowly gained in popularity in the countryside, so that by 1743, ninety-four percent of all parishes had some sort of lay devotional association. This phenomenon can be found as well in Alsace, where the largest number of rural confraternities was founded in the eighteenth century. Confraternities, then, could be adapted to a variety of religious purposes and their existence in various parts of Germany is not evidence of uniformity. . . .

Perhaps the most important development in Catholic Germany in the seventeenth and eighteenth centuries was the development of confessional identity. . . . Popular confessional identity began to develop in the late seventeenth century everywhere in Germany and continued after 1700.

. . . The characteristics of confessional identity, for Catholics as well as Protestants, were clear. They included the prohibition (in social practice, not only in legislation) of confessionally-mixed marriages and conversions and the creation of confessionally-uniform guilds and social institutions. Catholics further asserted their Catholic identity by buying Catholic religious books and by decorating their houses with Catholic pictures, statues, and devotional objects like rosaries, household altars, and the like. . . .

The origins of Catholic identity are harder to identify than its characteristics. Studies of confessionalism in German cities emphasize that confessional identity manifested itself in daily life. The importance of religious belief and practice in the daily life of early modern people is undisputed. Catholic identity, and the churchliness of the population, was based on the ability of German Catholicism to adapt to the needs and desires of the population; the success (or failure) of church reform and of a policy of confessionalization was only a secondary factor. . . .

IV. Conclusion: Varieties of German Catholicism

Overviews of early modern German history inevitably emphasize the diversity of the old Reich. Remarkably, however, Catholicism has often been treated as monolithic, or at any rate as very uniform across Germany, especially in contrast with the diversity of Protestantism. The tendency to overemphasize the unifying features of the Catholic Church, especially its institutional uniformity, the important role of the Jesuits, and the broad effort at reform is, at the very least, misleading. . . .

The ability of the Catholic Church to adapt to the diversity of conditions across Germany was one of its strengths. Put differently, the decentralization and relative disorganization of the Catholic Church at the national level left considerable room for the population to shape Catholic religious practice as it needed and desired. Each region, each *Landschaft*, even each city, town, or village could, within the general guidelines set by the church, adopt a kind of Catholicism that fit with local conditions. Even where the state took a major role in enforcing church discipline, as in Bavaria, the population retained autonomy in organizing everyday religious life, actually expanding its role after 1650. In the end, Catholic confessionalism was not imposed from above, but created at the intersection of church reform, state policy, and popular needs and desires. Because each of these factors varied across Catholic Germany, Catholic confessionalism varied in its character and origins.

Pieter Brueghel the Younger, "Dance Around the Maypole." (© *Bridgeman Art Library*)
Popular among the peasantry of early modern Europe, this celebration traced its roots to
ancient pagan fertility rites.

II Popular Religion

The confessionalization paradigm suggests that in their efforts to impose religious uniformity, magistrates aggressively tried to root out unacceptable beliefs and practices. One therefore might assume that the registers of consistories and other forms of morals courts might provide evidence of conflicts between the religion promoted by ecclesiastical and political leaders and that practiced by common folk. A number of historians have been most influential in the study of the relationship between the "official" religion and that of common folk. One major figure in the history of popular religion is Carlo Ginzburg, author of several path-breaking books. In *The Night Battles,* he analyzes the beliefs and mentality of certain peasants who served an important function in their native Friuli in northern Italy. These were the so-called *benandanti* or "good walkers" who, at designated times of the year, reputedly went out in spirit at night to fight witches in order to defend the crops and prevent famine. When they were first called before the Inquisition in the 1570s, the *benandanti* defended their actions as wholesome and beneficial, and Ginzburg concludes that this was a vestige of a pre-Christian pagan fertility cult, about which the priests and Inquisitor had utterly no previous knowledge. Through the persistent questioning of Inquisitors in trials spread out over three generations, the *benandanti* of the mid-seventeenth century accepted the view of the clerical elite that their nocturnal meetings amounted to devil-worshiping sabbats and that they themselves were witches. Ginzburg thus envisions an utter disconnect between popular and elite religion until the Reformation era when authorities, such as Inquisitors in Counter-Reformation Italy, aggressively sought uniformity in religious practices and beliefs. In effect, the Reformation would begin the process of stamping out various aspects of popular religion that had existed for millennia.

In 1971 Sir Keith Thomas published a very provocative work based on a vast amount of research, *Religion and the Decline of Magic: Studies in Popular Beliefs in Sixteenth and Seventeenth Century England.* As Thomas observes, a magician who casts a spell believes that his actions, if done properly, will work automatically, whereas a prayer is a form of supplication that will work only if God accedes to the request. According to Thomas, however, only in the sixteenth and seventeenth centuries did one begin to see in England a clear distinction between religion and magic, as the most educated people experienced a "disenchantment" of the world; no longer did the world seem permeated by spirits, demons, and other preternatural forces that could be manipulated through magic.

The same year in which Thomas's *Religion and the Decline of Magic* was published saw the appearance of Jean Delumeau's influential and controversial work, *Catholicism Between Luther and Voltaire: A New View of the Counter-Reformation.* He went a step further than Thomas, arguing that the bulk of the French population could not be considered truly Christian until the Counter-Reformation, when church leaders in France aggressively sought to eliminate the pre-Christian pagan and magical beliefs that were omnipresent among French peasants. Excerpted here is his fourth chapter, "Christianization," in which Delumeau discusses the French church's fight against paganism through missionary work to the countryside and mandatory religious instruction through the catechism. He finds that by the end of the seventeenth century, the French peasantry had largely been successfully "Christianized."

In his work on Germany, Robert Scribner reexamines the long held view—bequeathed to us by the sociologist Max Weber—that Protestantism took magic out of religion, promoted the "disenchantment" of the world, and ultimately led to the secularization of mentality (see Weber's *The Sociology of Religion,* first published as *Gesammelte Aufsätze zur Religionssoziologie,*vol. 1 [Tübingen: Mohr, 1922]). Although Thomas's findings in England could lend support to this stereotype, Scribner rejects it. Even though Protestants affirmed the absolute sovereignty of God and believed that humans could not have any direct knowledge of the divine, Luther and other Protestants were equally adamant in insisting that the devil and angels wielded real power in this world. They continued to believe that the supernatural intruded into the natural world, either as a sign from or punishment by God. Far from promoting belief in a desacralized world, Protestants espoused a "moralized universe," in which an unlimited range of events could be interpreted as evidence of divine approval or wrath. Since they continued to fear the acts of demons, Protestants may have actually suffered greater anxiety than did Catholics, who had more weapons, in the form of rituals and sacraments, to fight diabolical power. In any event, Protestants continued to employ the skills of a wide range of "magicians," to fight the demons, notwithstanding that such activities were strictly forbidden.

Many historians have seriously questioned the conception of a popular-elite dichotomy in the area of early modern religion. A case in point is Eamon Duffy, the author of *The Stripping of the Altars: Traditional Religion in England 1400–1580,* a work of magisterial proportions that traces changes in religious practices in England from the late Middle Ages down to the Elizabethan era. Duffy emphatically asserts that "no substantial gulf existed between the religion of the clergy and the elite on the one hand and that of the people at large on the other," nor does he find that the religion of most fifteenth-century English parishioners was "magical, superstitious, or semi-pagan" (p. 2). Duffy criticizes many historians, including Thomas, for paying short shrift to liturgy, which, he finds, was at the very heart of lay religious experiences. According to Duffy, the liturgy associated with the "traditional religion" of late medieval England resonated profoundly with the large majority of English people. The selection reproduced here is from chapter 17, which chronicles considerable resistance to Elizabethan reforms, as so many people resented the abolition of the mass and restrictions on pilgrimages, sacred images, prayers to saints, and so on. Eventually, though, the heavy-handed reform succeeded in eliminating many rituals that had meant so much to so many.

In *God in La Mancha: Religious Reform and the People of Cuenca, 1500–1650,* Sara Nalle provides a nuanced view on the issue of popular religion, a term that she too shuns. Rejecting the elite-popular and rural-urban cultural dichotomies that have been posited for other regions of Reformation Europe, she finds that in Cuenca, located in the heartland of Castile, the traditional religion practiced by everyone was "thoroughly mixed with magic." The Council of Trent brought about some very important changes to the church in this region, most obviously a much better educated group of parish priests, virtually all of whom were native to the diocese of Cuenca. Thanks to the ambitious efforts of the secular clergy, by the end of the sixteenth century the large majority of people living in this diocese embraced the basic precepts of the Roman Catholic Church, could recite appropriate prayers, and showed a good knowledge of the catechism. More important, the immense and growing popularity of Marian devotions, penitential confraternities, religious theater, and votive offerings palpably shows that Catholic authorities were effectively providing guidance to a most receptive audience. Counter-Reformation leaders also successfully promoted an inner spirituality among the rank and file, as witnessed by the new emphasis on silent prayer. Evidence from wills and testaments suggests, however, that by the first decades of the seventeenth century, the quest for personal salvation resulted in the increasing reliance on purchasing masses for one's soul at the expense of more communally oriented expressions of piety, no doubt an unintended consequence of the reforming efforts.

Tessa Watt examines popular piety in England through the medium of print for the years 1550 to 1640, an era that witnessed perceptible increases in literacy. Concentrating on "cheap print," Watt notes that many pamphlets, ballads, and broadsides were illustrated with woodcuts and employed rhymes, all geared for an audience on the "fringe of literacy"—rhymes and other mnemonic devices were useful since the printed word was often experienced orally, as literate people often read works aloud to friends who could not read. In these cheap publications, Watt sees a culture that was shared by the urban publishers and the consumers of cheap print, most of whom lived in rural settings. Moreover, the chapbooks and broadsides denoted more consensus than conflict in matters of piety. The literature did not amount to aggressive propaganda that promoted one confession over another; rather it upheld traditional religious ideals upon which Protestant precepts were superimposed, an apt metaphor for the transformations that popular piety itself experienced during this century. Thus, while print could be an important agent of change, it could also reinforce preexisting mores. The evidence from cheap print therefore suggests that the conversion to Protestantism did not introduce revolutionary changes in the religious practices of common folk in England.

Jean Delumeau

Christianization

The Fight Against Paganism

The Ban on Popular Festivals

Fr Boschet's life of Fr Maunoir, published in 1697, includes the following passage: "One must not be surprised to see in the missions something akin to what the pagans experienced when the first Apostles preached to them, because in many places of lower Brittany the mysteries of Religion were so little known it was a question of establishing the faith (kerygma) rather than of teaching Christian doctrine (paranesis)."

Are we to think, from this, of a Land's End (Finisterre) which the breakers of innovation reached only to die exhausted on the beach? It seems not. One of the main sources for superstitions in seventeenth-century France concerns not Brittany at all but Chartres, and it was in the diocese of Autun that in 1686 the peasants sacrificed a heifer to our Lady to obtain protection for their herds against the "plague." Truth to tell, before the Catholic Reformation gained momentum there seems to have been extreme religious ignorance in most of the country areas of the kingdom. When Fr Beurrier arrived at Nanterre (where he had been appointed curé-prior) in 1637 he was stupefied by the dearth of Christian

Jean Delumeau, "Christianization," in *Catholicism Between Luther and Voltaire: A New View of the Counter-Reformation* (London: Burns & Oates, 1977), 175–201. Reprinted by permission of the Continuum International Publishing Group.

education in "the local dignitaries of advancing years" who were ignorant "of even the commonest things that have to be known before one can receive the sacraments and be saved." In the second half of the seventeenth century, a bishop of Autun told the pope in a letter that the people in his diocese were "quite uneducated, hardly initiated in even the rudiments of the faith" and that they lived "in crass and deeply rooted ignorance."

As the classical age, then, dawned in France, and in Europe as a whole, the intellectual and psychological climate of the people was characterized by a profound unfamiliarity with the basics of Christianity, and by a persistent pagan mentality with the occasional vestiges of pre-Christian ceremonial. It would be an admirable historical exercise to group together, without regard for confessional barriers, the varied aspects of European churchmen's fight against superstition and paganized folklore at the time. Here we may content ourselves with selecting and comparing one or two of the more significant facts.

In 1579, a council at Milan forbade the manifestations of *calendimaggio* (Mayday festivities) in the north of Italy. These festivities included "cutting down trees, branches and all, parading them in the streets and squares of the towns and villages, and then planting them with wild and ridiculous ceremonies." These May-day antics were fairly widespread in Europe, and seem to have been, in Italy at least, a survival of the ancient *Floralia* on the calends of May. The consecration of the month of May to Mary (in the early eighteenth century) was probably not an attempt to Christianize the folkloric manifestations of that period of the year, but it may well have been a reaction against the widely-held belief that this month was an unlucky one: for example, it was considered unlucky to get married in May.

Still on the subject of May, and still in the late sixteenth century, "the dean, canons and other clergy" of Chalon-sur Saône used to process on Whit Monday to a meadow, where they "went several times round a dome in which was a mass of rounded stones with stone images round about it." This "dance of the canons" was abolished between 1593 and 1624 by bishop Cyrus de Thiard. At about the same time archbishop Pierre de Villars suppressed the so-called ceremony of the Blacked Men which took place at Vienne on 1 May. The four Blacked Men were chosen respectively by the archbishop, the chapter of Saint Maurice and the abbots of Saint-André and Saint-Pierre. Naked and blackened all over, they issued forth from the archiepiscopal palace early in the morning, ran round the whole city and then returned to the palace: on completion of which feat, the archbishop gave them a "king" and a guard. The cortege then went to the town hall to find St. Paul, dressed as a hermit, then to the abbey of the Dames of St. Andrew where the abbess gave them a "queen," decked out, like the king, in a quite grotesque fashion. "This ridiculous court processed round the city, the whole people running after it shouting and hallooing in the most fearful way." . . .

Missions: Their Popular and Rural Aspect

If Catholic Europe in the Tridentine period hummed with travelling missioners, it was because the parish clergy inherited from the previous period were so deficient. This was why Vincent de Paul founded the Lazarists. Here again France was the country in which the itinerant messengers of the faith worked most zealously and above all most methodically. However, their activity must ultimately be seen in a vast geographical and multiconfessional context in which Quakers and Methodists rubbed shoulders with Jesuits, Capuchins and Oratorians. . . .

If the seventeenth century was the golden age of Christianization, especially in France, it was because the missionaries tried to reach the rural world, whereas the preachers of the fourteenth and fifteenth centuries had contacted above all the urban public. The Oratory [a new French religious order founded by Cardinal Pierre de Bérulle] had hardly been founded, in 1613, when it set up a foundation of 500 francs to provide missions to prepare for the four main feasts of the year (Easter, Pentecost, All Saints, Christmas) in the villages of the Paris diocese. An Oratorian was to repair to a village near Paris for a fortnight, "going from one archdeaconry to another, and changing from year to year." The Oratorian Jean Eudes, who himself founded several congregations, was one of the best-known preachers of the seventeenth century. He gave celebrated missions in towns such as Rennes, Caen and Paris, but it has been calculated that about sixty-five per cent of his ministry was to rural parishes. He once said: "Mission being necessary everywhere, we shall preach everywhere, but with preference in the country." . . .

Although all social classes in seventeenth-century France were the object of the missionary apostolate, it was particularly the popular strata that the propagandists of the faith tried to reach (an additional proof that these were considered the least christianized, both in the towns and in the country). This explains St Vincent de Paul's advice to adapt the horary of the missions to the rhythm of peasant life. The first instruction of the day had always been early, before work started, and the "great catechism" (for adults only) late, at the end of the day's work. In the country areas the Lazarists preached in principle only from November to June, when there was least agricultural activity. The more spectacular side of the missions was evidently to impress a public whose mentality had retained its country roughness and who could learn most quickly from a direct, simple approach to religious teaching. There were autos-da-fé of books and superstitious objects, grandiose plantings of wooden crosses, allegorical pasteboard representations used by Fr Maunoir, and "living pictures" in his processions which evoked the principal scenes of the Bible and the gesta of eminent saints. Hymns were composed in the vernacular and made easy to remember by being set to the melodies of well-known popular songs. . . .

Missions: Their Methodical Approach

Unlike the great preachers of the fifteenth century, the missioners of the seventeenth were men of method. They descended on a parish in groups of four, six or eight, and would not leave until the entire population of the village or quarter had received the sacrament of penance. The daily exercises were numerous—sometimes four a day—and there would need to be quite a few religious to organize them properly. . . .

Because they were methodical, the itinerant preachers of the seventeenth century did not abandon a parish once they had been there. The foundations which contributed to the missioners' expenses were usually in the form of annuities which helped to keep the missions in a parish regular: every four, six or eight years, for example. Of what use was it, however, to work in a village if the surrounding areas and indeed the wider province were neglected? It was important to cover an entire region if it was to be brought to God. . . .

The itinerant messengers of the Catholic faith tried in any one parish to achieve limited but definite aims. First of all—and this is really revealing—the purpose was to teach the people four basic prayers: the *Pater Noster*, the *Ave Marie*, the *Credo* and the *Confiteor*, and inculcate the habit of reciting them twice a day, morning and evening: only long missions could do this. Secondly, the idea was to encourage an examination of conscience in the light of Christian doctrine, with special emphasis, and I quote from a Lazarist,

> "on repentance . . . man's last end . . . the enormity of sin, the severity of God on unrepentant sinners. . . .

The fear of God which resulted was meant to be salutary. It was designed to lead the faithful to a general confession, the basic legitimation of the mission. . . . The Eudist missioners guaranteed to be available for confessions from six o'clock to nine and ten to eleven thirty in the morning, and from two to six thirty in the afternoon; they had therefore to provide quite a team of confessors. "Lions" in the pulpit, they tried to be "charming" and "as mild as lambs" in the confessional. They covered their faces so as not to see the penitents. The mission ended with general communion, a suitable culmination to the purification brought about by the examination of conscience and absolutism. . . .

The Parish Framework: A Sacramental Life

The missions induced a sense of religious shock. Only a solid parish framework, however, could transform that shock into a durable spiritual life. As St Vincent de Paul wrote to the bishop of Périgueux in 1650: "We know by experience that the fruits of missions are very great, corresponding to the extreme needs of country people; but as their minds are generally rather rough and little educated, they readily forget what they have learnt and their good resolutions, unless they have good pastors who maintain the high standards they have reached."

St Vincent here exposes the nub of the Catholic Reformation: its permeation of the average Christian's daily life. . . . Tridentine Catholicism gave the faithful a feeling of security by surrounding them with protective sacraments, and consequently giving the sacraments a new depth. There was no difficulty in persuading the people of the need for baptism because there was general adherence to Augustine's view that "no one could be saved unless he were baptized." . . . [T]his meant hell (limbo) for infants who died without baptism. Tirelessly synodal statutes of the seventeenth century repeated the duty of parents to have their infants baptized within three days of birth. If necessary, negligent parents could find themselves refused entry into the church. . . . French parish registers reveal that lapses in the administration of baptism became rarer and rarer from the late seventeenth century onwards. Also the seriousness of the ceremony was brought out more; godparents had to be "practising Catholics" (which meant Catholics who fulfilled their Easter duties), and candidates who were "incapable or unsuitable because of their conduct and bad example" were to be turned down. . . .

More so than baptism, confirmation needed re-evaluating. According to J. Toussaert, in fourteenth- and fifteenth-century Flanders either the sacrament was a semi-superstitious rite or else no notice was taken of it. In 1665 Mgr de Péréfixe stated in a pastoral letter that "the people in the (Parisian) country areas and the poor have no knowledge of confirmation, either because of their pastors' negligence in omitting the relevant instructions, or because of their own laziness in not attending instructions." . . . Confirmation, then, did not begin to play a regular role in ordinary parish life until pastoral visitations became more frequent. From the late seventeenth century, the lists of confirmees which we have for the Parisian countryside include adults only by way of exception, which presumably proves that the sacrament was now being conferred systematically on children without undue delay. . . .

In the fourteenth and fifteenth centuries, the veneration of the Blessed Sacrament had developed enormously. However, the grandiose Corpus Christi processions and the magnificent monstrances that the late Gothic period has left us should not be allowed to give a false impression. Religious instruction being so deficient, the people venerated in the eucharist primarily a "miraculous object" and a "sensational element"; and such veneration was not necessarily extended into regular Easter duties. . . .

The Catholic Reformation tried to introduce regular Easter duties everywhere. It reminded the faithful that the Easter communion should be in one's own parish church (to make surveillance easier). The posting-up of the names of non-communicants on the church door, the threats of excommunication, the refusal of ecclesiastical burial amounted to so much social pressure that the number of those who did not fulfil their Easter duties does not seem to have exceeded one per cent of the Catholic population in the diocese of La Rochelle in 1648, and 0.22 per cent in the (rural) archdeaconry of Paris in 1672. Still, it is probable that the defaulters were more numerous than this in the towns, where surveillance anyway was more difficult. Of more interest from the point of view of gaining some ideas of the religious vitality of a population is the number of communions outside Easter time. It is certain that they increased, bringing with them a more frequent use of the confessional. At the beginning of his ministry at Ivry, Jean Jollain, who was curé there from 1669 to 1686, complained that even with his two curates he could not "manage to see to all the offices on feast days and confess 400 or 500 people who are accustomed to do their devotions at the big feasts such as the feasts of our

Lady and the parish's patron saint, the parish comprising nearly 800 communicants and 400 souls who do not as yet go to communion."

The combined action of the Jesuits, new congregations of nuns (Visitation nuns, Ursulines etc.), sodalities (especially the Blessed Sacrament and the Rosary) and missions, counterbalancing Jansenist reticence, brought in a change in the faithful's attitude to communion and confession. In 1687 at Lille, the Jesuits distributed more than 3000 hosts on some feast days. . . .

The Parish Framework: Sunday Mass

The new insistence on sacramental life was parallel with an effort to make the mass more important in the estimation of the faithful. Attendance at Sunday mass, which had formerly been a pious custom, gradually became a positive law; but to what extent was it observed before the Catholic Reformation filtered down to parish level? And what meaning did attendance at mass have in a generally slack and careless atmosphere? People sat on the altar-steps or chatted during the service; hats and coats were left lying around anywhere; gentlemen brought their hounds into church; the buildings in the country were often too small, and became crowded giving rise to "a thousand inconveniences and immodesties"; the lower people, excluded from the pews which the gentlemen and burghers had hired for their own use, had frequently to stand or sit on the floor; many of the men were content to attend mass from the porch, or divide the time of mass between this rather theoretic presence under the "roof" of the church and the neighbouring wineshop; even inside the church, scuffles and brawls were not uncommon (usually over precedence in seating); finally, the faithful were permitted no active participation in the liturgy. This is the picture that emerges from Jeanne Ferté's study on the religious life of the Paris country districts in the seventeenth century, before the impact of the renewal had made itself felt.

To personalize the sanctification of feastdays on which attendance at mass was obligatory, their number was reduced. . . . In 1657 the bishop of Autun wrote: "It is not appropriate to multiply holidays of obligation for fear of multiplying the occasions of sin," Christian festivals being the usual occasions of fairs, revels and debauches. . . . [Bishops] tried to see that the remaining feasts were more strictly observed: that no work was done, and that taverns were closed during "the divine service, the homily and the catechism." . . .

Did the mass of the faithful . . . take a greater part in the mass than before? . . .

A considerable number of priests raised their altars and at the cost of artistic sacrifices of which they were little aware replaced the Gothic rood-screens with simple altar-rails. At least now the faithful were less cut off physically from the eucharistic liturgy. Finally, a doctrine emerged encouraging a more active share in the mass. In 1651, François de Harlay, uncle of the future archbishop of Paris, wrote a work entitled *La manière de bien entendre la messe de paroisse* (Towards fruitful attendance at mass): "All the different private prayers should cease when the priest prays and offers the sacrifice in the name of all those present. You should be attentive to the prayer he is about to address God for you and for the whole congregation, and think of the sacrifice there present, by offering it—and yourself—through the priest with the mind of the Church and in union with the Church." . . . Despite these strong recommendations, congregations, especially in the country, remained more often than not passive, except during the congregational prayers and notices for the week. . . .

The Parish Framework: Catechism

The importance the congregational prayers and notices assumed in the mind of the faithful just shows how necessary preaching and catechism were. Yet it was only in the sixteenth century that the Protestant and Catholic Reformers—Luther, Calvin, Peter Canisius and the fathers of Trent—felt the urgent need for catechetical instruction. Even then it was slow to infiltrate religious habits, because it was unpopular with both clergy and laity. In Italy and the Low Countries, from the second half of the sixteenth century, sodalities of Christian doctrine multiplied, often at the initiative of the Jesuits who started catechism classes in the urban parishes. At Anvers in about 1610, 4000 children from nine to sixteen attended these religious instruction classes under sixty male and female teachers.

In the early seventeenth century in a diocese like that of Paris it was frequently foundations by pious laity which enabled a priest (effectively a curate) to be appointed to a parish with the specific role of teaching the catechism. The episcopate insisted and kept on insisting that parish priests should provide systematic religious instruction for the children. In 1652 Mgr de Ragny bishop of Autun urged his parish priests and curates to lay on religious instruction for the children every Sunday, "charitably" (without demanding payment). . . . This is the first allusion to catechetical teaching in the diocese. Three years later the new bishop, Mgr d'Attichy, told his clergy that people had complained to him because their pastors were neglecting the catechism. He therefore ordered them to teach children at least the Our Father, the Apostles' Creed, the commandments and the substance of the main mysteries of the faith. This religious instruction must be given on Sundays at midday, preceded by a long peal on the church bells to alert the people. . . . [R]epeated menaces show how novel catechism teaching still was, how it disrupted the traditional attitudes of parish clergy and faithful alike. To persuade the faithful that catechism was to their ultimate advantage, the archpriests of the diocese of Autun — in 1690–3 — resorted to a variety of expedients: they chose the most convenient time of day; attracted the children with small rewards, kindness and friendliness; put pressure on reluctant parents by threatening to bar them from the sacraments; in fact refused absolution and communion to parents and masters who did not send their children and young domestics to catechism; and limited the lessons to half an hour.

In the Low Countries and France, to take only these two examples, the seventeenth century saw the appearance of many catechism manuals. The Belgian ones were mostly off-shoots of Canisius' famous catechism; the French ones relied heavily on the experience of Bourdoise, who for forty years developed a catechetical method at Saint-Nicolas-du-Chardonnet. Between 1670 and 1685, a score of diocesan catechisms were published in France. One of the best-known was the one written by "the three Henrys": Henry de Laval, bishop of La Rochelle, Henry de Barillon, bishop of Luçon, and Henry Arnauld, bishop of Angers. It was first published at La Rochelle in 1676. . . . It included a "little catechism" of twenty-seven pages for young children, a "medium catechism" of ninety-three pages as preparation for first communion, and finally a "great catechism" of 382 pages for educated adults and priests, who could find in it sermon material in abundance. It was, in short, a theological vade-mecum for all ages and all levels of instruction, and a sign, among many others, of the new religious mentality thirsting for dogmatic clarity and doctrinal guidance. . . .

Robert W. Scribner

The Reformation, Popular Magic, and the "Disenchantment of the World"

For most college-educated people, one of the two or three things they commonly know about the Reformation is that it contributed, alongside the Enlightenment, to a process of secularization, often understood as the rationalization of modern thought-modes by the "disenchantment of the world," the elimination of magic from human action and behavior. This did not mean the repudiation of religious belief, but a separation of "magic" from "religion" in early modern Europe. The distinction between religion and magic had been blurred in the pre-Reformation church; indeed, for convinced Protestants the central act of medieval Christian worship, the Mass, with its doctrine of the transubstantiated Eucharist, had at its heart a form of magic. The Reformation removed this ambiguity by taking the "magical" elements out of Christian religion, eliminating the ideas that religious rituals had any automatic efficacy, that material objects could be endowed with any sort of sacred power, and that human actions could have any supernatural effect. Religion was thus freed of "superstitious" notions about the workings of the world and became a matter of internal conviction, enabling the rational human action characteristic of modernity.

The focus of this article is popular magic, which may certainly be used as a touchstone for judging the extent and manner in which the Reformation redefined the nature of religion. However, the problem is complicated because our modern view of the Reformation rests essentially on

Robert W. Scribner, "The Reformation, Popular Magic, and the 'Disenchantment of the World.'" Reprinted from *The Journal of Interdisciplinary History*, XXIII (1993), 475–494, with the permission of the editors of *The Journal of Interdisciplinary History* and The MIT Press, Cambridge, Massachusetts. © 1993 by the Massachusetts Institute of Technology and The Journal of Interdisciplinary History, Inc.

the ways in which it was constructed in the nineteenth century out of the characteristic intellectual concerns of that age (nationalism, scientific rationalism, and a preoccupation with evolutionary models of development). The Enlightenment and post-Enlightenment thought first positioned the Reformation as part of a long-term process of rationalization and secularization, whereas post-Enlightenment thought-modes failed to understand the essential characteristics of medieval Christianity, especially the medieval notion of the sacramental. The view that the Reformation was a logical stage on the road to modernization is now seen as problematic, as is the conventional wisdom of how it changed the notion of the sacred. In order to understand the relationship of "religion" to "magic" both before and after the Reformation, a good deal of rethinking is required. Thus, it is necessary to begin with the relationship of magic to pre-Reformation Christianity before we can go on to appreciate the problem magic posed for both Protestantism and Catholicism alike.

Let us begin with a definition of magic, which can be understood in the words of Flint as "the exercise of a preternatural control over nature by human beings, with the assistance of forces more powerful than they." Religion, by contrast, is the recognition by human beings of a supernatural power on whom they are dependent, to whom they show deference and are obligated. On the face of it we have a clear-cut distinction between religion and magic: on the one hand, human dependence on, and deference toward, the divine; on the other, human attempts to appropriate divine power and apply it instrumentally. Yet the contrast is not so simple when the reality of religion as a historical phenomenon is considered. Late-medieval European religion was complex and varied, and to grasp its totality we must be aware of its multidimensionality. There are at least seven major features of medieval European religion to consider. It was simultaneously soteriological, functional, pastoral, and concerned with piety, as well as having irreducible social, political, and economic dimensions. Only the first four will be mentioned here as most relevant to our theme.

Medieval European religion was "soteriological" in that it offered an understanding of, and a means toward, human salvation focused on the saving death and resurrection of Christ as revealed in the Bible, and, in particular, redemption from sin and its consequences for humans both individually and collectively. It was "functional" in that it gave meaning to daily life by marking out religiously the key stages in the human life cycle and in the cyclical rhythms of the seasons, thus providing a form of cosmic order for human existence. Its "pastoral" role was to offer consolation amid the anxieties of daily life and to provide a means of reconciliation for human frailty. The concern with "piety" refers to a consistent state or attitude about the religious meaning of life, expressed in actions symbolizing dependence upon and preoccupation with the divine, perhaps better signified by the word "godliness."

It was in the functional aspect of medieval religion that the line between religion and magic could become blurred. Religion functioned as a means of order in daily life because it was predicated on the assumption that all creation depended for its well-being on the sustaining power of the divine. Irregularities and discontinuities in the material world were understood either as a form of breakdown of this cosmic order or as a result of sacred power operating upon the world. Sacred power could entail the operation of either beneficent or malign supernatural forces, the divine and the angelic or the demonic. All manifestations of the sacred—whether in persons, places, or events—also entailed manifestations of sacred power and therefore the possibility of access to it. Saints, their bodies, their relics, and the places in which they were active; other holy places and charismatic centers; and moments of intense ritual significance all offered possibilities of sacred power manifesting itself. It was a power to which all persons sought access in their attempts to deal with the exigencies of the human condition—sickness, dearth, climatic variation, threats to human and animal reproduction, fear and anxiety, and the breakdown of human relationships.

The medieval church, as the institutionalized form of the organized community of believers, found itself under a twofold pressure. Its sacramental system, slowly developed over the course of several centuries of Christian practice, was primarily soteriological. Sacraments involved ritual actions which effected in the supernatural sphere that which they symbolized by their signifying performances in the natural: thus, the cleansing and purifying symbolic action of water in baptism brought about the purification of the soul from sin. But sacraments were also targeted on the whole person—body, soul and spirit—so that they were seen as offering consolation, succor, and nourishment for the body as well as the soul. Sacramental action thus had inner-worldly as well as transcendental efficacy. This was one field in which any firm lines between religion and magic could become blurred, but we can only appreciate the full complexity of the problem if we highlight another feature of sacramental action, the way in which it dealt with the demonic and the diabolical.

Christianity's view of the human need for salvation stressed the action of a perverted form of the supernatural in bringing about sin and human corruption from a preternatural state, personified in the shape of the Devil. The Devil represented and occasioned spiritual, moral, social, and material disorder in the natural world, and the sacramental system was primarily (soteriologically) directed at reversing the effects of his actions and offering future protection against them. Sacraments thus had a multiple efficacy—providing a means to salvation, offering succor for body, soul and spirit, and serving as protection against the temptations of the Devil. The Devil could, of course, work effects in the natural world, albeit only on divine sufferance, although theological opinion throughout the medieval and early modern period was divided as to whether these effects were real or imaginary. Be that as it may, the blurring of boundaries between religion and magic also extended along a second axis, the means through which one dealt with the this-worldly effects of the diabolical. The twofold problem for the church was, first, how to balance the soteriological with the functional and pastoral aspects of its sacraments; second, how to define the ways in which they could be employed to combat the wiles of the Devil. The problem was made the more complex by the medieval understanding that the sacraments' soteriological efficacy was automatic (*ex opere operata*); extending this notion to the other features of a sacrament would have brought it perilously close to a form of "magic."

The difficulty became yet more intricate with the development of the practices known as "sacramentals." In part, sacramentals were no more than ritual blessings of certain elements or objects used in liturgical action, a means of consecrating them to sacred use; for example, the water and salt used in the baptismal ceremony or the altar on which the Mass was performed. But they also involved an act of exorcism by means of which harmful spirits were expelled from these elements or objects. This aspect may have arisen from a Christianizing attempt to incorporate pagan amulets as non-Christian peoples were converted: the demonic beings from which they were believed to gain their efficacy were ordered to depart in the name of God as Creator, the Trinity, and Christ as Lord of the world, and they were then blessed so that Christians could use them without harm. Indeed, many of the blessed items used

as expressions of piety by medieval Christians had this character. However, by the later middle ages, sacramentals involved the exorcism and
blessing of a wide range of objects, the efficacy of which was held to be
analogous to that of the sacraments. The differences in efficacy were
nonetheless crucial. Sacraments were primarily soteriological and only
secondarily pastoral and consolatory, whereas the pastoral and consolatory aspects predominated in the sacramentals, which *could* be an aid to
salvation insofar as they were used in the right way and with the right
frame of mind (*ex opere operantis*).

There were three ways in which sacramentals could slide over into
the field of magic: the element of exorcism could be taken to impart
apotropaic significance to them, the blessing or consecration could be
seen to impart a sacred power, and their primarily this-worldly orienta-
tion could lead to their instrumental application. Moreover, the official
distinction between efficacy *ex opere operata* and *ex opere operandis* was
commonly ignored, and sacramentals in popular practice were regarded
as though they were automatically effective. Finally, these items fell more
easily than the sacraments outside the control of the institutional church,
since they became a matter of daily use by laypeople, rather than being
(as the sacraments were) under the control of the institutional church
in the person of the clergy. Sacramentals were enormously popular
and it was widespread demand which led to the mushrooming of such
blessed objects throughout the later middle ages and into the post-
Reformation period (indeed, up to the present day). They, above all else,
have earned the designation of "the magic of the late-medieval church"
and attracted the scorn and hostility of the Protestant reformers of the
sixteenth century. . . .

A consistent policy of demonization would have done much to keep
a firm boundary between religion and magic, but this was not always possible in practice, since it would have ruled out Christianizing strategies.
The most important area of the latter strategy was that of curing and healing charms. The persistence of non-Christian magical healing practices
led monks, as exemplars of sanctity and so as wielders of sacred power,
to adopt Christianized forms of healing charms in which the names of
Christ or other Christian figures replaced those of pagan gods. Healing
thus became a result of Christian prayer which, if not merely dependent
on the power of the cross as the most potent Christian symbol, could
be accompanied by magico-medical healing techniques, the success of
which could be made dependent on the innovation of Christian forms

of sacred powers. The ambiguity between prayer and the magical use of a spell or charm remained built into such Christianized forms, especially when they escaped the control of the monastic milieu and became the stock in trade of popular healers, cunning folk, sorcerers, and ultimately, of lay people. Thus, a third axis of ambiguity was created between religion and magic, along which ranged acceptable Christian practices based on notions like the healing power of prayer; mistaken or misguided "superstitious" invocation of Christ, the Trinity, and other Christian sacred persons; and being deceived into collaborating with the Devil.

This very crude sketch enables us to see why those approaching pre-Reformation religion through post-Enlightenment thought-modes failed to understand essential characteristics of medieval Christianity and popular magic or the troubled relationship between the two. What difference did the Reformation make to this complex and subtle structure of sacrality? The radical point of departure associated with Martin Luther and (even more radically) Ulrich Zwingli resided in their understanding of the absolute sovereignty and otherness of God, so that it was impossible for human beings to gain any knowledge of the divine by merely created means. This viewpoint destroyed the basis for sacraments and sacramentals, indeed for any kind of ritual by means of which this-worldly symbolic action could have any transcendental efficacy. All sacred action flowed one-way, from the divine to the human, and even salvation was but a recognition in the human heart of a grace apparently arbitrarily given by God. . . .

The consequence was in no sense, however, a desacralization of the world; quite the contrary. Luther had a powerful belief in the presence and activity of the Devil in the world, and believed that his age had finally unmasked the Devil's main agent, the Antichrist, the diabolical antithesis of Christ as Savior. He held his age to be the one in which the last great confrontation between Christ and Antichrist, between God and the Devil, was to be fought. It was an age witnessing a great outpouring of the Holy Spirit, guiding the world toward its providential culmination in the Last Days. Luther's thought was thus apocalyptic and eschatological, rather than desacralizing. Indeed, it can be said that the Word of God became for him the overwhelming sacramental experience, the sole means through which created humanity could come to knowledge of the divine. The world of Luther and the Reformation was a world of highly charged sacrality, in which all secular events, social, political, and economic, could have cosmic significance. The same was true of the second generation of reform, associated with Calvin and the followers of the "reformed religion," whose characteristic belief above all else was that Lutherans and Lutheranism had made too many compromises with the Antichrist by accepting that some matters were indifferent in the great cosmic struggle. Far from further desacralizing the world, Calvin and the reformed religion intensified to an even higher degree the cosmic struggle between the divine and the diabolical.

It is also incorrect to argue that the Reformation created an anti-ritual form of religion which dispensed with sacred time, places, persons, or things. . . . The attempt of the first generation of reformers to dispense with consecration or blessing as a means of setting sacred objects aside from the profane world proved futile. Throughout the sixteenth century and into the seventeenth, evangelical forms of consecration re-emerged and multiplied, and were applied to a wide variety of objects: church foundation stones, new or restored churches, pulpits, fonts, organs. . . . This was no matter of mere survivalism, the ignorant response of half-protestanized people incapable of understanding that sacred power no longer existed in a profane world. Protestant belief did not hold that the sacred did not intrude into the secular world, simply that it did not do so at human behest and could not automatically be commanded. . . .

Nonetheless, the Reformation, both in its first and second generations, could be said to have drawn a firmer line between magic and religion by its changed understanding of the sacraments, and its repudiation of Catholic sacramentals. The profusion of blessed objects (salt, water, palms, herbs, and so forth) that so often gave sacred meaning to the daily life of pre-Reformation Christians did largely disappear from the lives of those of evangelical belief. Yet this did not remove the popular desire for some kind of instrumental application of sacred power to deal with the exigencies of daily life, and Protestants often turned to distinctively "Protestant" remedies, using Bibles, hymnals, and prayer books for their healing and protective power. . . .

A further consequence of Protestant belief to which we must call attention . . . concerns what I have called the "moralized universe." Alongside belief in a sacramental world, pre-Reformation religion also believed that certain human actions could provoke supernatural intervention in the natural world, either as a sign or a punishment. For example, the birth of deformed children or animals was often understood in this way, either as punishment for human sin (for example, a monk fornicating with a nun) or as a warning of impending divine wrath.

Moral deviance, both individual and collective, was reflected in natural deformity, perhaps through belief in the links of microcosm and macrocosm, but more likely through a perception of a natural order influenced, via the supernatural, by the quality of human moral action. . . .

The Protestant elaboration of the moralized universe had the effect of increasing anxiety among those it affected. Deprived of the protective means inherent in the Catholic sacramental system, Protestants found themselves prey to anxiety that was hardly allayed by invoking the Protestant doctrine of providence. Indeed, anxiety may even have been increased by awareness of the omnipresence of a sacred order in and among the secular. . . . Protestant belief allowed for a whole range of supernatural beings to be active in the world, especially angels, demons, and various kinds of spirits, such as those of the revenant dead. Their activity was accepted as possible not so much because it was experienced but because such beings were mentioned in the Bible, although there was a tendency to trace many such phenomena back to the "tricks of the Devil." Indeed, it seemed to many observers as though the Devil and demonic spirits had become wilder and more incalculable, attested by the remarkable efflorescence of Protestant demonology, which by the second half of the sixteenth century attained the level of an obsession. . . .

Protestantism thus experienced problems along two of the axes of ambiguity we have identified for pre-Reformation belief: inner-worldly efficacy of sacred action, and the activities of the diabolical/demonic. The same was also true along the third axis—the "magical" power of prayer. As we might expect, practitioners of magic continued to ply their trade despite the implementation of religious reformation in any given territory. Indeed, we might well surmise that they received a double boost: the competition provided by the "magic of the medieval church" was in great part removed, while the anxiety about how to deal with the exigencies of daily life was often intensified rather than lessened. In the absence of a Protestant rite of exorcism, practitioners of magic who were able to deal with demonic possession or with poltergeists found themselves virtually in a position to monopolize the market. Indeed, they were able not only to survive under a Protestant dispensation but even to prosper, and they defied all attempts to eradicate them from the sixteenth to the eighteenth century and beyond. Practitioners of magic covered a wide range in early modern Germany, from purveyors of spells and charms . . . , soothsayers and diviners . . . , cunning men and women, [etc.]. . . . Such persons, men and women, were approached for a variety of reasons: to perform counter-magic against bewitchment, to divine lost or stolen objects, to discover the cause of human and animal illness, to heal, to protect, and to cast spells of various kinds, whether against human or demonic ill will, or simply to guard against disaster. . . . Recourse to blessings, spells and charms caused the most difficulty for the attempts of official Protestantism . . . to deal with forms of popular magic. . . .

If we were to lay a Protestant template on that formed by our three axes of Catholic belief, we would find one nestling inside the other like a pair of angle brackets. The relationship of Protestant to Catholic was a matter of degree, since the same axes were involved for both confessions in the three-dimensional relationship between religion and magic. . . . Protestantism was as caught up as Catholicism in the same dilemmas about the instrumental application of sacred power to secular life because it was positioned in the same force-field of sacrality. For this reason, Protestants experienced the same difficulties as Catholics when accusations of maleficent magic (and sometimes even of "white" magic) were laid in ways that turned them into accusations of witchcraft. The possibility of consorting with, and becoming implicated in, demonic activity was as real for Protestants as for Catholics. Thus, the puzzle of how a massive witchcraze could apparently arise in a period said to usher in the dawn of "modern rationality," . . . rests on a false dilemma. There was no inconsistency between Protestant thought-modes and a mentality that accepted diabolical efficacy in the world.

This is not to say that we could not find in Protestantism elements pointing in the direction mapped by those who see the Reformation as the first stage in the "disenchantment of the world," as the first step on the road to modernity. . . . It was the Enlightenment that first interpreted the Reformation as part of a long-term process of rationalization and secularization, an interpretation further reworked by the historiography of the nineteenth century until it constructed our modern view of the Reformation.

The paradigm of a secularizing and rationalizing Reformation has influenced many overarching interpretations of the ways in which the religion of Protestants contributed to long-term historical development, foremost among them that of Max Weber, who injected the notion of the "disenchantment of the world" into historical discussion. We may take Weber as a prime example of the ways in which nineteenth-century concerns were projected onto historical understanding of religion in the Reformation. Weber wrote from a background of nineteenth-century liberalism, claiming that he was himself "religiously unmusical." Many of the concepts he applied to the Reformation were arbitrary, if creative, adaptations of terms used in other, rather different contexts. . . . The notion of the "Protestant ethic" was an insight Weber arrived at less from historical research and more from observations of nineteenth-century Protestant behavior, which he then projected backwards in time in a classical example of the "regressive method." . . .

Whatever we may think of the sociological status of Weber's insights about the Reformation—and I must concede that I have always found them heuristically rewarding—I do not think that the thesis about the "disenchantment of the world" will any longer pass muster as a historically accurate description. It has certainly inspired many contemporary treatments of how the Reformation relates to the process of "modernization," not least the current interest among historians of the sixteenth century in social processes such as "confessionalization," social discipline and the "civilizing process" (alongside Norbert Elias and Michel Foucault, both of whom worked with the classic nineteenth-century paradigm of the Reformation). None of these interpretations, however, deal with, or show any understanding of, the nature of popular Protestantism. . . .

To explore the role of Protestantism in such processes, it is first necessary to construct a new understanding of the Reformation of the sixteenth century which takes account of those dissonant elements which falsify the paradigm that has been hitherto accepted, and then to write a new history of Protestantism which includes the religious experience and practice of ordinary believers, with all of their contradictions and misunderstandings. From the progress made so far on this task, I suspect that we would discover that Protestantism was as much a part of the problem as the self-evident solution to it; not a prime mover, but as subject as any other confession to secularization and desacralization, whatever set these processes in motion and whatever forms, stages, and modes of development they passed through. . . . It may also turn out that the "disenchantment of the world" played a marginal role in both the developing history of Protestantism and in advance toward "the modern world." This, however, is a story which still awaits its careful analyst.

Eamon Duffy

Elizabeth

The accession of Anne Boleyn's daughter in November 1558 launched the parishes of Tudor England on the third major religious transformation in a dozen years, though the extent and finality of the change was not at first evident to everyone. . . .

The Act of Uniformity, abolishing the Mass and reintroducing a slightly modified version of the second prayer-book of Edward VI, passed by the nerve-racking margin of three votes in April 1559, and came into use on 24 June. . . . Even after the passing of the Act of Uniformity, the introduction of the prayer-book, and the commencement of the draconian royal visitation with its attendant iconoclasm, traditionalists did not abandon hope of the continuance of something of the old order. . . .

In July 1559 Elizabeth issued a set of Injunctions for the "suppression of superstition" and "to plant true religion." Together with an accompanying set of articles of inquiry they formed the basis for a royal visitation of the whole country, which began in London on 19 July, and was extended to the rest of the country in August. Both the articles and the Injunctions were to a large extent modelled on those of Edward's reign, and required the recreation of the essential framework of Edwardine reformer—an English liturgy, the provision of Bible and Paraphrases, the abolition of images including those in window and wall, the outlawing of all vestments except the surplice and, at communion, the cope, the suppression of the parish procession and substitution of the English litany, and the abolition of the cult of the saints and of the dead. In particular, clergy were to discourage dying parishioners from making any religious obit provisions other than bequests to the poor and to highways. As in the case of the prayer-book and primer, the Elizabethan visitation articles and Injunctions in some respects took more account of Catholic sensibilities than the Edwardine provisions had done. The Rogationtide procession was to be retained as a religious thanksgiving for the fruits of the earth and a means of preserving boundaries, and a form of prayer for

Eamon Duffy, *The Stripping of the Altars: Traditional Religion in England 1400–1580* (New Haven and London: Yale University Press, 1992), 565–593. Copyright © 1992 by Yale University Press. Reprinted with permission.

the occasion was to be provided. Congregations were to bow at every mention of the name of Jesus. In removing images, those in windows were to be broken only if the window was to be reglazed. An addition to the Injunctions regulated the orderly removal of altars, forbidding the sort of iconoclastic activity which in fact took place in London, and declaring it to be in any case a matter of indifference whether the communion was administered at altar or table.

The Injunctions of 1559 have therefore been seen by some historians as markedly more conservative than their Edwardine models, and it has even been suggested that their draftsmen envisaged the preservation of non-abused imagery, such as Roods . . . , but the suggestion does not seem to be borne out by scrutiny of the articles which accompanied and glossed the Injunctions. . . . Despite the conciliatory signals in the prayer-book, primer, and Injunctions, the visitation of 1559 was to establish a pattern of rigorous suppression of the externals of Catholicism which was to preoccupy the episcopate for much of the next twenty years.

Some lessons had been learned from the Marian restoration. It would not now be enough to call for the surrender of Catholic liturgical books or the removal of images. There must be no opportunities for repetition of the scenes at Morebath or Long Melford and the hundreds of other parishes up and down the country where concealed or rescued images, vestments, and books had been restored at Mary's accession. . . . Commitment to the new order could only grow if all hope of a restoration of the old was extirpated, and that hope was recognized as inhering in the physical remains of Catholic cult, the "monuments of superstition." The commissioners were therefore to search out "any that keep in their houses undefaced" any such monuments and images "and do adore them, and specially such as have been set up in churches, chapels, or oratories." The progress of the visitation would be marked out by the smoke of bonfires of images and books in market-places and church greens throughout the land. And in what must have appeared an ominous preliminary to a re-run of the Edwardine confiscations, the Injunctions required the churchwardens of every parish to deliver inventories of "vestments, copes, and other ornaments, plate, books, and especially of grails, couchers, legends, processionals, hymnals, manuals, portuesses and suchlike." . . .

Attempts to prevent the destruction of images and ornaments were certainly very widespread. . . . [T]he Protestant authorities found themselves with an uphill task. Although the evidence of surviving churchwardens' accounts makes clear the essential conformity of most parishes, it was a reluctant and partial conformity. The removal of Roods and draw-ing down of altars which fill the pages of virtually every set of accounts from 1559 to 1561 were not in most cases the result of a landslide of Protestant fervour, but of weary obedience to unpopular measures. . . . [T]he majority of parishioners were firmly attached to "the observatyons and ryghtes of the catholyke churche," and many hoped, and most thought possible, a return of the old ways. They had seen all this before— the books and images burned, the altars stripped and demolished, the vestments sold for cushions and bed-hangings. That destruction had had to be reversed, with great difficulty and at enormous cost, and it was the rank and file of the parish who had borne the brunt. Now the newly ac-quired Roods and patronal statues, the untarnished latten pyxes and paxes and holy-water stoups, the missals and manuals still smelling of printer's ink, which Marian archdeacons had demanded from them, were to be once more pitched into wheelbarrows and trundled to the fire. And all this at the behest of a Queen still unmarried and young enough for child-bearing, whose prospects of a Protestant husband, and hence a stable con-tinuation of religious policy, were minimal. . . .

These preoccupations recur again and again in episcopal visitations and ecclesiastical court proceedings into the 1570s and beyond. In the diocese of Lichfield and Coventry in 1565 the bishop, under pressure from the Court, was driving his clergy to "call upon the people daily that they cast away their beads with all their superstitions that they do use," and the clergy to "cast away your Mass-books, your portesses and all other books of Latin service," and in any case to extinguish the lights which burned round the dead at every funeral. He demanded that wardens and sidesmen fine those using beads a shilling for every offence, and was also attempting to prevent the laity reciting the "De Profundis" Psalm for dead neighbours or laying corpses down by wayside Crosses as they brought them for burial. He was also demanding the surrender of holy-water stocks, sepulchres, and other ritual paraphernalia "which be laid up in secret places in your church."

Conditions in Lichfield and Coventry were no doubt worse (from the reformers' point of view) than in many other places, but the wide-spread survival of traditional practices and the equipment of Catholic worship was by no means confined to the dark corners of the land. The records of presentments in the Archbishop of York's Court of Audience, arising out of the visitation of 1567, throw a brilliantly clear light on this aspect of the state of the diocese, and demonstrate that it was not only in

Staffordshire and Derbyshire that images and holy-water pots, Rood-lofts, beads, and Latin primers survived to trouble the Protestant establishment. John Aylmer, Archdeacon of Lincoln, conducted a routine visitation of the diocese of Lincoln in 1565 which so horrified him that he lobbied Cecil, Throckmorton, and the Earl of Leicester for the establishment of a special commission for the country of Lincoln "for reforming this church and diocese . . . for undoubtedly this country hath as much need of it as any place in England."

The general outline of the picture presented by the returns can be crudely established by a simple count. If we take the destruction by the end of the second year of the reign of such major cult items as the altars, the Rood and other images, and the Mass-books, as an indicator of prompt compliance, just forty-five of the 180 parishes qualify as having complied promptly with the main requirements of the Elizabethan settlement. . . . Eighty-two parishes delayed the destruction or sale of important items like the images, books, and vestments for three years or more, many of them only complying after Aylmer's archidiaconal visitation of 1565, and some only within days or even hours of appearing before the commissioners in 1566. . . .

And even among those complying promptly by destroying images, books, and ornaments, obedience to "the lawes of the realme . . . and the procedyngs of the heyghe powers" was often the operative factor, rather than communal zeal for Protestantism. . . .

Episcopal visitations frequently singled out funeral ritual as one of the most recalcitrant areas of continuing Catholic practice, particularly the use of candles and Crosses about corpses, and the ringing of peals both before funerals and on All Souls' eve, to elicit prayers for the dead. . . . In 1590 the situation in the north-west had hardly improved, ministers complaining that throughout the county of Lancaster and in much of Cheshire whenever there was a death "the neighbours use to visit the Corse, and there everie one to say a Pater Noster, (or De profundis) for the Sole: the Belles (all the while) beinge ronge many a solemne Peale. After which, they are made partakers of the ded manse dowle or Banquet of Charitie."

Funeral practice was, inevitably, one of the areas where feeling remained most conservative. It was by no means the only one. . . . Those traditions were legion—crossing with the ring in marriage, and moving it from finger to finger as in the pre-Reformation service, . . . and a whole range of traditional actions in the communion service: standing while the Gospel was read, kneeling at the name of Jesus, refusing to receive the bread in their hands but insisting that the priest place it in their mouths, crossing themselves before receiving, or crossing themselves with the consecrated bread. . . . Such practices, of course, survived in some regions longer than others. . . .

Such meticulous removal of the externals of the old religion, "so that there remain no memory of the same in walls, glasses, windows or elsewhere within their churches and houses," was imposed as a matter of policy from above; as we have seen, it was for a time widely if quietly resisted. But it could not be without effect. As the memories of Catholic cultus faded, as even traditionally minded clergy read out week by week the fulminations of the *Homilies* against "papistical superstitions and abuses," and preached their quarterly sermons against the Pope, as the Commissions of the Peace were slowly purged of hinderers of religion, and wardens and sidesmen chosen to police the parishes who were ready to conform to and even to further "this religion," the chances of a reversion to the old ways faded. The process of destruction itself must have had its effect. . . . [H]oly-water stoups became the parish wash-troughs, sanctus and sacring bells were hung on sheep and cows, or used to call workmen to their dinner, pyxes were split open and turned into balances to weigh out coin or spice. The insistence of the authorities that all such sacred objects be defaced and "put to profane use" represented a profound recognition of the desacralizing effect of such actions. . . .

There were of course those for whom the Protestant gospel was a light on the Damascus road, the sense of a burden lifted from their shoulders. Their impact was certainly disproportionate to their absolute numbers, which were probably small in most communities in Elizabeth's early years. Time, the steady pressure of authority lending its weight to the reformed groups within local communities, and thereby ripping the balance of power in favour of the new faith, the impact of education and evangelization—all these would combine to change that. But for most of the first Elizabethan adult generation, Reformation was a stripping away of familiar and beloved observances, the destruction of a vast and resonant world of symbols which, despite the denials of the proponents of the new Gospel, they both understood and controlled. The people of Tudor England were, by and large, no spartans, no saints, but by the same token they were no reformers. They knew themselves to be mercenary, worldly, weak, and they looked to religion, the old or the new, to pardon these vices, not to reform them. When the crisis of Reformation came they mostly behaved as mercenary, worldly, and weak men and women will, grumbling, obstructing, but in the end taking the line of least resistance, like Bishop Stokesley lamenting his own helplessness in the face of advancing heresy and wishing that he had the courage to stand against it with his brother the Bishop of Rochester.

Their conformity was not always ignoble. Christopher Trychay on Exmoor conformed and conformed again, but he was no vicar of Bray. Reading his church book it is hard to see what else such a man in such a time could have done. For him religion was above all local and particular, "rooted in one dear perpetual place," his piety centred on this parish, this church, these people. It was not a matter of mere fear, though going with his wardens to be quizzed yet again by the commissioners for church goods in Exeter he would have seen the rows of rebel heads above the gates, and registered the fate of those who resisted the Crown. Some priests had led their people against the new religion, and had been hanged in their chasubles for their pains, and still the altars had come down, the royal arms replaced the Rood, the beloved images been axed and burned. . . . [F]or a man like Trychay there was nowhere to be except with the people he had baptized, shriven, married, and buried for two generations. A few years before Trychay had begun to minister at Morebath the wisest man in England [Thomas More] had written:

> *What part soever you have taken upon you, playe that aswel as you can and make the best of it: and doe not therefore disturbe and brynge oute of order the whole matter, bycause that an other, whyche is meryer and better commeth to your remembraunce . . . you muste not forsake the shippe in a tempeste, because you can not rule and kepe downe the wyndes . . . But you must with a crafty wile and subtell trayne studye and endevoure youre selfe, asmuche as in you lyeth, to handle the matter wyttelye and handsomelye for the purpose, and that whyche you can not turne to good, so to order it that it be not very badde.*

In parishes all over England decent, timid men and women set themselves to do just that. It was not for them to rule the winds: the conscience of the prince was in the hands of God, and the people must make shift to do as best they could under the prince. While Sir Christopher Trychay was priest of Morebath Protestantism would be long in making headway, and when it did it would be tempered, transformed.

But the price for such accommodation, of course, was the death of the past it sought to conserve. If Protestantism was transformed, so was traditional religion. . . . By the end of the 1570s, whatever the instincts and nostalgia of their seniors, a generation was growing up which had known nothing else, which believed the Pope to be Antichrist, the Mass a mummery, which did not look back to the Catholic past as their own, but another country, another world.

Sara T. Nalle

God in La Mancha: Religious Reform and the People of Cuenca, 1500–1650

In the second half of the sixteenth century, religious authorities guided conquenses' faith into devotions that reflected the priorities of the new age. For the religiously adept, the age's need for an interior life and direct contact with God could not be denied, but it could be supervised by ensuring that the materials and priests that could inform that interior life represented the latest teaching of the church. Devotion to Christ, the mass, the martyred saints, and of course the sorrowing Virgin were the watchwords of the period. The rapidity with which the penitential and eucharistic cults spread in the diocese indicates the great reservoir of faith among the mass of the people, who may not have been able to meditate but were prepared to offer their suffering and prayers instead. If the city of Cuenca was typical, most remarkable was the speed with which the new cults took hold and the old forms of religious life—the skits and banquets—were dismantled. Just as conquenses threw themselves into learning their catechism, they also seemed to embrace with enthusiasm the new holidays, cults, and religious organizations that religious and civic authorities introduced to the diocese. The most profound impact, however, of the new religious regime was not to be felt in the realm of the living, which, as every reader of the *Contemptus Mundi* knew, was filled with vanities. The Christian's true reward came after death. The question was how to obtain it. . . .

In the sixteenth century, members of the church and laity coincided in their goal to cultivate a more intense personal religiosity that included the desire to know God, to live according to Christ's example, and to prepare for death. Private devotions, penitential confraternities, and participation in the church's sacraments all increased. Judging by the types of devotions practiced and the suffrages ordered, people were not at all sure that their good works and faith would justify them. Conquenses prayed and read, punished their bodies, and bought perpetual masses in an effort to improve their merit. In the seventeenth century, however, this energy was channeled into very specific provisions for the afterlife. The question of personal salvation was transformed into a new religiosity, one that for many individuals substituted money and priests for prayers and community action. The church had succeeded in implanting a more personal faith, but one that became increasingly mechanical as time went on. If conquenses' wills are any measure of their faith, in the seventeenth century individuals no longer doubted the final destination of their souls or worried about the degree of glory they could achieve in heaven. Hell had receded into the background, and purgatory could be compassed in prayer. Conquenses seemed to ask, not *"Will* I be saved?" but "How long until I reach heaven?" and "How much will it cost?" The answer was a question of personal finances. The long-term consequences for Cuenca were plain to see: the subversion of faith and the investment of capital into enterprises that would yield no profit in this world. . . .

Late one Sunday afternoon in June 1654, four men waited to hear their death sentence pronounced. They stood high on scaffolding constructed next to the cathedral in the plaza mayor of Cuenca. Below them and fifty-three lesser prisoners sat officials representing the Inquisition, the bishop and the cathedral, the royal government, and the city of Cuenca. They all faced the crowd that had packed into the narrow plaza to watch the auto de fe. Perhaps the condemned men's gaze drifted from the excited but solemn crowd, made up of the city's parishes, cofradías, familiars, and religious, all carrying their standards, crosses, and candles, to the tall, stone houses that leaned into the plaza. From the open windows, which had been rented out for the occasion, the city's nobility returned the prisoners' gaze. The four condemned men, Portuguese conversos, had ignored previous warnings from the Inquisition and had continued to practice Judaism. The death sentence was obligatory. The city's doctor, who witnessed the auto de fe, wrote of the doomed men,

> *Lacking in faith, stubborn and obstinate,*
> *(whoever lacks faith lacks all)*
> *blind to the end, and rooted without reason,*
> *since they deny the truth which uplifts them,*
> *or better said, they are without hope —*
> *because hope and faith serve as a ladder*
> *to an action so uplifting as to save oneself —*
> *triumph despairs if one is without the other.*

But the city had not assembled to witness an execution. The actual sentences would be carried out later, down on the Campo de San Francisco. This was a joyous occasion, marred only by the Portugueses' intransigence. The city had gathered to see its faith renewed by the auto de fe. Except for the four resolute conversos, all of the prisoners had recognized their errors and now stood ready to embrace the church again. It was a triumph for conquenses, their church, and their city. Thanks to all of their efforts, the unity of the Catholic faith had been preserved.

Around them, the city and diocese, the empire itself, was in full decline. If the city's doctor, as he described the auto de fe, was aware of the contrast between the lavish spectacle and the city's abandoned houses, he gave no sign of it in his heroic poem. For the doctor, there was only one reality. Despite the fact that there was little to fear from heresy in Castile, and even less so in Cuenca, the doctor's idiom was the language of militant Catholicism. His turgid verse returned to the point over and over again: without the strong arm of the church, there would be no peace in Cuenca. The bishop of Cuenca, who reported on the state of the diocese a few years later, shared the doctor's uncritical vision. Even though by his own estimation the bishopric was desperately poor, in a report he sent to Rome in 1659, Fernández Pacheco concluded that all of his clergy were virtuous and well educated and the people were free of doctrinal errors and superstition. No synod had been held in over thirty years, but Fernández was confident that given the bishopric's reformed state, none was needed.

Elsewhere in Catholic Europe, the Counter Reformation was reaching full stride. In Spain, the heroic age of the church had run its course. Foreign visitors in the late seventeenth century described a country in which outward display of ceremony poorly disguised the emptiness of its interior life. By the eighteenth century, it almost seemed as if no reform of the church had ever taken place. Once again, important differences in preparation and vocation existed among the secular clergy. Now, however, reflecting the poverty of agrarian Castile, the rural clergy were the most poorly educated as well as the most poorly paid. The archbishopric of Toledo, where in the past developments had paralleled those in Cuena, presented a depressing picture of clerical absenteeism, ignorance, and concubinage. Jansenists and enlightened intellectuals in the government criticized local religion for its reliance on divine intervention, its processions, ex-votos, and miraculous images. What had once been the shared faith of all was becoming the devalued superstitions of "the people," and with time, increasingly marginal to the learned tradition of elites.

All this, however, lies in the future. If we return to our starting place, the late fifteenth century, we see that the reformation of the sixteenth century wrought profound changes in the religious life of Castile. However briefly drawn the picture of late medieval Cuenca, it showed that the only part of the Pre-Reform that affected the diocese was the outlawing of Judaism. Otherwise, the diocese reflected many of the traits of traditional Christianity: the confusion of religion and magic, the lack of clerical discipline, even the millenarianism. After the Comunero Revolt, however, the religious life of the diocese began to change rapidly. The push for a better clergy, the concern with religious education, and desire for an interior faith were all well established as the Council of Trent was entering its final session. Judging by conquenses' growing pious bequests and level of indoctrination, there seems to have been no sixteenth-century "slump" in commitment to Catholicism as there was in Lyon, divided between Protestants and Catholics, or in Renaissance Siena, where there was a "cinquecento collapse in piety and charity."

The forces of renewal and change were fourfold. First, between the reigns of the Catholic Monarchs and Philip II there was the sustained pressure of a century of reforms designed to bring local religious life in line with standards set in Toledo and Rome. However, what church authorities wanted should not be the sole criterion of religious life; we must also think in terms of the religious needs of the people who were the target of reform. One was the age-old demand for supernatural aid and protection, which reformers respected as long as the protection rendered was orthodox in nature. Alongside this traditional function of religion, however, there was a new one abroad in sixteenth-century Spain, the need for a more personal relationship with God. Ironically, this driving force for an interior life was one of the major challenges faced by Spanish religious authorities of the time. Although they wanted to encourage an individual faith, liberated from the compromises imposed by family and community, authorities feared the mystic. The tension between authority and interiority thus represents the second force of change. More peculiar to Spain was the third force of change, national identification with the Holy Mother Catholic Church. This identification took two forms: vindictive repudiation of Spain's religious and ethnic pluralism and the popular conviction, in Castile at least, that the church's struggles and priorities were the people's own. The final catalyst was not an idea or attitude but social crisis. The demographic crisis of the entire first quarter of the seventeenth century, coupled with economic hard times, reinforced both communitarian and individualistic aspects of sixteenth-century religious expression. For communities, economic and demographic catastrophe meant increased reliance on "survivalist" religious modes of propitiation. On the other hand, the sixteenth-century's emphasis on personal spiritual development meant that when death struck, individuals now turned *away* from the supportive network of kin and community to seek salvation on their own, via the offices of the church. Out of this crisis and the sixteenth-century reforms was born modern Spanish Catholicism: highly personal yet strongly conformist; localized yet nationalist; dogmatic yet proudly independent.

In practice, Catholic reform in Cuenca was an incongruous mixture of official compulsion and popular religious enthusiasm. The use of inquisitorial and episcopal edicts exhorting people to confess their transgressions and denounce those of others, as well as the public humiliations, drew alternately on consequenses' feelings of guilt and personal honor. Such emotional blackmail (to say nothing of trampling on unimagined human rights) effectively promoted compliance — if one's conscience did not suffice to combat sin, then the threat of losing one's honor was a powerful incentive. On the other hand, the insistence on asceticism, the sacramental view of religious practice, and the attack on "superstitions" and loose morals were trends that could be found among both groups of zealous religious and lay people seeking a more spiritual form of religious self-expression.

The religious reformation in Castile may be seen as two movements, spearheaded by different groups who were not always on speaking terms with one another. First, there was the essentially clerical attack on secular culture (sexual mores, public sins, magic) and heterodoxy, which was waged on all social fronts via ecclesiastical discipline. In this reformation of morals and ideas, the gentry were drawn into the Inquisition's net as frequently as were other Christians, and for very similar reasons. Don Alonso Pacheco de Guzmán, son of the duke of Villena, was penanced in 1562 as a great blasphemer. Doña Juana Pacheco (no direct relation) had to explain to the inquisitors why she said, contrary to the church's teaching, that being married was better than being celibate. The occult sciences, such as astrology, necromancy, and the like, were most popular among the upper classes, including Philip II himself, and it was not unusual for educated persons, even devout ones, to resort to love magic.

The second part of the reformation was the spiritual revival of the sixteenth century. Here, we can see the emergence of groups of self-conscious devout, primarily literate bourgeois, often of converso background, such as the conquense Juan de Céspedes (married to a conversa) and his group of "teatinos." However, it would be a mistake to insist too much on this association of religion with class, particularly in the latter half of the century. The Inquisition found people of all backgrounds making comments reminiscent of Erasmian spirituality; one did not have to be bourgeois to think that devotion to images was superstitious or that funeral pomp was a vanity. Many of the typically Tridentine confraternities were made up of working-class members or were founded in the diocese's small towns. The third estate could not afford as many suffrages as the gentry and clergy but was just as committed to the various forms of baroque funeral piety (friars, habits, special masses and indulgences), and a higher percentage of them gave to the city's charities. To complicate matters, there were clearly female and male forms of religious expression, which may, with further research, turn out to be just as significant as those associated with any particular social class.

By the seventeenth century, a new religiosity was laid over preexisting structures of faith. The catechization campaign had successfully taken root, and most conquenses fulfilled their minimum obligations as Catholics. Tridentine morality seemed to have won out for the time being. In the capital, during Lent conquenses avoided sexual intercourse, and illegitimate conceptions declined throughout the seventeenth century. The emphasis on personal faith can be seen in funeral strategies, which came to focus on the supreme moment of judgment between the individual and God. Local religion lost some of its autonomy, and

international Marian and Christocentric devotions were popularized.
What did not change in Cuenca in the late seventeenth century, however, was the pace of economic recovery. With recovery could come new
social structures, values, and priorities. Instead, the diocese remained
tied to a cruel subsistence economy, one that was as vulnerable to crisis
in the eighteenth century as it had been in the sixteenth century. Thus,
intertwined with the modern religion that took form through the
Catholic Reformation, there endured an earlier, resilient faith, the religion of preindustrial people dependent on the harsh and unpredictable
land of Castile.

Tessa Watt

Cheap Print and Popular Piety, 1550–1640

In 1626, John Taylor the Water Poet compiled his collection of *Wit and
mirth*. He claimed to have heard the anecdotes in inns and alehouses,
taverns and tobacco shops, and along highways and waterways. Even if
many of them were chestnuts from old jest-books, given Taylor's popularity the stories were likely to end up in these places once the printed
collection appeared. Some of the mirth touched on matters of religion.

> *A Poore County may [man] praying devoutly superstitious before an old
> Image of S.Loy, the Image suddenly fell downe upon the poore man, and
> bruised his bones sorely, that hee could not stirre abroad in a moneth
> after; in which space the cheating Priests had set up a new Image: the
> Country man came to the Church againe, and kneeled a farre off to
> the new Image, saying, Although thou smilest and lookest faire upon
> mee, yet thy father plaid me such a knavish pranke lately, that Ile beware
> how I come too neere thee, lest though shouldst have any of thy Fathers
> unhappy qualities.*

There were several jokes about sleeping in church:

> A *diligent and learned Preacher on a Sunday in the afternoone was*
> *preaching, whilest most of the zealous vestry men (for their meaner edifi-*
> *cation) were fast asleepe in their pues: in the meane space a young child*
> *cryed somewhat aloud at the lower end of the Church, which the Preacher*
> *hearing, called to the Nurse, and said, Nurse, I pray thee still thy childe,*
> *or else it may chance to awaken some of the best men in our parish.*

John Taylor's audience was amused by the backward image-
worshipper, but equally happy to laugh at the zealous vestry men. Both
the new Protestant culture of the word, and the traditional culture
of the image, were familiar reference points. Like the vestry men in
the anecdote, most of Taylor's readers were less likely to be hostile to the
Protestant preacher than simply bored by the sermon. Like the country
man, they had less faith than they used to in the power of icons (probably through education against idolatry, rather than the "knavish pranks"
of a statue), but the artefacts of this older system of belief were still part of
their visual vocabulary.

The sort of buyers we have identified for the cheap religious print
in our study were not the minority of godly "elect," but the ordinary
parishioners. If the sermon was soporific, and the old images of saints no
longer worked, the godly ballads and chapbooks caught the attention of
some of the audience which gathered around the pedlar in the church-
yard or marketplace.

Why should the historian be interested in these ephemeral pedlar's
wares? The development of "cheap print" is important as a chapter in
publishing history; acting both as an instrument and a measure of "typo-
graphic acculturation" in rural England. These paper artefacts also have
insights to offer us on some of the wider questions of the period, especially
on the impact of Protestantism, and of print, on traditional culture. We
will begin here with a brief summary of the development and specialization of the "cheap print" trade, before going on to address some of the
larger historical issues.

During the first quarter of the seventeenth century, a group of London
stationers developed publishing strategies which were increasingly re-
sponsive to the demands of the buyers, as they assembled and pruned
a stock of successful ballads and chapbooks, according to commercial
dictates. The nature of the ballad trade was transformed, as the "ballad

partners" organized themselves for efficient production and distribution. They increased the use of woodcuts, standardized the naming of tunes, and collected the copyrights to favourite titles, registered in 1624. Meanwhile, they translated some of the themes of the rising copper print trade into the cheaper medium of woodcut, producing large poster-size pictures which survive from about 1613. Most significantly for later generations of readers, they began to develop a new line of little books, to send along the same distribution network as the ballads. In the second and third decades of the century, they collected miscellanies and godlies in "penny" size; as well as the merry quartos which would later be sold as "double-books" and "histories." Finally, from the late 1620s, they began to stock new versions of these old merry tales, specially written or abridged for the 24-page octavo format.

Certain salient themes recurred in the successful ballads, broadsides and chapbooks, flowing freely between the different media. Partial substitutes for the outlawed saints were provided by new archetypes: Protestant martyrs and heroines like the Duchess of Suffolk and Anne Askew, Old Testament or apocryphal figures like wise Solomon and constant Susanna, pious women such as Katherine Stubbes or the Lady Jane Grey. Handy rules for social behaviour were available in the ballad of "Solomon's Sentences," in tables for the wall like "Finch his alphabet" and in the portable chapbook format of *Keep within compasse*. The fear of death was omnipresent, whether as the medieval vision of St. Bernard, the secularized image of the skeleton in the "dance of death" woodcut or the Protestant faith and repentance preached by John Andrewes, and practised by the clerk of Bodnam. The miraculous element of religion was still present in carols and woodcuts of the nativity and of Christ's miracles, as well as in ballads of Doctor Faustus, chapbook tales of magical friars and woodcuts of strange creatures ominously interpreted as divine portents.

These themes were packaged in forms which were suitable for the rudimentary reader, and attractive to an audience on the fringes of literacy. Ballads were set to catchy tunes, and given decorative woodcuts, which carried them beyond their readers to "illiterate" singers and viewers. Tables and chapbooks used mnemonic tricks adopted from oral habits of thought: numerical groupings like the "figure of three"; aphorisms, proverbs and short chunks of narrative (like the tiny chapters in *Patient Grissel*) which were easily digested and remembered. The structure of printed wares could also imitate familiar visible objects, such as the points, gloves and garters which may have been sold by the same petty chapmen who brought the broadsides into the countryside.

The new "publishing formula" of the chapbook was not an equation devised in the abstract. It was a response to the growing market of readers created by the rise of literacy. The specialization of "cheap print" coincided with the second phase of "educational revolution" which affected the school generations of James' and Charles' reigns. The publishers in London were not isolated from such developments, but linked to the rest of the country by a network of communications, which included the authors and the distributors of their products. . . .

This study has raised questions about the effects of two related forces in the century after the Reformation: Protestantism and print. Both have been credited with enormous, disruptive and even "revolutionary" impact on traditional English culture. According to Wrightson and Levine's study of Terling in Essex, a militant Protestantism "inserted a cultural wedge" in village society, as "distinctions of religious outlook, education and manners" were "superimposed on the existing distinctions of wealth, status and power." The godly parish notables led the attack on "a popular culture of communal dancings, alehouse sociability and the like" which "retreated before a more sober ideal of family prayer, neighborly fellowship, and introspective piety." Other historians have focussed on the logocentrism of this new Protestant culture; its emphasis on "the invisible, abstract and didactic word: primarily the word of the printed page." Thus, around 1580, according to Patrick Collinson, the English people crossed a watershed "from a culture of orality and image to one of print culture: from one mental and imaginative 'set' to another."

The evidence of cheap religious print does not contradict the cultural importance of either Protestantism or the printed word, but it does suggest that the confrontational models sketched above are unsatisfactory. In studying the relationship between these new forces and the existing culture, we need to see not only points of conflict and displacement, but also areas of consensus and gradual integration. Even to write of Protestantism or print as "forces" is misleading: we need to see them not as coherent and unchanging entities (one a set of doctrines, the other a technology), but as inseparable from and constantly modified by the cultural contexts in which they are found.

There were also, of course, points of disjuncture or disruption; situations and events in which conflicts flared. The sources to which historians have access tend to record these points of confrontation. Protestant tracts reveal a deliberate crusade against traditional visual images. Quarter sessions, assize and church court records document local conflicts over sexual morality, ale-selling and sabbath-day festivities. However, this bias in the sources can lead us to ignore areas of culture where these conflicts were either resolved or unarticulated. In some media, such as the narrative "stories" for walls, Bible-centered Protestantism and traditional visual piety found common ground. In other cultural forms, such as the ballads on death and salvation, old and new beliefs rubbed elbows without apparent sense of contradiction. These sources provide an oblique approach to the area of unconscious or semi-conscious values and assumptions; to the fragmentary mosaic of "commonplace mentalities."

The attempt to interpret cheap print in terms of consensual values, shared at many levels of society, is supported by Martin Ingram's investigation of church court records in Wiltshire during the same period. Ingram argues that the church courts enforced values which were "broadly consensual" and in line with the wide "spectrum on unspectacular orthodoxy" within which the beliefs of most villagers can be categorized. He argues that "the notion that religious commitment was conditioned by social class must be treated with caution." Rebellion against the church and its moral standards was more often a matter of youth culture than of economic standing, and established householders at all levels were normally guided by a sense of social morality. The church and religion

> were important as markers of status, respectability and belonging, if for nothing else; and though this may have been most true for the middle to upper strata of parish society (the groups from which churchwardens were usually recruited and which were most likely to possess family pews), it probably applied also to many "honest householders" of the poorer sort, who had a definite, albeit modest stake in the community. . . .

This evidence of a core of "honest householders," dominating village society at all social levels, indicates a solid market for the godly broadsides and chapbooks of the present study. The moderate piety of "100 godly lessons" or the woodcut "Christus natus est" would not seem out of place in the households (whether poor or prosperous) of Martin Ingram's Wiltshire village. It is less easy to see where they would belong in Wrightson and Levine's Essex village of Terling, where the atmosphere in the early seventeenth century was one of "strain and conflict" between the parish notables who tried to impose their values of "order and godliness" on the community, and the labouring poor who were indifferent, if not hostile, to the innovative Protestant culture. The evidence of cheap print questions the rigidity of this "polarization" of experience between godly and ungodly, elite and poor. In these cheapest of printed wares, Protestant doctrine and conservative piety were integrated, and "religion" continued to have a place in the world of popular songs and alehouses, which were supposedly the preserve of the irreligious multitude.

There is no doubt that religious and moral issues could often serve as a focus for parish rivalries. But, as Martin Ingram argues, these social diversions "were as much vertical as horizontal." . . .

[W]hile historians continue to argue over the correct ratio of conflict and consensus, even the exponents of the "polarized" society (such as Keith Wrightson) are agreed on the existence of "canons of good neighbourliness," "minimum standards" of behaviour and a "moral community" within which village society had to operate. The godly ballads, broadsides and chapbooks are artefacts of the process by which these standards were articulated, disseminated, absorbed, modified, adapted and reflected. They are the products of a dialogue between Protestant norms and traditional practices; between a centralized press and localized experience; between authors and consumers, through the profit-conscious publisher as middleman.

We need, then, to see belief-formation as a process: not a simple replacement of Catholic with Protestant doctrine, but a gradual modification of traditional piety. The resulting patchwork of beliefs may be described as distinctively "post-Reformation," but not thoroughly "Protestant." Piety retained a visual dimension, even if Christ in glory was now more remote, banished to the windows or roof of the parish church, or to the tiny woodcuts along the top of a ballad. Religious emotion still attached itself to heroic archetypes, even if these were increasingly Protestant martyrs rather than Catholic saints. Morality still meant good neighbourly behaviour, and hell was still the same fiery place, a final threat as direct punishment for sins committed in this world.

"Religion" cannot just be measured in terms of knowledge of particular doctrines, or attendance at church, or even adherence to the increasingly strict Protestant norms of sexual conduct. We must also look at the hazier area of images, emotions and fears; of the rules by which people ordered their lives (even if these were looser than the mostly "godly sort" might wish); and of how people placed themselves in history and the universe. Most historians would agree that the early sixteenth-century villager's representation of the world was inseparable from a Christian framework, even if this was infused with beliefs we would call "magical" or "pagan." The Protestant Reformation removed large chunks of the imagery and the festival calendar which had reinforced this framework, but the "mental set" was not so easily dismantled.

"Religion," even in Protestant England, was not a category isolated from other aspects of experience. If reformers abandoned their ambitious mid-sixteenth-century programme to create a Protestantized "popular culture" of song and imagery, this did not mean a sudden divorce of religion from these media. Artisans and writers could not help but continue to embed their products with religious values and themes. Even the broadside ballads written by the early Elizabethan reformers had a life of their own well into the seventeenth century, and sometimes beyond. A hardening of "puritan" attitudes in some places may well have alienated the young, the indigent or the transient from the parish churches, but we cannot assume that even these marginalized groups had no religious opinions. We must not think of religion as the exclusive preserve of the church, but look for ways in which "religious" beliefs in the broadest sense were encountered throughout local society: in popular songs, in cloths on alehouse walls, in tables pasted up in cottages, or in accounts of grisly executions chanted out in the marketplaces.

Just as Protestantism should not be seen as a coherent set of doctrines which simply replaces older belief, so print and literacy were not unchanging technologies which unilaterally replaced other forms of communication. . . .

[The] attempt to look at literacy in specific cultural contexts, and at "mixed" modes of communication, is appropriate to the evidence of cheap print in early modern England. The meaning of a printed ballad was not only in its text, but also in the melody of the tune it was sung to; its tempo and instrumentation; the location of the performance; the talent, character and social status of the singer; the people in the audience; the other songs sung before and after; even the other songs sung to the same tune, which resonated in the ears of the listener. The meaning could also be in the woodcuts along the top of the broadside; its location on the alehouse or cottage wall; the other ballads or painted cloths in the room; and the stained glass windows or paintings in the local church which recurred in the mind's eye of the viewer.

The "consumers" of cheap print brought certain habitual ways of seeing, reading, and remembering to the broadsides and chapbooks, such as the tendency to conceptualize morality in aphoristic packages, or to think of printed texts in terms of familiar objects like gloves and garters. Our interest in cultural "mentalities" on a broad societal level need not imply a deterministic attitude to the individual consumer. Unfortunately, we rarely have documents like those used by Carlo Ginzburg to show how a sixteenth-century miller constructed his own meaning from the books he read, filtered through the primarily oral culture he lived in. But by approaching obliquely, through an exploration of the various ways print could be used, we can suggest contexts in which an individual might encounter and interpret a given text. A crude woodcut of the holy family might trigger a visual response related to a favourite window in the parish church. A ballad of godly "Susanna" or the "Duchess of Suffolk" might be subsumed into a singer's stock of heroes and heroines; memorized and stored along with "Bonny Barbara Allen" and "The bailiff's daughter of Islington."

Indeed, whether or not the text was a song, it may have been treated as something to be *learnt*. Reading was taught as a form of rote-learning, with an emphasis on the ability to memorize set forms of words, such as the Creed, Lord's Prayer, Ten Commandments and catechism. Even when a pupil left school with what we would call full reading skills, this learning process may have helped to inculcate a habit of "intensive" reading: that is, contact with a restricted number of texts, which were slowly and closely perused, frequently re-read and often rendered aloud. A Bordeaux lawyer Pierre Bernaudau described this kind of reading amongst the French peasants of the late eighteenth century, whose reading matter consisted primarily of Books of Hours, almanacs and the *bibliothèque bleue*: "They have a mania for going back over these miserable books twenty times, and when they talk with you about them (which they do eagerly), they recite their little books word for word, so to speak. . . ."

[T]he study of cheap print in the early modern period does suggest that the relationship of reader to text was not the same as that of a twentieth-century literate scanning the morning paper. It appears often to have been more like the relationship of singer to song text, with the printed artefact acting as an aid to memory. The "godly tables" and painted sayings on walls were there to remind the viewer of things already known, not to bring new information. The ballads and chapbooks of Robin Hood, Patient Grissel and Guy of Warwick retold stories which had long been circulating orally, and were simply given a fixed form in print. Of course, we would not want to exaggerate this point: new stories of northern farmers, west-country tailors and London whores were constantly being added to the stock of timeless chivalric tales. But these acquisitions from print continued to enrich the oral culture, rather than simply replace it.

Literacy and print were not only "agents of change," but could also be forces for cultural continuity. Lucien Febvre and Henri-Jean Martin have shown how printing could reinforce a traditional world view:

> *Although printing certainly helped scholars in some fields, on the whole it could not be said to have hastened the acceptance of new ideas or knowledge. In fact, by popularising long cherished beliefs, strengthening traditional prejudices and giving authority to seductive fallacies, it could even be said to have represented an obstacle to the acceptance of many new views.*

A striking example of this persistence of old-fashioned beliefs is the length of time it took for the general reading public to take any interest in the discovery of the New World. Throughout the first half of the sixteenth century, works on the Americas circulated only within a small circle, and travel books continued to perpetuate a distorted picture of the world. This conservatism can be seen again and again in the ballads and chapbooks of the present study, which reprinted medieval chivalric stories and pre-Reformation visions of the after-life well into the eighteenth century.

We have been describing the conservatism of print in terms of the mental habits of orality: reading as remembering, reader as speaker or singer. The continuity of orality was, on the whole, accepted, unquestioned and ideologically unproblematic. Hearing and reading were both means of access to words; an oral sermon or a printed tract could bring an audience to the Word; and the Bible was the medium of revelation whether in printed form or real aloud. However, the continuity of the visual dimension was a more contentious matter. Here, in printed word and image, were two different ways of seeing, which seemed (from the extreme iconoclast's point of view) to be two incompatible ways of conceptualizing religious belief.

At the end of the sixteenth century, some reformers and writers in England became acutely aware of a tension between the verbal and the visual; between the iconic impulse of their inherited culture from Rome, and the iconoclastic implications of their new logo-centric religion. At its strongest, this awareness of cultural tension was directed inward, causing individuals to reflect on their sensory intake and on the value given to things read or heard, and things seen, in their construction of the world and its meaning. However, it would be a mistake to project this preoccupation of an educated minority onto the society as a whole. If there was a gradual suppression of the visual dimension in English culture, relative to the growing value placed on verbal or literate communication, it did not occur in one generation, nor even in several generations. The iconic and the verbal continued to exist in fruitful tension in the seventeenth century, finding new life in hybrid forms like the emblem, and in simpler "tables" which combined picture and text to meet the needs of a semi-literate audience. . . .

The profane and the pious, the verbal and the visual: all were accommodated within . . . the same mind, the same experience. It is only the historian who, like an iconoclast, wants to rip down all the images on the walls which do not seem to fit. We need to recognize how the culture could absorb new beliefs while retaining old ones, could modify doctrines, could accommodate words and icons, ambiguities and contradictions. There may have been Reformation and Civil War, riot and rebellion, but the basic mental decor did not change as suddenly or completely as historians would sometimes lead us to believe.

"Communion in Both Kinds." (© *Archivo Iconografico, S.A./CORBIS*) In participating in the Eucharist, Roman Catholic laypeople traditionally received the bread but not the wine; Catholic leaders feared that sharing the cup with the laity could result in spilling consecrated wine, which they considered to be the actual blood of Christ. As depicted here, by contrast, Protestant laymen and laywomen received both the bread and the wine of communion.

PART

III The Reformation of Rituals

Inspired to varying degrees by anthropologists, historians have paid growing attention to the importance of rituals in religious life. Many specialists in Reformation history have become convinced that for most believers rituals were deeply rooted in the popular religious psyche, and changes in rituals were among those that parishioners most noted and, at times, most resisted. In his research on the Genevan Consistory, an institution created by Calvin that served as a model for morals courts for Reformed Christians everywhere, Robert Kingdon found that at its creation in the early 1540s, the Consistory was initially most concerned with rooting out unacceptable "popish" religious behavior. Kingdon concludes that in this urban setting, popular religion was not tantamount to magic, as Delumeau and others have found for rural areas. Nor did Genevans appearing before the Consistory seem to think of religion as a creed—people for the most part were not being convoked because they had taken a stand against predestination or in favor of transubstantiation, for example. Rather, for rank-and-file Genevans religion was essentially a set of rituals. They were coming to grips with the fact that praying in Latin, fasting during Lent, and saying prayers to the Virgin Mary had to give way to praying in the vernacular to God the Father only, taking communion in both kinds (bread and wine), and singing the Psalms. The most obvious change that Genevans experienced was in the church service, as worship no longer centered on the mass, primarily a visual experience, but on the spoken word, delivered in sermons.

David Cressy looks at an important ritual that fell into disuse long ago: the churching of women. For a month after giving birth, a woman would remain isolated in her abode and would refrain from attending church. At the end of this period of confinement, the new mother went to church where she would be met at the entrance by the priest who sprinkled her with holy water, allowing her to participate again in the mass. Most Protestant critics dismissed this ceremony as a remnant of Judaism, which was based on the notion that women are ritually unclean after giving birth, and modern historians have deemed it misogynistic. Churching, however, continued to be celebrated long after the conversion to Protestantism in England. Cressy observes that, far from viewing it as degrading, women generally welcomed this ceremony, which they considered more a ritual of thanksgiving for surviving the perils of childbirth than a rite of purification.

In a very important work, *Reformation of Ritual: An Interpretation of Early Modern Germany,* Susan Karant-Nunn looks at a number of significant rituals, including those associated with communion. Luther found much to criticize in the Roman Catholic mass, finding particularly objectionable the belief that the Eucharist (or any sacrament, for that matter) worked automatically. For the Saxon reformer, the efficacy of the Eucharist or baptism, the only other sacrament he accepted, depended on whether the participant had faith, which was itself an unmerited gift from God. He also emphatically denied that the Eucharist was a sacrifice that placated God's ire and atoned for the sins of humanity. Be that as it may, Luther affirmed a belief in the real presence of the body and blood "in, with, and under" the bread and wine of communion. He also preserved a good part of the text of the mass in his Eucharistic service, including the singing of the *Kyrie* (the entreaty, "Lord, have mercy; Christ, have mercy"), the *Gloria* (the expression of praise, "Glory to God in the highest"), and the collects (a brief prayer preceding a reading from the Epistles). Karant-Nunn asserts that Lutherans' acceptance of images in churches, high altars, clerical vestments, and above all the belief that Christ was physically present in the Host, all conveyed the impression that the church was a repository of the divine where God seemed more accessible than elsewhere. In spite of his insistence that humans could do nothing to earn salvation, the rituals associated with the Lutheran Eucharist, unlike Reformed services, seemed to leave some room to believe that communicants' actions might please God to their advantage. According to Karant-Nunn, vigilant Lutheran pastors, who required most parishioners to take the Eucharist while excluding others from it for their misbehavior, fostered conformity in practices but did not strengthen community bonds, as worshipers became more segregated by class and sex.

The author of an important synthesis, *Ritual in Early Modern Europe,* Edward Muir has paid special attention to religious ceremonies. In the overview of the effects of the Catholic Reformation on rituals, excerpted here, Muir discusses important decrees of the Council of Trent that called for uniformity of practice. Trent mandated a uniform liturgy, for example, which was facilitated by, among other things, the introduction of a new universal missal—for the first time, the same mass books would be used throughout the Catholic world. Trent also reaffirmed the spiritual value of many rites that Protestants attacked, often instilling them with increased vigor. Masses for the dead, religious processions, the cult of saints, all were reaffirmed and thrived in post-Tridentine Catholicism. In general, Catholic leaders promoted rituals in which the experiences of the laity could be closely overseen by the clergy. Muir pays special attention to some rituals that were unique to Spain. The notorious and highly ceremonious *autos de fe,* to which heretics were subjected, promoted fear in the spectators and represented symbolically the Last Judgment. In the wake of Trent, bishops of the late sixteenth and seventeenth centuries sought to work through the parishes in order to ensure that the laity engaged in appropriate religious practices. Bishops enjoyed greatest success when they avoided confrontations with the laity, trying rather to channel lay enthusiasm through acceptable rites, especially those that reinforced community solidarity.

Robert M. Kingdon

The Genevan Revolution
in Public Worship

This [study] examines public worship in Geneva in the period of the Reformation. It develops the argument that there was a revolutionary change in public worship, a change that affected in important ways the texture of daily life of the entire population, for worship was much more central in everyday life than it is in modern days. It was a change from Roman Catholic forms of worship to Reformed Protestant forms of worship, specifically from worship centered on the Mass to worship centered on the sermon. [This argument] runs counter to a good deal of the most stimulating scholarship in the field of religious studies of the sixteenth century advanced over the past fifty years. That scholarship, as developed by men like Jean Delumeau and Keith Thomas, contends that Europe was not really fundamentally Christian at the beginning of the sixteenth century. Christianity was only a religious veneer, adopted and understood by a small elite of the educated and powerful. Most people, including most decisively the illiterate peasants who made up a considerable majority of the entire population of Europe, did not understand Christianity. Religion for them was a way of manipulating the environment. It was an ideology that had been there before Christianity arrived, and that survived under a thin Christian veneer. In many villages witches, cunning men, and other practitioners of primitive magic were as influential as the local priests.

The evidence from Geneva, most notably from the Consistory Registers, supplies almost no support for this theory. It demonstrates that Genevans, including the illiterate and most obviously women who were illiterate to a greater degree than men, before the Reformation were practicing Catholics and after the Reformation became practicing Protestants. Geneva was no doubt unusual in that it had been an episcopal city, dominated by several hundred members of the clergy. There may

Robert M. Kingdon, "The Genevan Revolution in Public Worship," *Princeton Seminary Bulletin* 20 (1999): 264–280. Copyright © 1999 by The Princeton Seminary Bulletin. Reprinted with permission.

be some evidence from the rural villages attached to Geneva that points in the direction of the Delumeau-Thomas thesis. Christianity was clearly not as dominant a force in the lives of the illiterate peasants in those villages as in the urban population. Even in Geneva's villages, however, while we find some evidence of folk religion or witchcraft, we find even more evidence of forms of Christianity.

The evidence I shall use to support my argument comes primarily from the study of religious ritual. I have come to the conclusion that rituals are a better index to the religious commitments of a community than institutional structures or systems of theology. . . . There is powerful evidence that religious rituals engaged deeply the entire population of sixteenth-century communities, more deeply than in many modern societies, and engaged both elites and the lower classes. By concentrating on rituals we can avoid the invidious distinctions between elite religion and popular religion that too many scholars have tried to make. Rituals no doubt meant different things to the intelligentsia and the illiterate. But they all accepted them and engaged in them. We do better to think of a spectrum of reactions rather than two sharply different categories of reaction. . . .

The key shift in public worship during the Reformation, as I have already suggested, was from a form of worship centered on the *Mass* to a form of worship centered on the *sermon*. Those are in fact the two words contemporaries almost invariably use for the two forms of worship, including most emphatically the secretaries who kept the Consistory Registers. . . . Catholic worship was built around the celebration of the sacrament most important to Christians. Protestant worship was built around an exposition of the Word of God cherished by Christians. . . .

A first thing to note is that celebration of the Mass was very common in Geneva before the Reformation. There were literally hundreds of Masses celebrated every week. [Thomas] Lambert estimates that there were as many as two hundred in the cathedral church of St. Pierre alone. Most of these Masses, to be sure, were requiem Masses celebrated by charity priests either by themselves or before small audiences. But in every one of the seven parish churches there was a high Mass on Sundays and on feast days that every adult in the parish was expected to attend. It is unlikely that everyone took this requirement seriously and actually did attend these Masses on Sundays and feast days, but it is clear that a fairly high percentage of the population took their religious obligations seriously and did.

The experience of attending Mass in those days was quite different from attending Mass in a Catholic church nowadays. One index to that comes from instructions to the faithful on how they should behave during Mass. The Mass was basically a visual experience, not an auditory experience. The average observer could not even hear much of what the priest said during a Mass, and could not normally have understood it if he did. The altar and its celebrants were separated from the congregation by a screen. The celebrating priest kept his back to the congregation. He spoke in a low voice that could not be heard by most of them. He spoke in Latin, a language most of them did not understand. The average observer was instructed not to even try to listen but rather to watch and to say prayers during the Mass. . . . [T]his instruction continues in French manuals for the faithful down into the eighteenth century. Most of the prayers one said during Mass were individual, not communal. They most often included the *Pater Noster* and the *Ave Marie*[, Latin versions of the Lord's Prayer and the Hail Mary, respectively]. Sometimes they included the *Credo* . . . , other formulaic prayers [or] free prayer. The Mass reached a sharply defined climax with the presiding priest's consecration of the elements, announced by a sacring bell, followed immediately by the elevation in which the priest lifted the host high above his head so that everyone could see. With that consecration, devout Catholics believe, a miracle occurs and the host in the priest's hands becomes the body of Christ. The host, in fact, becomes God. Theologians may quibble that there is a difference between the body of Christ and God, but that is a nuance of which most believers in the sixteenth century were unaware. They were convinced that God had entered the church in this form. They knew that were expected to display due reverence, to adore this God among them.

There was, to be sure, more to a typical High Mass than the simple celebration of the sacrament. There was a greeting at the beginning and a benediction at the end. There were prayers by the priest. There were prayers by the congregation, often led by a priest, for specific individuals, living or dead, or for specific ends, like a good harvest or a successful pregnancy. There were readings from Scripture, in Latin, usually a selection from an Epistle, and another, this one sung, from a Gospel. There was the kiss of peace, usually administered to a peace board, first kissed and passed among the clergy, then among the entire congregation. There was aspersion with holy water. There was the distribution of Blessed Bread, usually after the sacrament. Communion for the laity was not a part of the normal Mass. The elements of the sacrament themselves were on most occasions offered to the clergy alone. Only on Easter was every member of the parish welcomed and expected to receive communion, following a careful season of preparation, including a full and proper confession and then absolution for each person intending to receive the sacrament. The only part of the service that resembled a Protestant sermon was the prone, a brief oral presentation in the vernacular rather than in Latin by the parish priest, usually including some announcements and occasionally some catechistic instruction. There was almost never a proper homily or sermon. Most priests did not know how to preach and were not expected to try.

This did not mean that medieval Christians did not hear sermons. They just did not hear them within normal church services. Preachers were usually itinerant professionals, normally friars, who came to a city to preach a series of special sermons during special seasons, most commonly Advent or Lent. They usually preached them in a friary or public building, not in a church. . . .

The sacrament, however, remained at the very heart of medieval worship. The primary importance of the crucial consecration and elevation of the host and the miracle of God's arrival was recognized by everyone. People who were pressed for time often came only for this one crucial moment and left soon after. That did not please the clergy, and there were frequent warnings that one's religious obligation to attend Mass weekly meant an entire Mass, not just part of one. The very fact that the warnings were issued, however, reveals that a number of people in fact were not attending entire Masses.

This means that the average medieval Christian received what was most essential for his faith primarily through the sense of sight, through watching the Mass and particularly the elevation of the host attentively and in a proper frame of mind, often bolstered by the smell of incense and the touch of rosary beads. He or she did not receive this essential information through the sense of sound, through listening to a verbal discourse.

All of this changed dramatically with the Reformation. To begin with the very number and appearance of the churches changed. In Geneva four of the parish churches were closed, and only three remained open. . . . The interior of the three surviving parish churches also changed. Partitions were removed, including the rood screen that had separated the sacred space around the altar from the lay congregation, and other partitions that had blocked off parts of the interior into chapels. The altars on which the sacrament had been performed during Mass were all removed, along with the tabernacles containing the blessed sacrament and the lights signalling its presence. Statues and other traditional visual aids to worship were removed. The walls seem to have been whitewashed, to cover over paintings. The stained glass in the windows was not destroyed, but not maintained either. The cathedral organ was locked up and no longer used. The city government tried to sell it, but could find no buyer, so it simply stood there unused. In the resulting large open spaces, Protestants installed pulpits and benches. A high pulpit for the preacher at the best acoustic location in each church was set up, high enough so that all could see him, with a sounding board above his head to make it easier to hear him. There may have been as well a lower pulpit for the cantor, hired to lead the congregation in the singing of psalms. . . . [A]uditors sat on benches, with most of the women and children together near the pulpit and most of the men behind them. There were exceptions to this segregation by gender, however, for those who were hard of hearing. . . .

These parish churches, furthermore, were staffed with entirely new ministers. . . . The new preachers were almost all immigrants from France. They were highly educated, although not always in theology. Both Calvin and Théodore de Bèze (Beza), for example, had taken university degrees in law and abundant training in what then was called the humanities and what today we would call classical literature. . . . These new ministers were chosen primarily for their skills as preachers, because they were well trained in rhetoric and had experience in public speaking. They also had to have good strong voices. . . . Each prospective minister had to appear before the Geneva Company of Pastors and deliver a sample sermon. . . . Of the ministers appointed in the period three stand out in the effectiveness of their preaching. One was William Farel, originally from the French province of Dauphiné, but trained in Paris and Meaux, who was famous for his passion and his fury. His sermons could be really inflammatory, even provoke riots. He arrived in Geneva before the Reformation, in 1532, and preached there regularly from 1534 to 1538, in the years the Protestant regime was being established. . . . Another was Pierre Viret, from another French-speaking part of Switzerland but trained in Paris. His sermons were particularly eloquent and were highly appreciated by Genevans, perhaps in part because he spoke in a dialect closer to theirs. Most of his ministry, however, was spent in nearby Lausanne. He preached in Geneva with Farel briefly in 1534, but then moved on to Lausanne where he directed a sizable Reformed church until

1558, when the Bernese, who controlled that area directly, threw him out. He was then appointed as minister in Geneva but served only from 1559 to 1560. He then left Geneva again, this time for France, and concluded his career in various parts of that country and in neighboring Béarn. The third, of course, was John Calvin himself, and most of his ministry was in Geneva. Calvin was as capable of passion as Farel and Viret, and could both inspire and enrage people in his audiences. The traits that particularly distinguished Calvin's preaching, however, were the sense of authority he managed to convey and his clarity. . . . He . . . used the French language with uncommon skill. One specialist in language of the period, Francis Higman, claims that Calvin invented the short French sentence. The argument is certainly plausible when one compares samples of Calvin's writing in French with the writing of such famous literary contemporaries as Rabelais. Their French seems very complex and convoluted compared to Calvin's. Calvin's preaching, to be sure, was not as concise and direct as his published prose. It was always extemporaneous and often contained a certain amount of digression and repetition. But it was always simple and clear. Whatever the secrets of Calvin's success, there is no doubt that he was the most respected preacher in Geneva throughout most of his career. There would be bigger crowds of local Genevans whenever and wherever Calvin preached. . . .

[In church services] the worship leader looked very different. Instead of a priest in colorful vestments changing with each part of the liturgical year, he was a preacher dressed for every service in a plain black robe with a starched white collar, the so-called bands of Geneva. To contemporaries he did not look like a clergyman. He looked like a lawyer. The service was built not around a sacrament but around a sermon [which] was in [the] form [of] a commentary on Holy Scripture. The preacher would read a passage ranging from one to twelve verses, on average between two and four, from a selected book of the Bible and then use his allotted time to explain it. He would read it directly from a Bible before him in the pulpit. . . . After explaining terms, a preacher would then go through the entire passage explaining its sense to contemporary listeners, occasionally adding some rather pointed applications to current events. Now and then these applications made listeners angry, even furious. Fairly often the preachers of Geneva were told to stick to the Bible and stop meddling in politics. . . .

Calvin followed the discipline of *lectio continua* in much of his own preaching. He would pick one book of the Bible and spend most of a year going through it, passage after passage, day after day. He would normally preach on a book from the New Testament or on the Psalms on succeeding Sundays. He would normally preach on a book from the Old Testament on succeeding weekdays, every other week. (In the alternate weeks he delivered lectures in Latin that were commentaries on books of the Bible, similar in form to his sermons but more erudite in content.) He interrupted this routine to preach sermons appropriate to the season on Good Friday, Easter, and Pentecost. On those days his sermons were based on appropriate texts from Matthew's Gospel or the Acts of the Apostles. . . .

This type of service clearly surprised and baffled many people in Geneva. There are frequent cases heard by the Consistory in its early years of people called in and accused of babbling in church, even during a sermon. The majority of those facing this accusation were women. Often they were elderly, no doubt illiterate. When pressed they would say in some distress that they were simply saying their prayers. They were doing in church exactly what they had been taught to do as children by their parents. . . . The Consistory would [admonish them to keep quiet] and listen. These same people then would be called back in later sessions to find out what they were gaining from sermons. They would be asked when [they last attended] a service? Who was the preacher? What was the Bible passage upon which he was commenting? If they had trouble answering these questions they would be told to go to church more often, to listen to even more sermons, to become more fully acquainted with this new way of gaining religious truth.

Geneva provided plenty of opportunity to hear sermons. On an average Sunday there were eight full services, plus three catechism services. There was an early service at 4 or 5 in the morning, depending on the season, intended primarily for servants. There was the main service at about 8 in the morning. Catechism was always at noon. Then there was a final service at 2 or 3 in the afternoon, again depending on the season. Two of the parish churches had this full complement of services, [while the other] had only two of the three services. There were also several services on Wednesday, a day of prayer, when the hours of work in many establishments were curtailed. And there were also single services every other day of the week. It was thus possible to go to church every day, and several times on some days. There was furthermore an obligation laid on everyone in town to attend service at least once a week, ideally on Sunday. While not everyone lived up to this obligation, a good many did.

There is plenty of evidence that the churches were usually crowded, some times so crowded that there was not room for everyone who tried to get in, especially toward the end of Calvin's career, with the doubling of the city's population due to a flood of religious refugees. . . . There remains the question of what people actually gained from listening to these sermons. Some complained to the Consistory that they could not understand sermons, that they were hard of hearing, or simply had a "fat head" that kept them from following an oral argument. The Consistory's normal reaction to these reports was that they should try harder, that they should attend more sermons, that they must gain the habit of finding out about religion in this way. It may be true that for many it became a ritual without much personal meaning, that many people went to sermons for sociability or because it was expected of them. But they did attend. There is strong evidence, moreover, that many Genevans did learn from these sermons, that they did absorb some theology. A few could even absorb the essence of debate on doctrines as complex and abstruse as predestination. . . . [Be that as it may, the evidence from the Consistory Registers indicates that for most people in Geneva, religion was not defined by theology; rather, religion was a set of rituals, and men and women in Geneva eventually accepted that Reformed sermons were replacing a host of Catholic rituals.]

Just as the Catholic service did not consist solely of the sacrament, however, the Protestant service did not consist solely of the sermon. It included individual bidding prayers by the minister. Even more striking, it included a number of congregational recitations, the most important of which were the Creed and the Our Father, now in French rather than in Latin. Their use took a somewhat different form than in Catholic services. The Our Father, in particular, was no longer repeated in a low voice by individuals as they observed a sacramental celebration. It was now rather repeated in unison by the entire congregation, led by the preacher of the day, usually two times within each service. Calvin resisted suggestions that it be repeated more than twice, on grounds that this would be a step toward superstition. He felt that Catholic practice had turned this prayer and others into mantras or spells with magical properties, not petitions the meaning of which the penitent really comprehended, [in part because of] its use in Latin, a language most Europeans did not understand. . . . [R]ecommended according to the text of the Bible by Jesus himself, . . . [the recitation of the Lord's Prayer continued to be an essential part of Protestant services].

The Reformed service also included a cappella singing by the entire congregation. Some of this singing was of texts originally written in prose. There was a setting to music of the Ten Commandments, for example, that was widely used in services. Most of the singing, however, was of Psalms taken from the Old Testament. Arrangements were made to translate the entire Old Testament book of psalms into French, by translators of considerable eminence, most notably Clément Marot, a poet from the French royal court who had turned Protestant and fled, and Théodore de Bèze, famous as a Latin poet before his conversion to Protestantism, and Calvin's eventual successor as leader of the Genevan church. These translations were then set to music by composers of some stature. . . .

Psalters containing these psalms and usually a few additional songs were printed for use in Protestant worship. They became best sellers of the period. They probably outsold even Bibles. The Bible, after all, is a fairly long book and thus fairly expensive, especially in a period when by far the largest cost of a book was the cost of the paper that went into it. Tens of thousands of copies of psalters were printed in Geneva at the height of Calvin's ministry, for sale all over Protestant Europe. . . . [Under the tutelage of cantors, the ability to sing psalms eventually became widespread in Geneva. Once it took hold, the singing of psalms] came to mean a great deal to lay Protestants. It was often something they could embrace more fully than they could embrace some of the doctrines they heard explained from the pulpit. . . .

Genevan services were often accompanied by other rituals. Baptisms had to be celebrated in church, before a congregation, not in private as before the Reformation. An ordained minister had to preside, never a midwife. They usually took place after the sermon toward the end of a service, most commonly one of the very early or late Sunday services, not the main service. Marriages also were celebrated during a service, usually before the main service began. Another ritual often accompanying a service was a ceremony of reconciliation, in which people who had been involved in public quarrels formally forgave each other and were welcomed back into the general community.

The sacrament of communion also became a part of Protestant services. But it was no longer a daily or weekly part of the service. Communion was offered only four times a year. There were elaborate preparations for each communion service, a part of which are detailed in the Consistory Registers. Elders were assigned to each parish church and charged with assisting the ministers in distributing the communion elements. . . .

Of special importance in preparing for quarterly communion was the drawing up of lists of people who should be denied communion, who were excommunicate. A number of these people were routinely called before the Consistory in the weeks before a communion service to see if they were now qualified to receive the sacrament. A significant percentage were usually found ready, having acquired the additional information they needed to be good Christians, or having purged themselves of the misbehavior that had led to their excommunication. A sentence of excommunication, thus, often did not last more than three months. . . . [Some others] judged to be too ignorant or too stubborn, . . . could remain excommunicate for long periods of time, [occasionally] even banished from the community altogether.

After each communion service, furthermore, there would be additional discussion of the ritual before the Consistory. People who had not taken communion would be called in for questioning and asked to explain their abstention. People who had ignored sentences of excommunication and contrived to receive communion anyway, perhaps in a parish church other than their own where they would not be recognized immediately, would be called in for scolding and punishment. . . .

Calvin would have preferred communion more frequently than once every three months [b]ut . . . bowed to the will [of the city government] on this point. . . . [The frequency of communion] was not as important [to him] as the maintenance of discipline. Indeed it can be argued that Calvin made a virtue of necessity and made communion of greater importance than before by demanding that everyone receive it, by insisting that everyone who received it be judged worthy, and by going to considerable lengths to see to it that recipients were in fact worthy.

Even though there was more to a Protestant service than the sermon, however, just as there was more to a Catholic service than the sacrament, everyone recognized that the sermon was the climax of the normal service. Busy Protestants would now come late to service but in time to hear the sermon, then leave early after the sermon but before the benediction, just as busy Catholics had come only to witness the consecration and elevation of the host. And Protestant preachers, just like their Catholic predecessors, would complain and insist that people were obligated to attend an entire service, not just a selected part. . . .

[All told,] the forms of public worship were changed dramatically in Geneva with the Reformation, [and] this constituted a kind of revolution, a religious revolution to accompany the political revolution that

had led to the beginning of the Reformation there. People went to worship in buildings that looked radically different. They were led in worship
by ministers of a very different character and appearance. Above all they
had to deploy a different set of senses. They were expected to absorb what
is most essential in religion through hearing rather than through seeing.

David Cressy

Purification, Thanksgiving, and the Churching of Women

. . . Churching was a ritual process that connected the semi-secret
domestic world of women and childbirth with the public ecclesiastical
and communal business of religion. Like the related ceremony of baptism, churching became embroiled in the liturgical and disciplinary
contests of English protestantism and the struggles of religious politics:
but it also had social, sexual, and festive associations that lay beyond the
reach of the church. As a post-partum ceremony, churching occupied a
special space in the womanly world of fecundity and matronhood. . . .

What little discussion of churching one finds in the secondary
sources has largely been shaped by Keith Thomas. In *Religion and the
Decline of Magic* Thomas emphasized the split between the official position of the church, which "chose to treat the ceremony as one of thanksgiving," and the views of people at large, for whom "churching was
indubitably a ritual of purification closely linked with its Jewish predecessor." Popular superstitions, so-called "taboo" and "magical elements"
in the ceremony, and puritan objections to the eccleiastical service,
all confirm that we are witnessing a ritual of purification. . . . Some

David Cressy, "Purification, Thanksgiving, and the Churching of Women," in *Birth, Marriage, and Death: Ritual, Religion, and the Life-Cycle in Tudor and Stuart England* (Oxford
and New York: Oxford University Press, 1997), 197–229. Copyright © 1997 by Oxford
University Press. By permission of Oxford University Press.

scholars have also adopted the anthropological language and interpretive schema of van Gennep, and see churching as a rite of reintegration after the ritual isolation of childbearing, the ritual closure to a period of liminal transition. . . .

The most common view seems to endorse those early modern puritans who criticized churching as an unreformed purification, while at the same time arguing, with certain feminists, that churching was a patriarchal or misogynist instrument for the subjugation of women. My reading of the evidence leads me to neither of these conclusions. Indeed, an alternative case can be made that women normally looked forward to churching as an occasion of female social activity, in which the notion of "purification" was uncontentious, minimal, or missing. . . .

The documentary material that might permit a re-examination of purification, thanksgiving, and the churching of women comes from several sources. It includes biblical exegesis, religious debate, and sermons; liturgy and the arguments for liturgical revision; ecclesiastical visitation articles and the records of visitation processes; accounts of parochial administration covering fees and church fabric; and family papers, diaries, and letters. The majority of this evidence comes from male clerical authors, of course, and it reflects their concern with worship and discipline; only a few sources depict churching in practice, and rarely from the viewpoint of the woman in the pew. As usual, people's behaviour and thinking must be inferred from fragments. None the less, we can construct a history that traces several clusters of issues from the mid-Tudor Reformation to the later seventeenth century. . . .

In the short review that follows I want to suggest that religious and disciplinary concerns altered over the course of the Elizabethan and Stuart periods, and that changing attempts to regulate churching produced varying responses at the local level. . . .

The formal religious ceremony of thanksgiving formed part of a larger social ritual with complex secular dimensions. One did not have to be a devotee of the Book of Common Prayer to celebrate the social reappearance of a woman recovering from childbirth, or to join in offering thanks for her safe deliverance. Like the christening feasts that celebrated baptisms, the wedding suppers that accompanied marriages, and the funeral dinners following burials, the "gossipings" associated with the churching of women provided opportunities for hospitality, conviviality, and display. . . . The scale of the celebration varied according to circumstances and social status, but usually included feasting and drinking. . . .

In some towns the corporation attempted to control expenditure on "dishes, meats and wines" at churchings as well as baptisms, as part of their campaign of reform. Thanksgiving gossipings and associated childbirth gatherings had allegedly got out of hand. At Leicester in 1568 it was ordained that, "for the eschewing of the superfluous charge and excess of the inhabitants . . . there shall be no feasts made at any churching within the said town saving only one competent mess of meat provided for gossips and midwives." In 1575 the aldermen of Kirkby Kendal restricted to twelve the number of wives accompanying a woman to her churching, and set limits on the drinking and feasting that followed. . . .

References to thanksgiving gossipings in diaries indicate that they were often mixed occasions, though generally dominated by women. . . . For the woman and her friends, churching provided a social occasion, a sisterly outing with wives and midwife escorting the newly delivered mother. The same women who had gathered to attend the birth — "those who serve the child-bed mysteries" in Herrick's supple phrase — would now share in the thanksgiving for the mother's deliverance. Midwives, as we have seen, served as keepers of custom, and may have helped organize the traditional parts of the ceremony; their prominence at churchings also advertised their skills in the birthroom. Dressing for the occasion, wearing fresh clothes, gadding with gossips, and consuming food and drink, were important accompaniments to this ritual. . . .

Churching marked the end of the woman's privileged "month," and for the man the end of what contemporaries sometimes called their "gander month." It concluded a period of physical recovery, and also a time of sequestration and abstention during which (at least in some cases) the husband took charge of domestic duties while being excluded from the matrimonial bed. . . .

Throughout this time, in popular opinion, the woman in childbed was considered to be "green." The term was used partly with the sense of her being unwell or unready, but was primarily related to the condition of "greensickness," amenorrhoea, the stoppage of the menses or terms. Sixteenth-century folklore held that an unchurched "green woman" should stay at home, refrain from sexual intercourse, and not participate in the sacraments of the church. . . . The ceremony of churching established a ritual closure to this state of affairs, allowing the resumption of sexual relations between husband and wife and the restoration of normal domestic order. . . .

From the earliest times, the churching service was attended with ambiguity. In pre-Reformation practice the ceremony was as much a blessing as a cleansing, a comfort as well as a purification. In some versions of the Sarum Missal one finds the "ordo ad purificandum mulierem," in others, and perhaps more commonly, "benedictio mulieris post partum ante ostium ecclesie." Some have the priests saying "Thou shalt purge me, O Lord, with hyssop," after sprinkling her with holy water, and before leading her into the main part of the church; others omit those words. The priest recited psalms, spoke of deliverance from the peril of childbirth, and concluded with the prospect of eternal life. In traditional catholic practice the woman to be purified wore a white veil, carried a lighted candle, and was accompanied by two married women, but this was not formally required by any rubric.

Protestants maintained that this ceremony was a continuation of Jewishness, a superstitious adherence to Mosaical and Levitical law. From the progression from the church porch, through the sprinkling with holy water, to the reference to purging with hyssop (the herb used to cleanse sacramental vessels), the ceremony was filled with priestcraft and popish superstition. Though the service was substantially rewritten for the Church of England, puritan agitators of the 1570s (and later) asserted that little had improved.

Edward VI's reign saw important changes in the liturgical conduct and in the larger religious significance of this service. What appeared in 1549 as an anglicization of the Latin "ordo ad purificandum mulierem" (the order for the purification of women) became in 1552 and all subsequent editions of the prayer book, "the thanksgiving of women after childbirth, commonly called the churching of women." The three words circulated around each other, each with their attendant connotations. Officially, after 1552, the service was no longer a purification; all notion of a penitential cleansing was disclaimed. . . .

The service announced the woman's deliverance and preservation from "the great danger of child-birth." . . . Could the impulse for its retention in England have come from women's delight in the social and religious attention they received at their churching, rather than from male or clerical anxieties about unpurified women? We should at least keep open the question whether purification was something done *to* women, or *for* them.

In the old catholic service the priest met the woman before the church porch, and only moved inside the church after sprinkling her with holy water. In the rubric of 1549 "the woman shall come into the church, and there shall kneel down in some convenient place, nigh unto the choir door." By 1552 that convenient place had moved from the threshold and margins of the church to its ritual centre: now the woman should kneel "nigh unto the place where the table standeth." These may seem like minor adjustments, but they were enormously significant. They transformed the woman from a penitent to a celebrant (or "gratulant"), from a petitioner at the margin to the focus of community attention. There was no more sprinkling with holy water, no mention at all of veils or candles, and, after 1552, no reference to the customary offering of chrisoms, the cloth wrapped round a newborn child at baptism. . . .

The *Admonition* controversy of the 1570s raised alarms about the Jewish and popish remnants in the Book of Common Prayer. The widely read puritan *Admonition to the Parliament* claimed that "churching of women after childbirth smelleth of Jewish purification." . . . An unauthorized pamphlet of 1601 continued the puritan attack. Churching, it insisted, contained "no one word, matter or form of thanksgiving," but was rather a "Jewish or popish purifying shadowed and varnished over" and continued "under the pretence and colour of a service of God."

But this was never a popular argument; its most vocal adherents were radical churchmen. Few lay people knew or cared whether their religion had Jewish analogues or Jewish ancestry. Some might object to particular aspects, like the use of Psalm 121, the veil, or the offering, but few were prepared to dismiss churching altogether as the relic of an alien religion. . . .

Most of the brief ceremony of churching was taken up with recitation of Psalm 121. This was a psalm of praise and thanksgiving for divine protection, which included the strange promise "that the sun shall not burn thee by day, neither the moon by night." Puritans could not denounce these words of David, but claimed instead that they were "childishly abused" in the context of women recovering from childbirth. . . .

To radical Elizabethan puritans the churching of women was "heretical, blasphemous and popish foolerie . . . knavish presumption and presumptuous knavery . . . idle babblement" and altogether unnecessary. . . . But there was little popular support for this position. There is, on the other hand, strong evidence from visitation processes that many women wanted the ceremony in some form or other, and that in most cases they conformed to the Book of Common Prayer. Susan Wright's calculations from a remarkable "chrisom book" show churching rates of 75 to 93 per cent in late Elizabethan Salisbury. Similar evidence from Jacobean London indicates that 92 to 96 per cent of all "women who gave birth and had their child baptised underwent the ceremony of churching"; even among women whose babies died before they could be baptized the churching rate exceeded 76 per cent. Jeremy Boulton finds that "neglect of the ceremony, either from religious dissent or simple indifference, appears to have been insignificant." And this high level of participation prevailed among rich and poor, "across the social structure." . . .

In the Elizabethan period, objections to churching came more frequently from the clergy than the laity, when reforming ministers set their scruples against community expectations. . . .

Rather than evincing hostility to churching, the records show some families so eager for some version of the ceremony that they risked offending against ecclesiastical discipline. William White of Charlbury, Oxfordshire, explained to the court in 1596, "that his wife being delivered of a child, could not be churched for that she was excommunicated, and he, being desireous that she shall serve God, did say and read certain prayers unto her." For a husband to church his wife was most disorderly, but it is not clear from the records whether this took place in church or at home. Other records point to churchings by irregular ministers, or by clergy from outside the parish, and occasionally by laymen such as the parish clerk.

In a remarkable case from Bedfordshire, the wife of Richard Chaw of Elstow was presented to the archidiaconal court in 1617 "for churching herself." The court heard "that she coming to the church to thanksgiving, and the minister having warning overnight and not coming to church accordingly, she did take the Book of Common Prayer and read the thanksgiving herself openly in the church." Here was a woman who was determined to have her moment, and whose literacy is attested as well. . . .

One issue which brought together anxieties about Jewishness, popery, and superstition, the lingering stain of purification, and the exercise of ecclesiastical authority, was the wearing of veils. There was nothing in the rubric of the Book of Common Prayer requiring a woman to wear a veil at her churching, and to leading Elizabethan churchmen it was a matter of indifference. When Thomas Cartwright alleged that the customary wearing of a veil smacked of Jewish purification, John Whitgift responded that the veil was the woman's affair, and the puritans were making a fuss over a trifle: "let the women themselves answer these matters." . . .

Elizabethan and early Jacobean bishops made no mention of veils in their visitation articles, and few took action over what women wore for their churching. Discipline was haphazard, and the traditional headgear became a matter of discretion and custom, and perhaps even widespread neglect. . . .

By the 1630s the high ceremonialists had again made the veil a crucial part of churching, and refocused the ceremony on the woman at the high altar instead of the more comfortable custom of churching in pews. . . . The new episcopal policy was intended to promote gravity and decorum. Instead it generated friction. Women who were perfectly content to be churched according to the directions in the prayer book now found themselves at odds with the church if they neglected to wear a veil. . . .

Churching Continued, 1645–1700

Officially the churching of women came to an end in 1645 when the prayer book was superseded by the Directory of Public Worship. But we know from diaries and family papers that some people, especially royalist gentry, continued to seek out ministers to perform the office, following as closely as possible the Book of Common Prayer. . . .

Churching was restored at the Restoration, and soon again became a test of conformity to ecclesiastical discipline. Anglicans insisted that participation in the ceremony signified adherence to law and custom, quite apart from any spiritual benefits that might be thought to accrue from it. . . .

An annual opportunity to preach on the subject of churching occurred each 2 February with the festival of Candlemas, or the Purification of the Blessed Virgin Mary. Mary herself, of course, was "without the least spot or impurity in the whole business of conception and childbirth," explained the Cambridge churchman Mark Frank, but she none the less went through the Levitical business of purification, and made her customary offering at the temple. If *she* could subject herself to such conformist discipline, so now could Christian mothers follow this "good example of church duties." . . . Mary's devotion would serve as an example to all mothers to make their dutiful thanksgiving. It also served to rebuke nonconformists and "schismatics" in the continuing struggle over religious authority and discipline.

Restoration bishops commonly enquired about churching as they attempted to secure conformity to the Book of Common Prayer, and their visitation questions were often modelled on those of the 1630s. But after 1662 they were more likely to face nonconformist refusal to be churched at all than disputes over adiaphora and externals. Challenged by more fundamental problems of membership and discipline, later Stuart churchmen seem to have abandoned the divisive insistence on veils. . . .

Adherence to canonical requirements may have slackened somewhat in the later seventeenth century as some families drifted away from the established church and others sought to domesticate or privatize ecclesiastical ceremonies. . . .

An educated guess might be that compliance drifted down to perhaps two-thirds of the population, with enormous local variation. Scattered evidence from the eighteenth and nineteenth centuries points to active churching, and in some districts it is still performed today. Churching continued because women wanted it for religious, cultural, and emotional reasons of their own; custom maintained it, and the established church performed the office in the interests of duty and conformity. After the diminution or exhaustion of post-Reformation controversies the practice seems to have become routine and unremarkable. Most episcopal visitors stopped asking questions about churching by the 1680s, and the issue was allowed to die down. . . .

It is important to stress the multiple meanings of churching, and consider how the ceremony operated differently, or carried different connotations, according to different points of view. Among protestant controversialists—both critics and apologists of the Church of England—there was long discussion about the Jewish aspects of "purification," and whether it was honourable or dishonourable to God. The debate was academic, theological, and casuistical, and had little bearing on liturgical practice, and impacted only indirectly on the social and cultural experience of women.

Episcopal disciplinarians saw the enforcement of churching as part of the task of securing conformity to the Book of Common Prayer. . . . There was no canon regarding churching, nor was the rubric definitive or clear; but every deliverance from childbearing allowed the church to assert its authority over the laity, and particularly over women.

For the minister who performed the office, churching may have had spiritual or disciplinary connotations, but it was also a supplementary source of income. So whether the clergyman was performing the service for the woman, or imposing it on her, he was also doing it for himself. Parents who failed to make their customary offering—the chrisom cloth or its cash equivalent—were considered as debtors, and could be subject to disciplinary action.

The central actor in churching, of course, was the woman who had recently given birth. What did churching do for her? It involved the church and the community in her recovery from childbearing. It signalled her new status as a mother (after a first birth), or confirmed her status as a breeding woman. The ecclesiastical ceremony and the gossips' feast that followed marked her formal public reappearance after the conventional month of seclusion. The ritual put her on display, as the centre of attention. Normally she would sit to the rear of the church or in a segregated section (although seating plans varied, and some women sat with their husbands), but at her churching she came forward to the most prominent seat or pew by the altar, all eyes upon her.

The ceremony celebrated her survival, and offered the comforts of religion. It recognized her endurance of the pains and the perils of childbearing, and focused on the woman rather than her baby. It was, fundamentally, a thanksgiving. Was it also a purification? Only if she thought herself unclean. Most clergy taught, following Timothy, that the woman was sanctified by childbearing, that the child was the joyful offspring of the marriage bed. If some preachers harped on the curse of Eve or the sinfulness of conception it was to argue that all humankind was corrupt, not simply recently delivered women. In any case, parishioners could take what they wanted from such sermons, and did not necessarily agree with the theological beliefs of their ministers. If the mother shared the superstition that a "green" woman was out of grace with her neighbours, the ceremony released her from that anxiety, and restored her to her normal condition. . . .

Susan C. Karant-Nunn

Repentance, Confession, and the Lord's Table: Separating the Divine from the Human

. . . Going to church before the Reformation was a sensuous experience. Indeed, the Mass (together with the sacred space within which it was celebrated) made use of every human sense. Even in rural churches and chapels, the devout heard the sound of the bell, the intoning of the ritual prayers—mesmerizing in their unintelligible, monotonous Latin—and the special words of consecration, *"Hoc est corpus meum"* and *"Hic est sanguis meus,"* by which the mundane elements of the bread and wine underwent transubstantiation. They often saw the altar with its cloths and retable, the corpse-laden crucifix, the sheen of paten and Chalice, the glint of candlelight, the ceremonial vestments sometimes even in simple parishes worked by nuns in flowers or scenes of the Savior's life, the transfixing motion of the priest's hands as he raised up the Host and by God's permission effected a miracle. They smelled the sweat of their neighbors and at the same time the heavenly fragrances of beeswax and incense. They felt holy water on their fingertips and the very flesh of Christ sacrificed as the priest placed the wafer into their mouths at the rood screen or the altar steps. And they tasted, besides the plume inhaled as the acolyte swung the censer, the body of God's Son as they closed their lips. . . .

Just as important, church interiors conveyed the lives of Christ and the saints. They did this explicitly by means of paintings, frescoes, pictures in stained glass, sculptures, and seasonal artifacts such as the baby Jesus for use in the nativity scene. . . . They achieved this implicitly by means of layer upon layer of symbolism that informed the churches themselves and every object in them. . . .

The focal point of every church was the so-called high altar, a term used to distinguish it from the numerous side or low altars that coexisted in the nooks and niches of every affluent church. From the early Middle Ages the altar had been thought of as the tomb of Christ, that sturdy plane upon which the parish priest offered up the repeated sacrifice of the Lord, called the Mass. . . .

The priest, as the instrument of this wonder, bore a heavy responsibility. . . . The celebrant was supposed to be cleanly, carefully attired, aware of the significance of the alb, the long, plain linen underdress to be worn at Mass; the chasuble, the sometimes ornately decorated overgarment worn over the alb; and the stole. . . . In a small church, he entered without fanfare, but in a prominent church with some pomp and choirsong. Two candles burned on the alter. All was ready for the oblation, near the alter—the wine and the water with which it would be mixed, and the wafer of bread, round like a giant coin and usually impressed with a crucifix. The acolyte would bring them to the priest. The first part of the Mass included the priest's greeting the people, a penitential rite based upon the clergyman's confession of sin (*Confiteor Deo*, "I confess to almighty God") and the *Kyrie eleison* ("Lord have mercy, Christ have mercy," uniquely retaining the Greek phrase, not its Latin translation); usually a recitation of *Gloria in excelsis* ("Glory be to God on high"); a prayer or prayers (*collecta*) before a reading from an Epistle and thus varying with the occasion; a reading from the Gospels; and a brief homily if the priest was capable of delivering or reading one. . . .

During the second part of the Mass, the creed was now sometimes pronounced, followed by the offering of the bread and the wine, the officiant's washing his hands before touching the elements that would become Christ's body and blood, and the priest's "secret" and silent recitation of preparatory obsecrations. After a prefatory thanksgiving and recitation of the *Sanctus* ("Holy, Holy, Holy"), the long Eucharistic canon began with prayers for the living. A small bell was to be rung before transubstantiation occurred so that the onlookers could prepare for the miracle. The people knelt and the men removed their hats. Facing the altar, the priest then softly intoned the words of consecration of the bread and wine. He kept the formula to himself. . . . His back to the onlookers, he held each element aloft so that all could observe the Son's arrival and his simultaneous sacrifice, with the eyes of faith even if the visible accidents remained unchanged, and could adore Him. . . . [T]he priest's every gesture, indeed his extended posture during the elevation, contributed to his reenactment of the Crucifixion. These were charged moments.

Next usually came prayers for the dead and the Lord's Prayer. After the *Agnus Dei* ("Behold the Lamb of God that taketh away the sins of the world"), members of the congregation, particularly (but not exclusively) those who had confessed the day before, came forward to receive the Host. The Chalice, as we know, was reserved to the clergy. The priest and his helpers seem in the early sixteenth century to have placed a smaller wafer in each person's mouth, though this may have varied from place to place. The pictorial evidence suggests that this practice continued within the Lutheran Church. A special cloth was held under each person's chin in turn, to catch any precious crumbs that might inadvertently be allowed to fall. One could not degrade the Body of the Lord. . . .

The Wittenberg divine's rejection of salvation by works carried with it categorical denunciation of the Mass as Catholic theologians understood it. As Luther examined the complex implications of his reading of Romans 1: 17—as he thought further about his insight concerning first his own and then others' salvation—he found it necessary to carry the teaching of justification by faith alone over into all the subdivisions of his doctrinal worldview. If works could avail a person nothing toward salvation, then the Mass as *opus operatum*—that is, as an act with salvific validity in and of itself—was dead. . . .

Nonetheless, in his "Formula missae et communionis" of 1523, Luther wrote, "We are not able to deny that Masses and the rite of the communion of bread and wine were divinely instituted by Christ." . . . He advised . . . keeping (in this order) appropriate Sunday introits, the *Kyrie*, the *Gloria*, untainted collects, and readings from the Epistles that could not be understood superstitiously but that prompted faith in Christ. Next should come the gradual, a pair of verses sung after the Epistle, perhaps the *Alleluia*, but the officiant might choose others that pertained to the church calendar. Then was to follow the reading from the Gospels. Here Luther added, "We do not prohibit either candles or incense nor do we decide on them. This matter is free." Pastors might exercise their judgment in including or excluding these parts of the divine service. At this point, Luther became much more directive and, indeed, emphatic. Above all, everything suggestive of oblation must be removed, and only that which is "pure and holy" should remain. . . .

Finally, Luther admitted that local variations were many, and he did not rule them out. One of the salient features of his "Formula missae" is its flexibility. Pastors should, above all, be guided by the Gospel and dispense with every hint of the Mass as sacrifice. In addition, pomp and luxury must be pared away. He did not insist on priestly vestments. . . .

One of Luther's chief concerns in bringing the Mass into German was to render the often traditional words well sung. For to Luther the Mass was a musical event, and it would be so all over Lutheran Germany by mid-century. Masses in the late Middle Ages could be said or sung, and priests often did sing them, or rather considerable parts of them. Luther sought the advice of the elector's experts on music in deciding which notes to use, and he departed from Catholic practice, which made his version literally less monotonous. . . .

The most drastic contrast with the pattern laid down by Luther was, of course, that introduced as part of the Calvinization of a few territories during the sixteenth century, most notably in the Rhenish Palatinate in 1563. . . . [H]ere the prince, Friedrich III, an imperial elector, . . . forbade the wearing even of simple cassocks (*chorrock*, literally a choir robe) by presiding clergy; the use of Communion napkins that in some places were still being held under communicants' chins; turning in the direction of the Eucharistic elements during the words of institution; any exorcism; Latin songs; altars; all images including crucifixes. In Calvinist services, only psalms were sung, and organs were silenced and removed (though restored in some places at the end of the century). In the Sunday service, instead of the Epistle, any suitable part of the Bible could be read. Latin was eliminated. Reformed liturgists, then, broke more completely with Catholic precedent, as they were aware. . . . In Reformed churches, the sensuality of the Catholic Mass was now entirely gone. Church interiors were whitewashed and every seductive image removed. The experience of the worship service, finding no outward distraction, had to concentrate on the Word preached—hardly a tangible object—and on individual interiority. What is more, during the course of the century, in many Reformed churches the focal point—the Eucharistic table—shifted to one side of the nave, as though to underscore the papist superstition inherent in altars. The people could no longer contemplate even a bare remnant of the site of earlier devotion. This kind of service was much more intellectually demanding than that in which visible symbols were rife; and whether average people, including the masses of the uneducated and not particularly motivated, were able to rise to the challenge of the theologians is unavailable to our scrutiny. . . .

How successful were Reformation leaders and their successors in persuading the populace that the Eucharistic elements and attendant acts did not have supernatural powers? Once again, we are thrown back upon clues that initially seem rather small until one perceives that they recur. In a rural parish in the Rhineland, the congregation was distressed when the pastor dropped some Hosts at the altar. In a village pertaining to Halberstadt in 1589, the people were upset by the sexton's having seen that he was running out of wafers (Hosts) during Communion and having broken some of the remaining ones in half. They reported it to the visitors, who interrogated the culprit—for they, too, thought it wrong, but probably for different reasons. To the members of the congregation, it may well have seemed that the cleric was desecrating Christ's body, while the visitors probably regarded this act as too reminiscent of Catholic practice. Nonetheless, officiants were to know in advance how many communicants there would be, so that they did not prepare too many Hosts. This suggests a traditional concern with the treatment of extra consecrated wafers (which is to say, with the Body of Christ). One could not easily affirm the bodily presence and at the same time ascribe no special status to the embodying bread. The Lutheran retention of the specially formed wafer also doubtless reinforced the tendency to ascribe the same miraculous properties to the Protestant Host as one had to the Catholic. The Zwinglian and Calvinist use of common table bread marked a radical visual break with the past that helped to bolster their leaders' respective theologies of the Eucharist. . . .

Taken altogether, Luther's Mass was shorter and more edificatory than its Catholic predecessors. It was designed to be comprehensible to the masses and not to enchant them. Yet its provenance was clearly visible. The sequence of its parts remained almost entirely as under Catholicism, though Luther emphasized pastors' right to elect one prayer, one hymn, one biblical passage over another as well as the adiaphoristic nature of such matters as whether to retain candles, altar cloths, images, and vestments—even the ringing of the altar bell before elevation. Nevertheless, as is well known, Luther made two radical changes: the elimination of the Mass as sacrifice and the expansion of the homiletic moment into a prominent, time-consuming aspect of worship. . . .

. . . The visitation protocols leave the distinct impression that the main Sunday sermon was supposed to be no more than one hour in length—but even this greatly surpassed the Catholic homily. On the one hand, it is true that the priest was demoted to the level of parson, whose role was now strictly to be played out on earth and among men, without mediatory access to the divine. On the other, however, as we who have followed the discussion concerning confessionalization are aware, Protestant pastors compensated for their loss in two ways: through their responsibility to carry out—not just to pay lip service to—the religious education of each person in their charge; and through their alliance with the authorities of both church and state. What they sacrificed in the supernatural sphere they made up for in the earthly. Everywhere in Germany, pastors were integrated into a disciplinary network that combined church and state, and this showed itself in ritual. . . . Everywhere admission to the Eucharist came to depend on individuals' fulfillment of moral and ritual prerequisites. . . .

Officially, the Reformation completely undid the fundamental assumption that human beings could in any way wield or influence divine favor. Even where such traditional phrases as *the power of the keys* remained, when we look at the *configuration* of penance and the Mass, when we study it in the context of theology, liturgy, and political environment, we see that the confessor and officiant could in no way sway God. Even speaking "in God's stead," the pastor pronounced his conviction, grounded in doctrine, that the deity would regard kindly the truly repentant sinner. Christ's atonement would cover those who sorrowed and struggled against sin. The clergyman did not *cause* God to look kindly or to mitigate punishments due the living and the dead, for in contrast with Catholic views, God had never relinquished any of his authority to human beings—not to Peter, not to St. Francis. . . .

No human activity could affect or effect outcomes. This theologically based conclusion, however, is hardly useful in the mundane sphere. In everyday earthly society, rewards and punishments must exist as incentives. In the early modern there-and-then, people could not avoid attributing illness and deformity to personal sin, and collective tragedy (such as war and epidemic) to God's wrathful response to human disobedience. Thus, sensitive educated mortals could have been torn between the teaching that works availed them nothing, and the socially influenced value that works were essential to the individual as well as the collective wellbeing.

This ambiguity played itself out in the Lutheran sanctuary. . . . [T]he images, the colors and textures, the candlelight, the Latin, the vestments, the organ music, and above all the real presence of Christ's body and blood in the Eucharist, particularly in the traditional wafer-shaped Host, conveyed semiotically to worshippers that the divine was still among them and likely to be concentrated more in the church and its grounds than outside. . . . The Lutheran service writ large held out to the individual access to God far more than the Reformed one did.

Inherent in this still recognizably Catholic-derived Mass, then, was the message not only that God was still approachable (if in a more limited way than before), but also that human beings, including but not exclusively the clergy, could still act in ways that obtained His benefit. In abolishing the sacrifice of the Mass and the priesthood as a separate caste, Luther on one level concentrated all *action*, all *effect*, in the god-head, thought of most of all as the Son. But on another level, by leaving a generous residue of sensuous cultic objects and processes behind, he allowed his followers to go on affirming a more diffuse and available sacrality. Calvinism, by contrast, presented congregations, in their sternly ordered ranks, with the unadorned Word, free of distraction. . . .

[W]hile at the formal level late medieval clergy and laity constituted two separate castes, in the domains of background and outlook the parish priests had a great deal in common with their parishioners. Despite the drawing apart of elite and urban clergymen, in other settings the people and those who cured their souls understood one another well. In coming together for Mass, and in the celebration of it, they formed, as ministrants and recipient/observers, a complementary whole. They had quite a successful symbiotic relationship, until in the later Middle Ages that relationship began to deteriorate under the pressures of excessive clerical populations and jurisdictions, and of economic competition.

As for the laity, the sociological assumptions of late medieval society could serve as fault lines along which eruption occurred, or they could facilitate cooperation. Laypeople constituted no unified whole, nor in towns did they wish to. Princes and magistrates were the first groups demanding and receiving acknowledgment of their special status in the form of views and pews (and burial places) inside the sanctuary, and they came forward first to receive the sacrament. But the hoi polloi stood, knelt, and sat around the late medieval church interior, shifting their weight, physically unconstrained (and likely also socially so). . . .

The Masses of the Reformation occurred somewhat further along in the processes of social differentiation (hierarchization), discipline, and condoned clericalism. Increasingly in the sixteenth century, with the full consent of Protestant authorities, church interiors were divided up into rows of pews, which the burghers often personally owned but sometimes leased, and the flowing social body now became the ordered, ranked, gender-separated *bodies* containing individual souls. . . . People were forbidden to leave the church before the final benediction without good reason. At the same time, as popular confraternities were banned and many types of craft gatherings were forbidden or closely overseen, social subdivisions (a basis of medieval identity) broke down. This is a secular concomitant of changes in the Mass that cannot be overlooked. At least men increasingly faced God as individuals just as they were individually answerable to the magistrates. For most purposes, women were subsumed under them. All were now to come forward to the Eucharist according to sex, standing, and marital status. This tendency may have existed in the late Middle Ages, but after the Reformation regimentation grew apace. Although in one sense falling into line and barely distinguishable, their places in that line coincided with inner and outer circumstances that the pastor, through his confessional role in the Lutheran Church, knew well. No one could slip through to the Lord's Supper without his approval. . . .

Even though the reformed liturgy included a collective confession and, sometimes, absolution, its purpose in the context of the whole was to abase oneself before God, not to foster cohesion on earth. [John] Bossy has noted that the unison singing of vernacular hymns "did surely achieve something of the immediate and unproblematic unity at which they [the Reformers] aimed." However, we need to think about this seeming unity in the light of intense confessionalization, which used congregational singing, and specifically the carefully crafted lyrics, to indoctrinate the people and to gain their conformity to the elite-defined norm. . . . In the form of parish inspection and synodal oversight, the urban elites carried out their *Drang nach außen* in the countryside. Through the forcible improvement of the clergy—which was much more successful than their efforts among the laity—authorities of church and state separated the pastors and deacons from their congregations at least as much, and in rural parishes far more, than Catholicism ever had. The ministry became an implement of official control (though it doubtless comforted as well) and the laity a mass of potentially eruptive, daily disorderly underminers of the Christian polity. Ordinary Christians became objects to be acted upon by the publicly admonishing, disciplining deliverers of the Word. These shifts of intention are evident in the reformed Mass and service of worship.

Edward Muir

The Reformation as a
Ritual Process

Although the humanist critique of ritual abuses began within . . . Catholicism . . . , an official Catholic reassessment of the role of ritual in the
church was long delayed until the waning days of the Council of Trent,
which met with several long interruptions between 1545 and 1563. . . .
[M]ost Catholic prelates thought radical change neither possible nor
desirable. It was one thing to acknowledge the consequences of lay ignorance and the cupidity of those who benefited financially from celebrating the sacraments, but it was quite another to go along with the
[Protestant] reformers' rejection of the sacramental edifice of the church
and the elimination of the special status of priests as ritual specialists.
When the Council finally issued its decrees it reaffirmed traditional
Catholic dogma regarding the mass, retaining transubstantiation and the
mass as a sacrifice, and refused to allow any consideration of the Eucharist
as merely a sign that promised salvation or even less as a simple commemorative meal that served as a reminder of Christ on the cross. Even
as they were brought under stricter regulation, commemorative masses,
relics, sacramentals, saints' days, and all the seven sacraments were not
only reaffirmed as efficacious but reasserted as essential guides for the
road to salvation. Instead of rejecting the role of liturgical rites, the Council of Trent reinvigorated their celebration.

Most of the Tridentine reforms concentrated on technical matters
of ritual practice, especially in promoting uniformity throughout the
church. In 1562 in its twenty-second session, the Council passed a
decree on the correct observation of the mass that attempted to limit
abuses arising from avarice, superstition, and irreverence. For example,
stipends for the saying of masses were to be regulated by the bishops.
Most of the pronouncements concerned matters external to the mass
itself, such as guaranteeing that masses be celebrated only in consecrated

Edward Muir, *Ritual in Early Modern Europe* (Cambridge: Cambridge University Press,
1997), 178–180, 204–212. Copyright © 1997 by Cambridge University Press. Reprinted
with the permission of Cambridge University Press.

places, rowdy conduct be banished, unsuitable music be prohibited, the celebration of many simultaneous masses be curtailed, and the observance of fixed numbers of memorial masses be eliminated.

The most contentious issues arose from attempts to bring consistency to the bewildering variety of mass rites celebrated across Catholic Europe. To create order out of the ritual chaos, the church needed a uniform missal, but the Council relegated the completion of this task to the pope. A papal commission under Pius IV (1559–65) and Pius V (1566–72) eventually solved the problem by issuing a new universal missal based on a revised version of the old Roman missal. In effect, the entire church with its enormous variety of local saints' days, special practices, variant prayers, and adaptations to historical change had to conform to the liturgy as it had supposedly been practiced in the city of Rome in the eleventh century. As a consequence many of the additions and perceived abuses of the later Middle Ages were eliminated. Votive masses, which had supplied the vast industry of masses for the dead, were greatly reduced. Numerous feast days were dropped from the liturgical calendar, especially the profusion of local saints' days, but special provisions were made for those churches that could prove a feast day had been in practice for at least 200 years. . . .

The governing principle of the commission seems to have been to create clarity by stripping away distorting additions to the basic forms of the mass and liturgy. Nevertheless, much of what the more radical Protestants considered to be distractions and unjustified additions were retained, such as polyphonic music, sumptuous clerical vestments, saints' images, holy water, and multiple altars. The Catholic reform impulse was consistently clerical and elitist. . . . Few concessions were made toward creating a stronger ritual bond between the priest and laity: the chalice continued to be reserved for the priesthood, and the mass text was still in Latin. Rather than making the priesthood bend down to the level of the simple laity, the reforms required the laity to raise themselves in obedience to clerical directions and in rigid observance of liturgical rites. . . . Perhaps the most innovative provision was the recommendation that the laity should receive the Eucharist every time they came to mass rather than the yearly communion that was normal before Trent. To enforce uniformity Pope Sixtus V established in 1588 the Congregation of Rites, which was charged with enforcing the celebration of the mass and liturgy in the prescribed forms.

The Catholic reform avoided the austere intellectualism of the Protestants despite the erudition of the prelates at Trent, but they hardened practice into an obsessive ritual rigidity that fettered the marvelous liturgical creativity of the later Middle Ages. Both Reformations produced unintended ironies. While the Protestants found it difficult if not impossible to escape the hold of collective rituals on religious practice, the Catholics promoted ritual observances in which the ritual experiences of the laity could be carefully controlled and correctly interpreted by properly trained clergy. . . .

The ritual processes of the Reformation in the Catholic world followed two distinct tendencies: one, regulations imposed from above and the other, pietistic practices expressing lay enthusiasm for Christian renewal. The regulatory path was set out by the decrees of the Council of Trent, which attempted to standardize liturgical practices in order to eliminate abuses and the confusing variety of rites. The Council charged bishops with putting into action what had been determined at Trent, but the effective implementation of the Tridentine decrees varied enormously across Europe and the Americas. They were perhaps most thoroughly enforced in the papal state itself and northern Italy where the interests of the landed elites and the church hierarchy often coincided, but even there implementation was controversial and uneven. . . . Outside of Italy the decrees were welcomed without significant official resistance only in Portugal and Poland, but even there actual compliance lagged behind stated goals for many years.

The pietistic strain of the Catholic Reformation appeared independently of the Council of Trent and evolved from the extraordinarily abundant repertoire of late medieval ritual practices that the laity and clergy reinvigorated and redeployed, in part as a Catholic response to the Protestant threat and in part as a general revival of Catholic piety that coincided with the Reformation but was not entirely dependent on it. At every point where Protestant reformers had criticized traditional ritual practices—the non-biblical sacraments, proliferation of sacramentals, use of images, cult of the saints, liturgical processions, masses for the dead—Catholics responded by reasserting the spiritual value of such rites, producing more processions, more elaborate decorations for churches, more side altars, more images, more magnificent music, more bejeweled chalices, richer liturgical vestments, even more saints. The pietistic trend consisted not just in the enforcement of liturgical uniformity but in the elaboration of a distinctively Catholic ritual vocabulary that contrasted with Protestant rituals, especially in the emphasis placed on the miracles of the saints and the Eucharist.

The principal Catholic strategy was to employ liturgical processions to demonstrate community cohesion and conformity. As early as 1528 in Paris King François I personally joined a procession designed to compensate the Virgin for a sacrilegious act committed against a statue of her in a public street. After hearing mass in the local church, the party proceeded to the location of the desecration where the king replaced the defaced statue with a new, silver-plated one. When the substitute statue was itself defiled it had to be replaced anew, and the repeated defacement of these images of the Virgin gave them miraculous qualities in the eyes of local Catholic women who considered them especially efficacious for difficulties in pregnancies. One woman reported that after praying before the original broken statue, she felt the dead baby in her womb come back to life. Catholics had answered Protestant iconoclasm by reasserting the miraculous potential of image veneration.

Protestant polemics against the Eucharist made defending the sacrality of the communion wafer a goal of many Catholic processions. In 1535, also in Paris, the king joined as a bare-headed, humble penitent a vast procession devoted to combating Protestants who had tacked up posters that "blasphemed God of the blessed Sacrament of the altar." Along the processional route residents were obliged to stand in front of their houses holding a lighted torch while they watched pass the procession in which priests and acolytes carried an impressive array of precious relics including, besides the host, which was given pride of place, the remains of six saints, the crown of thorns, a piece of the cross, a drop of Christ's blood, and a drop of the Virgin's milk. Ending with a high mass at Notre-Dame, the procession was followed by the public execution of six Protestants convicted of heresy.

By the last decades of the sixteenth century, newly founded or revived confraternities composed of lay brothers institutionalized the rejuvenation of Catholic ritual through regular processions. In the pietistic atmosphere after Trent the most favored of these was the Confraternity of the Holy Sacrament, most chapters of which had been established in towns long before the Reformation era. In periodic processions these brothers displayed the host for public veneration in an elaborately decorated pyx carried beneath a canopy as the relics of saints would have been in earlier times. The cult of the Eucharist became so vital that witnessing the miracle of the mass as often as possible began to displace other forms of pious activity. . . .

More disturbing than reassuring for many viewers were the penitential companies whose members wore hoods over their faces as they whipped themselves bloody while processing through the streets several times a year. Although flagellant companies had spread widely as a menacing phenomenon during the fourteenth century, the practice had died out except in a few pockets in northern Italy and southern France until the Wars of Religion, and the Catholic Reformation encouraged a widespread revival in the late sixteenth century, especially in France and Spain. By disguising identities and reminding viewers of convicts facing execution, hoods made the flagellants anonymous. The bloodied bodies of unrecognizable friends and neighbors stumbling down the street could cause widespread terror. . . . As a French apologist from the early seventeenth century put it, such severe self-discipline became a form of self-martyrdom: "In the eyes of the world made effeminate by its pleasures, [the penitent] will appear to be possessed by a hatred for himself and seem to act as an executioner of his own life, but though it be said that he is lost for the earth and damned in the opinion of men, he will grow in God's esteem." . . .

Perhaps the most powerful accomplishment of Catholic Reformation rituals was their ability to go beyond representing abstract truths such as Eucharistic doctrines, to evoke deeply disturbing emotions, especially fear and grief. The ritualized summoning of painful experiences was especially marked in Spain with the Holy Thursday rites, which Maureen Flynn has called a "spectacle of suffering." From sunset to midnight young and old, men and women, flooded the streets of Spanish towns to bemoan the impending death of Christ. According to the Gospels of Matthew and Luke, as Christ contemplated his crucifixion while praying in the garden of Gethsemane his apostles asked to share in his suffering. Emulating these first Christians, Spanish companies of female and male *disciplinantes* re-enacted the gospel scenes more emotionally than literally by sharing a simple meal together, then walking barefoot through the streets as they flagellated themselves. The rite created a memory of the last supper and the agony in the garden by leading penitents to discover God through the extreme limits of physical suffering, concentrating all the mundane miseries of the participants on their own self-tortured bodies, which through flagellation became akin to the tortured body of Christ. Pain became a medium of exchange with God, a means of making a sacrificial offering to him. The Spanish Holy Thursday rite exemplified the critical difference between Catholic and Protestant ritual vocabularies. For the Catholic evoking an emotional response and discovering God through intense physical sensations garnered spiritual merit. For the Protestant concerned to understand the biblical text correctly, the imitation of Christ came less through the body than the mind.

The most dramatic of Catholic rituals extended penance, the sacrament so disputed by the Protestants. The elaborate ritual of penance, the Spanish *auto de fe*, which literally meant a theater of faith, was performed during the height of the Catholic enthusiasms of the seventeenth century. The *auto* symbolically pre-enacted, in effect, the last judgment, stimulating deep anxiety among viewers over how they would fare when they stood before God on the last day. Everything about the *auto* seemed designed to promote fear and to offer the possibility of relief from fear by asserting that suffering bodily pain in this life would relieve the soul from worse punishments in the next. Organized through the cooperation of ecclesiastical and secular authorities, *autos de fe* brought together an assortment of sinners and criminals for a vast public rite of penance that displayed in a dramatic fashion the essential elements of the sacrament: contribution, confession, and satisfaction or punishment. The prisoners usually consisted of persons alleged to have been blasphemers, bigamists, witches, Judaizers (in the Spanish sense of the word, former Jews who had reverted to the old faith), or Protestants who were forced to march in a procession of sinners that usually went through the streets of the city from the cathedral to the town hall or place of punishment. These processions would typically include some thirty or forty convicted souls, but in moments of intense crisis they could be far larger. In Toledo in 1486 alone there were three *autos*, one parading 750 sinners and two displaying some 900 each.

A 1655 *auto* in Córdoba illustrates the abundant symbolic character of the rites. Soldiers bearing torches that would light the flames for those to be burnt led the procession, which included three bigamists who wore on their heads conical miters or hats painted with representations of their sin, four witches whose miters depicted devils, three criminals with harnesses around their necks to demonstrate their status as captives, and a group of barefoot, bare-headed repentant sinners dressed in yellow tunics that were marked with bands the width of which indicated the seriousness of their transgressions and carrying unlit candles to represent their lack of faith. Criminals who had escaped justice were represented in the procession by effigies made in their likeness, and those who had died before punishment were carried in their coffins. Each of these sinners appeared before their neighbors and fellow citizens stripped of the normal indicators of their status, dressed only in the emblems of their sins. Among them walked a few who wore the infamous *sanbenitos*, a kind of tunic or vest with a yellow strip down the back, and a conical hat painted with flames. These were the *relajados*, the unrepentant or relapsed sinners who were going to be "relaxed," that is strangled and burned at the culminating moment of the *auto*. The procession ended in the town square at a platform from which the prisoners would perform their penances before the public as if on the stage of a theater: forced to their knees the sinners were asked to confess and to plead for readmission into the bosom of the church. For those who did confess, a sentence was announced that would rescue them from the pains of purgatory and the flames of the *auto*. The penalties depended upon the crime and displayed a great variety that included joining a penitential procession for a number of Fridays, requiring self-flagellation in public, or demanding that the penitent continue to wear the badges of shame for a prescribed period of time.

The most horrendous scenes of suffering awaited those who refused to repent or who had relapsed into sin or heresy, which meant that even if they chose to confess, they would not be considered sincere. If holdouts repented prior to the reading of the sentence, then the *auto* was a success, a triumph of the Christian faith over its enemies, and everything that could possibly elicit a confession was attempted, including haranguing, humiliating, and torturing the accused until their stubborn will broke. If the accused finally repented after the sentence was read then they would be strangled before burning, but if they held out to the very end, they would be burned alive. From the ecclesiastics' point of view, the refusal to repent was a disaster for the entire church because the flames opened a window into hell, and they would certainly prefer to see the church's authority acknowledged through confession than to see the power of Satan manifest in such a public fashion. It is reported that crowds witnessed the violence of the *autos de fe* with silent attention in a mood of deep dread not so much of the inquisitors, it seems, as for the inevitability of the final day of divine judgment that would arrive for them all. The core assumption of the *auto* ritual was that the infliction of bodily pain could save a soul from damnation. . . . It was assumed that the public ritual framework for the sacrament of penance would have a salutary effect on those who witnessed the *auto*, encouraging them to repent before they too faced the divine scourge. . . .

[Bishops who, in the wake of the Council of Trent, attempted to re-form the parishes and the rituals practiced in them faced considerable challenges.] . . . Making parishes undisputed religious and social cen-ters required considerable cooperation and negotiation between church authorities and the laity. Those bishops who were most successful were those who found the means to link their obligations to regulate ritual practice with the pious inclinations of the congregations. Especially in rural areas religious worship took place in many different locales, and even the parish church itself was a highly segmented space, with different social and kinship groups using the space in different ways. . . . [T]here was a profusion of side altars, scattered haphazardly throughout the church, some placed against columns in the middle of the church, some backed up against the main altar, crowding it with an abundance of ex-votos (mementos of miracles granted) hanging from the ceiling. . . . Second, much of what appeared and went on in the church did not conform to accepted church practice; 250 parishes have been studied in three dioceses in southern Piedmont in the late sixteenth century; in only two of these was the baptismal font correctly placed in the pre-scribed location. . . Third, it was often unclear exactly what or where the parish church was. In some places the ancient parish had been aban-doned, in others there were disputes between churches for the title, and in yet more cases the parish had disappeared entirely. . . .

The visits of bishops to the parishes, as required by Trent, resulted in endless disputes as the ecclesiastical authorities attempted to define who in the community, whether an individual or family or political institution or corporate organization such as a confraternity, had legal responsibility for each ritual object and church furnishing. . . . [I]n their visitations to parishes, bishops showed great sensitivity to the exact details of ritual practice, especially the rites of confraternities and families at their pri-vate altars, because the ritual act itself conferred status on individuals, groups, and even buildings. In the diocese of Asti in 1626, for example, the episcopal visitor was furious when he discovered that the local con-fraternity of flagellants had presented their crucifix for the people to kiss in exchange for alms. He was angry not because of the implications of idolatry but because the flagellants had taken money for a ritual service, which was the exclusive prerogative of priests. . . . Any attempt to change any ritual had implications for the distribution of power within the community and the prestige of individuals and groups. . . .

Although bishops might be censorious about the crudest abuses of ecclesiastical property, such as using parish churches as stables or taverns, they had to avoid head-on confrontations with parishioners sensitive to their ritual rights. The most successful reforms came when bishops co-opted the laity by redefining or restructuring established lay practices. The conciliatory bishops often succeeded when they limited themselves to three areas. First, exercising control over the multiplicity of side altars eliminated some of the most obvious distractions from the centrality of the high altar in the parish church. Side altars tended to segment the public church into the private spaces of aristocratic landlords, kin groups, or confraternities, and bishops had to make these groups responsible for maintaining a part of the church without allowing them to destroy the public character of the parish and its forms of worship in what was often a delicate balancing of private and collective interests. Second, bishops had to redeploy existing forms of collective worship into the parish organization, eliminating semi-private cults and the display of ex-votos, which distracted worship from the high altar. The cult of the Virgin of the Rosary, preached by the Dominicans, assisted this effort by redirecting prayer away from private altars to the collective repetition of the rosary at the high altar under the direction of the parish priest. Third, bishops enhanced rituals that assisted in developing a community identity. By promoting the cult of the host at the high altar, the thaumaturgical appeal of many of the saintly cults on side altars diminished, and the host itself served as a metaphor for the unified body of the community, whose competitive and envious members joined together for worship at a single altar. Confraternities devoted to the body of God assisted in translating private interests into communal ones. The elaboration of the cult of the Eucharist achieved far more than a response to the Protestants. It became a synecdoche—the part that stood for the whole—of the community, strengthened by a reinvigorated, bishop-controlled, parish-based reformation of worship.

Bernini, "The Ecstasy of St. Teresa." (© *Bridgeman Art Library*) The future saint and the most prominent female religious figure of the sixteenth century, Teresa of Avila experienced a vision in which an angel appeared to her and repeatedly pierced her heart with an arrow of divine love, resulting in mystical ecstasy.

PART

IV The Reformation and Gender

In recent years gender analysis has had a huge impact on historical research in general and has added a vitally important dimension to our understanding of the Protestant and Catholic Reformations. The author of several books, Merry Wiesner has had an enormous influence on the study of the Reformation and gender. In "The Reformation of the Women," Wiesner endeavors to look briefly at both how women participated in Reformation movements and how male church and political leaders tried to "reform" women by closely controlling their behavior. Some women showed determined independence, such as those who converted to one faith against their husbands' wishes or the German nuns who willingly embraced Protestantism but insisted on remaining in their convents. Some females attained a certain prominence in reforming movements, such as Argula von Grumbach, a German noblewoman who actively promoted the Lutheran cause; Marie Dentière, a former abbess who left her convent to advance the Reformed church in Geneva; the Catholic Angela Merici, founder of the Ursulines, a group of unmarried laywomen who served the poor, ill, and orphans and who supported themselves through teaching and weaving; and Teresa Avila, the Spanish mystic and reformer of her Carmelite order who was sanctified not long after her death. In short, while male authorities defined women primarily as sexual creatures and accordingly sought to supervise their sexuality carefully, many females identified themselves less by their biological nature than by their spiritual gifts and intellectual capacities and enjoyed a degree of success in defining themselves spiritually.

Lyndal Roper's "'The Common Man,' 'The Common Good,' 'Common Women': Gender and Meaning in the German Reformation Commune" is a seminal article that explores how women fit into the notion of the "community" in the German Reformation. Certain scholars of the Reformation have placed considerable emphasis on the "community" as actor in the early Protestant movement. Bernd Moeller wrote an important essay, "Imperial Cities and the Reformation" (in *Imperial Cities and the Reformation: Three Essays,* ed. and trans. H. C. Erik Midelfort and Mark U. Edwards, Jr. [Philadelphia: Fortress Press, 1972]), in which he claims that Protestantism resonated with so many urban inhabitants because German citizens, in any of a number of cities in the Holy Roman Empire, considered themselves to be part of a political and religious community. Studying the German Peasants' War of the 1520s, Peter Blickle considers this revolt to be the "Revolution of the Common Man," asserting that it involved not just peasants but also miners and underprivileged urban dwellers, all of whom desired greater rights and appealed to a concept of community that was independent of the prevailing political and religious powers (*The Revolution of 1525: The German Peasants' War from a New Perspective,* trans. Thomas A. Brady, Jr., and H. C. Erik Midelfort [Baltimore: Johns Hopkins University Press, 1981]). Since these and other historians made no mention of women in their discussions of community, Roper examines the concept of community in different contexts with the aim of identifying women's place in it. She finds that in urban public processions, especially those conducted for swearing oaths, women in fact played no role whatsoever, reflecting that there was no place for females in the "official" understanding of community. When women did try to initiate political actions, their activities were deemed subversive because they violated the social mores that were prescribed for their sex. In short, as a political concept, the community was exclusively male and, as the Reformation took root, appeared to be tied more to the notion of fatherhood than to the bearing of arms.

In "From Prophecy to Discipline, 1450–1650," Gabriella Zarri looks at the different experiences of female religious, including those regarded as saints. The fifteenth century witnessed an increase in the number of female religious orders, most notably the growth in the number of Third Orders for women. At first, women who joined the Third Orders generally continued to live in their own homes and participated in a form of religious life without taking formal vows. Angela Merici's founding of the Ursulines, groups of laywomen who initially did not take the vows of nuns, bore witness to the important contributions women were making to the renewal of religious life in early sixteenth-century Italy. The reforms of Trent introduced unprecedented rigor in regard to female religious orders. Convents were more cloistered than ever before, and the Third Orders were in effect dissolved, as their members were now required to become nuns and reside in convents. On a positive note, Tridentine discipline did provide greater educational opportunities for nuns, evidenced in a growing number of works written by them. While female saints reached their apogee in terms of power and prestige in the late fifteenth century, Martin Luther of course rejected the very notion of sanctity for both women and men. From the mid-fifteenth to the mid-seventeenth centuries, the number of women who were canonized declined considerably, and the new female saints were more likely to be reformers of religious orders than mystics, formerly the most common type of female saints.

Sherrill Cohen has a more sanguine assessment of the impact of the Catholic Reformation on some Italian women. "Asylums for Women in Counter-Reformation Italy" investigates new types of institutions that were established for women. Beginning in the mid-sixteenth century, institutions for "fallen" women were founded in many Italian cities. An excellent example is the Casa del Soccorso di San Paolo, established in Bologna in 1589, which was a home for women who allegedly were guilty of illicit sexuality, including prostitutes. This home had a strong punitive character, but a stay in such an institution amounted to an act of purification, allowing women to regain their lost honor. Although divorce was not an option for Roman Catholics, other havens were created for women who suffered from miserable marriages, providing refuge from abusive or negligent husbands.

Gender analysis has played an essential role in the history of the family, and many historians have pondered the Protestant and

Catholic Reformation's impact on the family, including women's place in it. The author of several influential books on the history of the family, Steven Ozment has consistently argued against the view that the Reformation, particularly the Protestant reform, was detrimental to women by enhancing patriarchal power, making females more subordinate to their husbands and fathers. He insists that Protestants enhanced marriage by making it the "normal" state for almost all adults and denying that the celibate life was morally superior. According to Ozment, though believing that the husband was to be the head of the household by biblical mandate, Protestants viewed marriages as partnerships and supported a form of equality within marriage, the most important expression of which was the introduction of divorce and remarriage.

Examining the control of marriage and its impact on women, Jeffrey Watt does not see much change for the better for women. To be sure, the introduction of divorce was an important innovation—in large part because they considered marriage a sacrament, a vehicle of God's grace, Roman Catholics to this day do not recognize the possibility of divorce. But centuries would pass before it had much of an impact on marriage and the family. Divorce remained quite rare in almost all parts of Europe throughout the early modern period, and the recognized grounds for divorce were very limited, essentially restricted to adultery and abandonment. In particular, the consistent rejection of cruelty as a ground for divorce throughout the sixteenth and seventeenth centuries showed that Europe's matrimonial courts offered little relief to the wives of abusive husbands. Moreover, Catholic and Protestant courts rejected the majority of suits filed by women who sought to enforce marriage contracts with men who had allegedly seduced them; and a double standard prevailed in many Catholic and Protestant areas, whereby a male's sexual indiscretions were punished more mildly than a female's.

All told, the Protestant and Catholic Reformations affected women in ways that varied according to place and class. It is difficult to argue that the status of women in general declined or was enhanced with the Protestant and Counter-Reformations. For those with a religious calling, the Protestant and, to a lesser degree, the Catholic Reformations probably meant a step backward. For others, modest increases in educational opportunities in Reformation Europe, especially among Protestants, represented a step forward. The large majority of women probably saw little change in their lot. Having no political voice and fewer economic opportunities than males, they were subject to their fathers and husbands whether they lived before or after 1517, in Lutheran, Calvinist, Anglican, or Catholic territory.

Merry E. Wiesner

The Reformation of the Women

"Since it were very pernicious that the opinions of men, although good and holy, should be put in the place of the commandment of God, I desire that this matter may be cleared up for the well-being and the concord of the churches." These are words spoken by Charlotte de Mornay, a French noblewoman and Calvinist Protestant, in 1584, to the consistory of Montauban, where she was residing. The matter in question was the consistory's excommunication of her and her entire household because she wore her hair in curls. Such matters, de Mornay continued, were no grounds for the exclusion of someone from church ceremonies and services, and she as a noblewoman was certainly not going to obey the middle-class pastors on an issue that had nothing to do with her or anyone else's salvation.

This conflict and de Mornay's comments about it highlight many of the issues involving women's religious life in the Reformation period. First, though we may view the arrangement of women's hair as trivial, it had tremendous social and symbolic importance. Immediately upon marriage, women covered their hair, for long flowing hair was the mark of someone who was sexually available, either as a virgin or prostitute. Protestant woodcuts often contrast pious women listening to sermons with their hair carefully covered with women buying indulgences whose heads only bear a few feathers or ribbons. Both the New Testament and

Merry E. Wiesner, "The Reformation of the Women," in *Gender, Church, and State in Early Modern Germany*, Pearson Education Limited (London and New York: Longman, 1998), 63–78. Copyright © Addison Wesley Longman Limited 1998. Reprinted by permission of Pearson Education Limited.

church fathers such as Tertullian had ordered women to cover their heads, not simply as a gesture of respect but also specifically to lessen their sexual attractiveness. Thus the pastors claimed biblical authority for their position, and at the heart of the issue was the control of female sexuality and the maintenance of a moral order in which women were subservient. These factors will emerge in nearly all the religious conflicts involving women in the Reformation period, even when the participants did not articulate them.

Second, the key question for women was often the conflict between the authorities de Mornay mentions: the opinions of men and the commandment of God. Women had to choose between what male political and religious authorities, and sometimes even their fathers and husbands, told them to do, and what they perceived as God's plan for their lives. Third, de Mornay's confidence in challenging the pastors, and the source of some of her irritation, came from her status as a noblewoman; the women whose religious choices had the most impact in early modern Europe were usually noblewomen or rulers, whose actions affected their subjects as well as themselves and their families. . . .

Finally, this incident nicely captures the ambiguities of the title of this session, the Reformation *of* the women, an ambiguity fortuitously present in the German "die Reformation der Frauen" as well. By her actions, de Mornay transformed the consistory's attempts to reform *her* into a more far-reaching theological discussion in which *she* played a role. She was not alone in this, for the Reformation period saw Protestant and Catholic women throughout Europe doing the same thing, taking new or traditional ideas about their place and role expressed by men and using these as a call to action. Most studies of women and the Reformation (my own included) have focused on either one or the other sense of "of"—i.e., either Luther's or Calvin's or Bullinger's or some other man's ideas about women, marriage, and the family and the legal and social changes that resulted from these, or women's actions in support of or opposition to the Reformation. Here I would like to highlight some examples from both the Protestant and Catholic Reformations where the two senses of "of" are in tension, where moves to "reform" women were suddenly faced with "reformed" or "reforming" women who often had very different ideas about the type of reforms necessary.

My first example is also the best studied, women who took the Protestant notion of a priesthood of all believers literally and preached or published polemical religious literature explaining their own ideas. Women's preaching or publishing religious material stood in direct opposition to the words ascribed to St Paul (1 Timothy 2: 11–15) which ordered women not to teach or preach, so that all women who published felt it necessary to justify their actions. The boldest, such as Argula von Grumbach, a German noblewoman who published a defence of a teacher accused of Lutheran leanings, commented that the situation was so serious that Paul's words should simply be disregarded: "I am not unfamiliar with Paul's words that women should be silent in church but when I see that no man will or can speak, I am driven by the word of God when he said, He who confesses me on earth, him will I confess and he who denies me, him will I deny" (Matthew 10, Luke 9). . . . Marie Dentière, a former abbess who left her convent to help the cause of the Reformation in Geneva, published a letter to Queen Marguerite of Navarre in 1539 defending some of the reformers exiled from that city, in which she gives ringing support to this view: "I ask, didn't Jesus die just as much for the poor illiterates and the idiots as for the shaven, tonsured, and mighty lords? Did he only say, "Go, preach my Gospel to the wise lords and grand doctors?" Did he not say, "To all?" Do we have two Gospels, one for men and the other for women? . . . For we ought not, any more than men, hide and bury within the earth that which God has . . . revealed to us women?" Katherina Zell, the wife of one of Strasbourg's reformers and a tireless worker for the Reformation, supported Dentière in this, asking that her writings be judged, "not according to the standards of a woman, but according to the standards of one whom God has filled with the Holy Spirit."

Zell's wish was never granted, and women's writings were always judged first on the basis of gender. Argula von Grumbach's husband was ordered to force her to stop writing, and Marie Dentière's pamphlets were confiscated by the very religious authorities she was defending. Once Protestant churches were institutionalized, polemical writings by women supporting magisterial churches largely stopped. The reformation of women (their being made Protestant) was not to become a reformation which included female voices, other than those singing (and very occasionally writing) hymns.

A second example is provided by women whose religious convictions came to disagree with those of their husbands. Should a woman whose own faith had been reformed (either Protestant or Catholic) be encouraged to reform that of others within her household, including her husband? This issue was tackled in theory by both Protestant and

Catholic authors, with Catholics and English Puritans generally encouraging active domestic missionary work on the part of women, and continental Protestants prayer and forbearance. Jesuits encouraged the students at their seminaries to urge their mothers to return to confession and begin Catholic practices in the home and other Catholic writers approved of daughters inspiring their parents as well: "Young girls will reform their families, their families will reform their provinces, their provinces will reform the world." . . .

Should a woman's religious convictions provide just grounds for her leaving her spouse? In terms of general principles, neither Catholic nor magisterial Protestants recommended that wives leave husbands with whom they disagreed; a few Anabaptists did, but they expected the women to remarry quickly and thus come under the control of a male believer. In practice, Catholic political authorities put fewer blocks in the path of a woman who did. Protestant city councils in Germany were suspicious of any woman who asked to be admitted to citizenship independently and questioned her intently about her marital status. Catholic cities such as Munich were more concerned about whether the woman who wanted to immigrate had always been a good Catholic than whether or not she was married, particularly if she wanted to enter a convent. Protestant reformers were actually more willing to praise or accept individual women who had left their husbands than Protestant political authorities were, because they did not have to translate this into policy. Elisabeth of Brandenburg, the wife of Joachim I, lived for a while in the Luther household after leaving her Catholic husband, and even John Knox, hardly a friend of independent women, accepted English married women without their husbands in his entourage in Geneva. Economic and social realities meant that leaving a spouse for religious reasons remained within the realm of theory for most women. . . . For most women, any religious reformation which she experienced would remain a private matter.

The one exception to this provides our third example, the case of women rulers, those women for whom the reformation *of* the women led most clearly and least problematically (in the eyes of male reformers) to a reformation *by* women. Though none of the reformers differentiated between noblewomen and commoners in their public advice or writings, in private they recognized that noblewomen had a great deal of power and made special attempts to win them over. . . . Their efforts met with results, for female rulers frequently converted their territories to Protestantism or influenced their male relatives to do so. In Germany, Elisabeth of Brunswick-Calenberg brought in Protestant preachers and established a new church structure; in France, Marguerite of Navarre and her daughter Jeanne d'Albret supported Calvinism through patronage and political influence; in Norway, Lady Inger of Austraat, a powerful and wealthy noblewoman, led the opposition to the Norwegian archbishop who remained loyal to Catholicism. In all of these cases political and dynastic concerns mixed with religious convictions, in the same way they did for male rulers and nobles.

A female ruler's ability to transform her private religious convictions into the official religion of her territory *was* problematic in the case of one special type of female ruler, the abbess. Abbesses, particularly those of free imperial convents, provide a fourth and especially instructive example of women who transformed efforts to reform them into efforts to carry out reforms. Many free imperial convents, and also those established by regional ruling houses, had undergone reforms in the fifteenth century to bring them back to high standards of spiritual observance. These reforms were sometimes introduced by bishops or male leaders of the order to which a convent was affiliated, but the ones that were most successful were those which gained the enthusiastic support of the abbess. Some abbesses made careers of travelling from house to house carrying out reforms, and at times their zeal for strict observance far surpassed that of the male members of their order.

Reformed convents proved to be the most vocal and resolute opponents of the Protestant Reformation. This was recognized by their contemporaries: Bishop Heinrich Julius of Halberstadt, who was Lutheran, noted that the continuation of Catholicism in the convents was "the result of the resoluteness of the nuns . . . the monks, though, are very lukewarm in the practice of their religion." A papal nuncio reported that "the four women's convents [in Magdeburg] have remained truer to their beliefs and vows than the men's monasteries, who have almost all fallen away." Nuns were often subjected to verbal abuse, denied confessors, required to hear Protestant sermons daily, forcibly removed from convents because of the will of their families or even had their convents physically dismantled around them. They were the only adults treated in this manner, in part because territories could not expel them the way they could monks who rejected Protestant teachings; cloistered nuns were generally members of prominent local noble and patrician families whereas monks were more socially diverse and often came from another part of Germany. In many areas, political authorities simply stopped trying to convert the nuns and instead confiscated their lands and refused to allow new novices. In other areas, political authorities gave up completely, and the convents survived as Catholic institutions within Protestant territories until the nineteenth-century secularization of all church lands. . . .

Not all convents and abbesses fought Lutheran teachings, however; some accepted the new theology and energetically introduced it into their territories. Anna von Stolberg, for example, was the abbess of the free imperial abbey of Quedlinburg, and so governed a sizable territory including nine churches, a hospital and two male monasteries. She accepted the Protestant Reformation in the 1540s, and carried out a number of moves that were standard for Protestant authorities, including closing the monasteries, requiring clergy to swear to the Augsburg Confession, and setting up a primary school. Though her actions gave clear proof of her religious ideas, she continued to receive both imperial and papal privileges, for Catholic authorities were unwilling to cut off support from what was, at any rate, still a *convent*.

Protestant authorities were ambivalent about Lutheran convents, and class and gender both worked to aid the abbeys' ability to survive. Gender stereotypes about female weakness may have provoked opposition to female rule in theory, but they also enabled men to take actual examples of that rule less seriously, at least at the local level. These abbeys were not viewed as as great a threat as male monasteries because their residents were, after all, women. Most of the residents were also noble or patrician, whose families not only resented any insult to their female members, but were also unwilling to bear the consequences of closing the abbeys. Dowries were getting larger, and even wealthy families were often not able to find appropriate partners for all of their daughters. As six noblemen writing to one of the Dukes of Brunswick when he was contemplating closing the convents in his territory put it, "What would happen to our sisters' and relatives' honour and our reputation if they are forced to marry renegade monks, cobblers, and tailors?" These, by the way, were Lutheran nobles. The women's class status not only gave them support from beyond the convent walls, but provided a large part of their internal motivation and self-conception as well, in the same way it did for Charlotte de Mornay. They realized that there was no place for female leadership within the new Protestant churches unless they kept abbeys open. Former monks could become pastors, but for former nuns the only role was a pastor's wife, an unthinkable decrease in status for a woman of noble standing. Anna Sophia, a later abbess of Quedlinburg, wrote a book of meditations which included a long introduction and afterword discussing the special duties which virgins had to praise God and comparing the women in her convent both to the vestal virgins and to biblical women such as Deborah, Hannah, Judith and Mary. She makes no statements about the capabilities of all women the way the middle-class . . . Marie Dentière did, but does stress those of her noble co-residents; she clearly recognized that identification with her class would take her further than identification with her gender.

Though I have discovered no actual moves against Lutheran abbeys on the part of political authorities, some Protestant theorists were troubled by these institutions both because of Luther's and others' critique of monastic life and the fact that they were places where women held power directly and passed it on to other women, rather than simply ruling in the absence or during the minority of a man, as was the case with female secular rulers. Some Lutheran writers chose a legalistic way out, noting that many of these abbeys were not convents in the technical sense of the word, but secular endowments (*Stifte*) in which the women took no final vows; therefore they weren't *really* monastic establishments. Others used even more convoluted reasoning, commenting that though Isaiah appears to view female rulership as a curse (Isaiah 3: 12, "I will give you children to be your oppressors and women to be your rulers"), he was talking not about the female sex here, but about those of the feminine temperament (*Gemuth*) which did not include such brave and virile abbesses. The most common way for both Catholic and Protestant theorists to resolve the issue of Lutheran abbesses was simply to ignore them; in the Ecclesiastical Reservation of the Peace of Augsburg, for example, the language is completely male-specific. This avoidance is firmly entrenched in both Protestant and Catholic historiography of the Reformation, so that female religious are viewed as willing recipients (à la Katherine von Bora) or heroic opponents (à la Charitas Pirckheimer) of a reforming message they in no way shaped. The residents of the Lutheran abbeys which still exist in Germany today would no doubt be surprised to learn that their forbears are described as so passive.

So far I have been talking largely about women who responded to Protestant ideas with their own writings or actions, but the same thing happened in the Catholic Reformation. A fifth example of women who transformed efforts to reform them into efforts to carry out reforms is provided by the numerous women in Europe who felt God had called them to oppose Protestants directly through missionary work, or to carry out the type of active service to the world in schools and hospitals that the friars and the new orders were making increasingly popular with men. For example, Angela Merici founded the Company of St Ursula in Brescia, Italy. The Company was a group of lay single women and widows dedicated to serving the poor, the ill, orphans, and war victims, earning their own living through teaching or weaving. Merici received papal approval in 1535, for the Pope saw this as a counterpart to the large number of men's lay confraternities and societies being founded at that point.

Similar groups of lay women dedicated to charitable service began to spring up in other cities of Italy, Spain, and France, and in 1541, Isabel Roser decided to go one step further and ask for papal approval for an order of religious women with a similar mission. Roser had been an associate of Loyola's in Barcelona and saw her group as a female order of Jesuits which would also not be cut off from the world but would devote itself to education, care of the sick and assistance to the poor, and in so doing win converts back to Catholicism. This was going too far, however. Loyola was horrified at the thought of religious women in constant contact with lay people and Pope Paul III refused to grant his approval. Despite this, her group continued to grow in Rome and the Netherlands, where they spread Loyola's teaching through the use of the Jesuit catechism.

The Council of Trent responded to these efforts and to Protestant critiques of convent life with the same move that had been part of church reforms since the Gregorian—compulsory claustration for all women's religious communities. Enforcement of this decree came slowly, however, for several reasons. First, women's communities themselves fought it or ignored it. . . . Second, church officials themselves recognized the value of the services performed by such communities, particularly in the area of girls' education and care of the sick. Well after Trent, Charles Borromeo invited members of the Company of St Ursula to Milan, and transformed the group from one of lay women into one of religious who lived communally, though they still were not cloistered and did not take solemn vows; in terms of their status, they were much like the secular endowments of Germany. From Milan, the Ursulines spread throughout the rest of Italy and into France, and began to focus completely on the education of girls. They became so popular that noble families began to send their daughters to Ursuline houses for an education, and girls from wealthy families became Ursulines themselves.

The very success of the Ursulines led to the enforcement of claustration, however, as well as other Tridentine decrees regulating women religious. Secular endowments were not a tradition in France the way they were in Germany, and wealthy families were uncomfortable with the fact that because Ursulines did not take solemn vows, their daughters who had joined communities could theoretically leave at any time and make a claim on family inheritance. (Solemn vows bound one permanently to a religious establishment, and made an individual legally dead in the secular world.) Gradually the Ursuline houses in France and Italy were ordered to accept claustration, take solemn vows, and put themselves under the authority of their local bishop, thus preventing any movement or cooperation between houses. They were still allowed to teach girls, but now only within the confines of a convent. Class and family interests had worked in favour of women's independent religious actions for convents in Protestant Germany, but against them in Catholic France.

Extraordinary circumstances occasionally led church leadership to relax its restrictions, but only to a point. The situation of English Catholics under Protestant rulers was viewed as a special case, and a few women gained approval to go on their own as missionaries there. One of these was Luisa de Carvajal y Mendoza, a Spanish noblewoman who opposed her family's wishes and neither married nor entered a convent. She was quite effective at converting non-Catholics and bolstering the faith of her co-religionists, and later commented that being a woman helped her, as the English never suspected a woman could be a missionary. Paul V, pope from 1605 to 1621, was relatively open to female initiatives and in 1616 granted Mary Ward, who had run a school for English Catholic girls in exile in the Spanish Netherlands, provisional approval for her Institute of the Blessed Virgin Mary. She wanted women in her Institute to return to England as missionaries, for "it seems that the female sex also in its own measure, should and can . . . undertake something more than ordinary in this great common spiritual undertaking." She openly modelled the Institute on the Jesuits and began to minister to the poor and sick in London, visiting Catholic prisoners and teaching in private homes. The reports of her successes proved too much for church leadership, and she was ordered to stop all missionary work, for "it was never heard in the Church that women should discharge the Apostolic Office." Undaunted, Ward shifted her emphasis, and the Institute began to open houses in many cities throughout Europe in which women who took no formal vows operated free schools for both boys and girls, teaching them reading, writing, and a trade. . . . Her popularity and independence proved too much for the church hierarchy, however, and the year after the Bull was published against Ward's schools, most of her houses were ordered closed, and Ward herself imprisoned by the Inquisition in Munich. "Jesuitesses," as Ward's Institute was termed by her enemies, were not to be tolerated, and similar other uncloistered communities of women, such as the Visitation, started by Jeanne de Chantal and Francis de Sales, to serve the poor, were ordered to accept claustration or be closed.

Female religious were thus blocked in all of their efforts to create a community of women dedicated to reforming the world, but beginning in the seventeenth century, lay women in some parts of Europe were slowly able to create just that. The first example of this was the Daughters of Charity begun by Vincent de Paul and Madame de Gras; though both founders privately thought of the group as a religious community, they realized that outwardly maintaining secular status was the only thing that allowed them to serve the poor and ill. The Daughters took no public vows and did not wear religious habits, and constantly stressed that they would work only where invited by a bishop or priest. This subversion of the rules was successful, for the Daughters of Charity received papal approval and served as the model for other women's communities which emphasized educating the poor or girls; by 1700 numerous teaching and charitable "congregations" were found throughout Catholic Europe. They explicitly used the Virgin Mary as their model, stressing that she, too, had served as a missionary during the Visitation. The congregations were often backed by larger women's religious confraternities, in which elite women supported a congregation financially or engaged in charitable works themselves. The choice which the Council of Trent had attempted to impose on women, "maritus aut murus" (a husband or a cloister), had finally been replaced by a range of options. These intermediate groups provided lay women with companionship, devotional practices, and an outlet for their energies beyond the household, and may partly be responsible for women's greater loyalty to the church with the growing secularism of the eighteenth century.

For female religious in Catholic Europe, however, the only way they could act as reformers was by instructing girls, and that only within the convent. No nuns were sent to the foreign missions for any public duties, though once colonies were established in the New World and

Asia cloistered convents quickly followed. The exclusion of women from what were judged the most exciting and important parts of the Catholic Reformation—countering Protestants and winning new converts—is reflected in the relative lack of women from the sixteenth century who were made saints. Luisa de Carvajal was raised to the status of Venerable, the first rung on the ladder to sanctity, but only 18.1 per cent of those who reached the top of the ladder from the sixteenth century were women, whereas 27.7 per cent of those from the fifteenth century had been female. Most of the women who did achieve sainthood followed a very different path, one of mysticism or of reforming existing orders, a path in some ways set by my sixth and final example, the most famous religious woman of the sixteenth century, Teresa of Avila. If any woman made a reformation of her own, it was Teresa.

Teresa took her vows as a Carmelite at twenty, and then spent the next twenty-five years in relative obscurity in her convent at Avila. During this time of external inaction, she went through great spiritual turmoil, extremes of exaltation and melancholy, and suffered physical effects such as illness, trances, and paralysis. The mystical path which she created during these adversities was one of union with God not through mortification of the flesh, but through prayer, purification of the spirit, and assistance to the women of her convent. Teresa's confessors ordered her not only to describe her mystical experiences in writing, but to reflect on them and try to explain why she thought these were happening to her. Though Teresa complained about having to do this, she also clearly developed a sense of passion about her writing, for she edited and refined her work, transforming it into a full spiritual autobiography. Writing had been imposed on her as a way of demonstrating she was not tainted with Alumbrado, Lutheran, or other heretical ideas, but her autobiography became a document designed to keep others from heresy or convert those already lapsed.

Like Angela Merici and Mary Ward, Teresa also yearned for some kind of active ministry, and explicitly chafed at the restrictions on her because of her sex: "Nor did you, Lord, when You walked in the world, despise women; rather, You always, with great compassion, helped [or favoured] them. And You found as much love and more faith in them than You did in men. Is it not enough, Lord, that the world has intimidated us . . . so that we may not do anything worthwhile for You in public?" In part she solved this by interpreting her prayers and those of other nuns as public actions: "we shall be fighting for Him [God] even though we are very cloistered." When she was fifty-two, she also began to reform her Carmelite order, attempting to return it to its original standards of spirituality and poverty. To do this, she travelled all around Spain, founding new convents, writing meditations, instructions for monastic administrators, and hundreds of letters, provoking the wrath or annoyance of some church authorities; a papal nuncio called her a "fidgety, restless, disobedient and obstinate woman, who under the guise of devotion invents evil doctrine and breaks cloister."

Teresa's success in reforming the Carmelites won her more supporters than critics within the church, however, for, unlike Angela Merici and Mary Ward, she did not advocate institutionalized roles for women outside the convent. Her frustration at men's alterations of Christ's view of women did not lead her to break with the male church hierarchy, and the words I just quoted which expressed that frustration were expunged from her works by church censors. In the same way that Lutheran convents disappeared from German Reformation history, the version of Teresa which was presented for her canonization proceedings, held very shortly after her death, was one which avoided inconsistencies and embarrassments. She was fitted into the acceptable model of woman mystic and reformer, assuming a public role only when ordered to do so by her confessor or superior; only recently have we begun to understand that Teresa thought of herself as a Counter-Reformation fighter, viewing the new religious houses she established as answers to the Protestant takeover of Catholic churches elsewhere in Europe.

What conclusions can we draw from these six rather disparate examples—Protestant polemicists, wives who disagreed with their husbands, reforming rulers, abbesses, Catholic activists, and Teresa?

In many ways, they sound exactly like their male counterparts. Protestants find biblical examples of great women or use Paul's words in one place to argue against those in another, while Catholics build traditions, using the life of Mary to serve as an example for activism. Rulers and abbesses took their right to make political decisions for their territories as the self-evident privilege of their class, and only spoke about their gender when others made an issue of it. Both men and women agreed that women are morally and mentally weaker, and that female religious authority is possible only in times of extraordinary need. As long as women worked within (or subverted, depending on how you look at it) male-defined limits, they received some support for their acting in support of a Reformation.

In other ways, however, these women approach things very differently. In our terminology, male religious and political authorities thought of women as a sex, while the women who have left us their thoughts thought of women as a gender. The "Reformation of the women" in the intellectual and institutional constructs of men—marriage and funeral sermons, treatises on celibacy, laws regarding prostitution, adultery, marriage, inheritance, and morals, the *Hausvater-* and much smaller *Hausmutterliteratur*—not only was one imposed on women, but one which largely concerned their physical and sexual status. Both sexes were urged by Protestants to give up the monastic life, but for women this was automatically expected to lead to marriage; the claustration of women ordered by Trent explicitly aimed at preventing all sexual contacts; the ultimate critiques of Teresa, Mary Ward, Marie Dentière, and others like them were always sexual, not theological—"they undertook and exercised many other works unsuitable to their sex and their capacity, their feminine modesty and, above all, their virginal shame." Sixteenth-century male religious reformers, like nineteenth-century male social reformers, thought of women as "the sex."

Reformation women, however, . . . saw being a woman as not simply a matter of biology and sexuality, but of traditions, laws, customs, political systems, economic relations and emotional linkages—in other words, though they would never have expressed it this way, they saw gender as socially constructed. They saw themselves (and sometimes other women) as less determined by their biology and sexual status and more by their intellectual capacities, spiritual gifts, and, among noblewomen, social class. Because they thought that such things could to a degree overcome or make irrelevant their gender, they felt driven not simply to *be* reformed, but to *do* reforms. . . .

I have concentrated here too much, perhaps, on the second sense of the "Reformation of the women." Current research also suggests that if any Reformation was successful in the sixteenth century, it was that "of the women" in the first sense, a restriction of women's sphere of independent actions and an increase in the power of male heads of household, both temporal and spiritual. . . . A concentration on the first sense alone, however, negates the subjectivity and historical agency of women, making the Reformation yet another example of the oppression of women. There are plenty of examples of that, so I have chosen to examine some women who made the Reformation their own. . . .

Lyndal Roper

"The Common Man," "The Common Good," "Common Women": Gender and Meaning in the German Reformation Commune

This paper originated in a diffuse feeling of unease about what has become a platitude of recent Reformation scholarship—the role of the "common man" and of the community in the Evangelical movement. The orthodoxy seems to offer an almost visually specific identification of the Reformation actor: we think we can see him looking out at us from the early Reformation woodcuts, dressed in his sturdy peasant boots, gesturing confidently with the certainty of his Evangelical faith, or sometimes posing with his ally, the trusty soldier. But was the social reality addressed by polemicists and imagined by modern historians truly so homogenous, so folksily familiar? What did such images mean to women? Did they consider themselves to be addressed by artist or pamphleteer? What was the community to which pamphleteers appealed—was it one which included women? Indeed, how useful is the term "community," so apparently crucial to Reformation rhetoric, in an analysis of the Reformation itself?

The Reformation rhetoric becomes still more puzzling if, for a moment, one inverts the male gender of the "common man," the seemingly gender-neutral abstraction. By *gemeine Frau* or *Gemeinerin*, sixteenth-century hearers would have understood the prostitute. The domain of the civic prostitute was the *Gemeinhaus*. Gender thus appears to reverse the word's associations, for while the *gemeiner Mann* is the community's representative and the Reformation's hero, the prostitute was by symbol and tradition excluded from the commune. . . .

Lyndal Roper, "'The Common Man,' 'The Common Good,' 'Common Women': Gender and Meaning in the German Reformation Commune," *Social History* Vol. 12 (1987): 1–21. Copyright © 1987 Taylor & Francis Ltd. Reprinted by permission of Taylor & Francis Ltd. http://www.tandf.co.uk/journals.

Yet both the *gemeine Frau* and the *gemeiner Mann* were central terms in the speech of the early Reformation movement. Propagandists for a morally reinvigorated Reformation called for the abolition of the civic brothels and the ending of the common women's trade. In pamphlets and images, the common woman was frequently aligned with the Reformation's enemies, the loose-living, lecherous priests and monks. . . . [W]hen Reformation polemicists used the biblical figure of the Babylonian Whore of Revelation to such devastating effect as a symbol of the papacy, the older tradition on which they drew was sharpened by the contemporary interest in the evils of prostitution. . . . Thus, while the common woman stood for all that was papist and ungodly, the common man embodied what was decent, upright and populist in the early Reformation movement. . . .

[T]he rhetoric consistently invoked a male-defined notion of who the community included, what sexuality consisted in and whose sexual "needs" ought to be perceived and served. In this universe, women are sexual objects rather than subjects, resources to which access is either to be denied, secured to one man alone or allowed to all men, depending upon the status of the woman as virgin, matron or prostitute.

The imagery of the common man, the Reformation hero, and the rhetoric of community which underlay it, were relentlessly male. In woodcuts, he is shown either with an agricultural implement of some kind, frequently a flail, rake, hoe or pitchfork, tools identified with male agricultural labour and strength; or with a short sword, a socially recognized phallic symbol. Most often, he is depicted as a peasant, and sometimes he is explicitly identified as Karsthans, Jack Hoe. . . . He alone can embody the peasants' struggle and tragedy. The female presence is only implicit, in the baskets of eggs and cheese, the butter churn and milk can of women's work, which stand among the male agricultural implements forming the base of the monument.

But though the common man is most often depicted as a peasant, the images are often either inclusive of common city men or ambiguous between peasant and city-dweller. No ambiguity, however, attaches to his gender. When he features in pamphlet dialogues he is often given a name, thus fixing him as a male personality. Frequently he is identified by his work or social position. In the few cases in which women are the actors in such dialogues they represent not the universal voice, the common character, defined by work or class, but add a more marginal, piquant flavour to the dialogue, often because they are defined by their sexual status first. Thus we meet the man who is "the" peasant, "the" priest, "the" weaver; while the infrequent woman may be identified as the priest's concubine, or as an old, post-sexual woman and so on. The rhetoric of the early Reformation movement, with its insistence on "brotherly love" as its touchstone, conjures up the bonds of loyalty, equality and fellowship which would have been most present for the men in their membership of guild or journeymen or peasant associations— structures of belonging which were not available to most women. This rhetoric in turn shaped the forms of political association: thus during the Peasant War, "Christian brotherhoods" emerged, a potent translation of the language of male bonding into political grouping and action.

It might also perhaps be argued that the grievances of the urban and the rural "common man," articulated in the course of civic unrest during the Peasant War in 1524 and 1525, reflect a male set of political priorities, focusing as they do on demands connected with labour services, fishing, hunting and timber rights, commons, beer and its taxation, ground rents, the power of particular officials, the abolition of cartels, the taxation of clergy. . . .

There is current an explanation of the Reformation, particularly its early years, which lays great weight on the importance of the community as actor in the evangelical movement. . . . We need an account of what community means in this period, and who it might include. As I hope to show, this will also be related to the different contexts in which "common" might be used. I shall proceed by examining three occasions on which "community" is constituted: first, in the public processions of the city, especially those related to oath swearing; second, at moments of crisis, particularly the years 1524 and 1525; and third, I shall examine how chroniclers use the term as they write their own historical accounts of the period.

From the descriptions of the annual oath swearing at Augsburg which have survived, it is clear that the ceremony was mainly structured around guild houses. At points around the centre of the city, near the town hall, outside the patricians' houses and at the major guild houses actors were to assemble, in their groups. According to one ordinance, all citizens, and their sons or servants are to attend, together with those who do not have citizenship or guild membership but merely live in Augsburg. The order also notes that as soon as the storm bell rings, the women must stay indoors. The inhabitants must swear an oath of loyalty to the mayor (*Bürgermeister*); and various civic ordinances are to be read out.

If any *Bürger, Bürger's* son or manservant were not present . . . they are to come at a later date and perform the ceremony. No one should employ a man who has not been sworn in this fashion.

This apparently detailed description, however, leaves it unclear precisely where women were during these ceremonies. But the insistence on *Bürger, Bürgers sune oder knecht* (citizens, citizens' sons or manservants), all exclusively male forms, stand in marked contrast to the usual carefully repetitive male and female forms of each of these words. The assembly points listed clearly rest on the primacy of craft loyalties in this physical demonstration of the collectivity of the city. . . . As an enactment of community, then, it appears to have been a quintessentially male drama. . . .

The contemporary accounts of the ceremony of [oath-swearing] in other cities also suggest the non-participation of women. Thus, in the preamble to the Nördlingen oath-formula, we read that "all those, who are citizens here or have citizenship, men young and old (*mans namen*), who have come of age." In Rheinfelden, in 1530, those who must swear are defined as "the citizens and citizens' sons, who have reached sixteen years of age"; in Schaffhausen, they are "citizens and citizens' sons"; while in Schlettstadt, "every citizen's son who lives with his father and is eighteen years of age, he must swear each year with the *gemeind.*" Others, such as that of Ulm, do not specify whether only men are present, but refer simply to "the whole *Gemeinde.*"

Women, then, could not be councillors, could not vote in elections to office, and appear, even as widows, to have had neither a formal say in the conduct of guild affairs nor a place in the social life of the guild. Though non-citizen males could be incorporated into this vision of community, women, it seems, could not. Celebrations to mark the entry of the emperor into the city reveal similar patterns. . . .

These occasions represent the official, sanctioned view of who comprised the community and how its divisions should be articulated. But, as I hope to show through analysis of the disturbances of 1524–5, other groups might subvert these concepts, using the rhetoric and symbolism of community to different ends. . . .

In 1524, when the Augsburg Council attempted to have the pro-Reformation monk Schilling banished from the town, a group of evangelical folk massed on the Perlach, the square outside the town hall, at the time of the Council meeting and demanded that the preacher be brought back to the city. Three days later they assembled again, but this time the Council was prepared. It had arranged for those who supported the Council to be armed, positioned them at all the crucial points of the city, and distributed the muskets from the arsenal to forestall any attempt by the evangelicals to arm themselves. It hired foreign mercenaries and maintained them for almost a year after these initial disturbances so as to ensure order.

The Council managed to quell the unrest, but it then carried out a full and elaborate series of interrogations of those whom it suspected of being ringleaders or even of having "murmured against the authorities." By the middle of the next month, the Council felt strong enough to proceed against two men who were implicated. It had them executed on the Perlach, in the early morning, without the customary sounding of the bell. . . .

So far as we can tell, no women were present on the Perlach at this enactment of communal protest. . . . Though in 1524 the Council resolutely interrogated women who had murmured against the Council, it did not charge any in connection with the Perlach incident; nor did those men who were interrogated mention any women having been present. The Council's own report-list of "those who acted at the town-hall" together with details of their remarks does not include any women.

However, this is not to say that women were not actively involved in Reformation disturbances of other kinds. Women took part in some of the acts of disruption in churches: a girl threw blessed salt in the front; women made sure they were in church when they knew "something was going to happen"; and women are frequently named as the sources of rumour or the channels of information about action against urban Councils, in favour of the Reformation.

We have a particularly rich account of what one woman was supposed to have said. She was interrogated . . . because of words she was overheard to have said. . . . Anna Vasnacht admitted saying, "Why do they not let poor people do the guard duty, who don't get more than 1 batzen daily pay; it would be better to do that than to take foreigners," and to have argued that the money which paid these mercenaries came from the taxes Augsburg people paid. It ought therefore to be spent on buying corn and *schmalz* (dripping) for locals. And, finally, she admitted to having said, "If one is going to act in an ungodly manner, then an honourable community (*gemein*) is as good as a Council." Despite torture, and over several days, however, she resolutely denied having said that the Council alone is nothing unless the community (*gemein*) acts with it; or that, "When our men don't act, then we women will, or must take action; for they are acting under cover, and that will not happen in future"; or that, "The community (*gemaind*) will know, what is afoot, . . . and our men must have a chance of sitting up there. Oh that they might all be struck by leprosy."

Both what Anna was believed to have said, and what she admitted to saying, are significant, and have a bearing on concepts of community. Clearly she took an interest in politics and operated with a definite political theory. She seems to have believed that the Council was not superior to the *Gemeinde*; and that money paid in taxes should be used for the benefit of the community which paid it. She appears to have thought of men as the natural political actors.

Yet she was also alleged to have put forward the idea that if men did not take action, then the women must do it for them. At one level, this can be interpreted as an argument parallel to Luther's claim that secular authorities must act where religious authorities have failed, that princes can be emergency bishops. Similarly, Vasnacht would be claiming that women may act as emergency men. Yet Vasnacht's alleged words had a more disturbing resonance. Even to imagine women as political actors was to reverse the categories of political life, to envisage a world where women ruled men. This prospect of a gender order turned upside-down was redolent of visions of a topsy-turvy world. It was an image which the spy who sat behind her could believe in seriously enough to inform the Council. But it was also one which underlined the divisions between the political worlds of women and men. Whether Vasnacht thought that women were included in the concept *gemaind* is unclear, but she undoubtedly conceived of women being able to act politically (if she did at all) only if men had proved themselves utterly incompetent. Yet women's action could only be imagined in terms which made it seem profoundly subversive of political order itself. Even so, this was a vision of women as political actors.

Interestingly, the Council noted a brief description of her beside her accuser's testimony: "The woman which the Jungfrau reported is reputedly from Ulm and is not living with her husband. She is the sister of the woman barbersurgeon in the corner house and is a tall black-surly haughty-tongued wife." Perhaps it is not coincidental that a woman who was independent, clearly powerful within her own district, who certainly would have had access to networks of gossip through her sister (whose occupation and corner-dwelling would have been extremely conducive to such networks) and was given to speaking her mind on political topics, should have been perceived not as a statesmanlike speaker, or as a dangerous inspirer of revolt, but as an ill-tempered gossip. She was "*hoch maulets*," an insult which uses the term for animals' mouths, thus implying that her speech was not really intelligent discourse.

A different example from the city of Mühlhausen may illuminate how problematic the relationship between women and the field of the political might be. In 1525, at the end of the Peasant War, the defeated city of Mühlhausen tried to secure terms from the princes in a last attempt to avoid the prospect of a massacre of all its inhabitants. The "citizens" instructed the city's women to gather and go as a delegation to the princes' camp to beg for mercy. This public representation of women as a collectivity—arranged at the "citizens" request rather than, it appears, the women's initiative—took a very interesting form. The unmarried women were dressed in wormwood wreaths, the married women in humble clothes as if to stress the city's own humbling and resignation of resistance. The use of wormwood in the wreath, a herb particularly associated with women as well as with sorrow, may have been meant as a reference to the wreaths worn by virgins at weddings: unlike the wedding wreaths, these are crowns of sorrow for the virgins of a city whose young men may be massacred. The procession of unarmed women, carefully divided into pre-sexual and sexual classes, towards an army of vengeful, weaponed soldiers, was a stark enactment of the fact that these were females who were no longer protected by their menfolk, and were directly confronting the possibility of rape. It was a statement by the men of Mühlhausen that they had given up all resistance, even to protect their women. And, at another level, it may also have signified the unmanning of the city which surrender involved: instead of the city being represented by proudly armed men in ritual, it was represented by mere women, the ultimate enactment of its degradation.

Interestingly, the princes apparently refused to accept that these women could hand over the commune or act on its behalf, and a second procession of all the males of the city, "bare-headed and barefoot, with folded hands" had to journey out to surrender "themselves, their wives and children, city, possessions and goods." In this ritual exchange between groups of men, women appear to have functioned as cypher. Yet even the terms of the political drama in which they are used can allow them only a contradictory role: while they can be used to signify the collapse of the city, they do not have the political capacity to offer its surrender. In the end the men must speak for them and offer surrender on their behalf. The exchange underlines the extent to which women, whether as actors or symbols, could be excluded from public political language: even when it is men who speak through them, women cannot quite be used to represent the commune. . . .

What do these very different usages of *gemein* and *gemeiner mann* reveal about the meaning of community? First, they suggest that *gemein* is a term which derives its meaning in its use. Community is not an existent entity which can simply be invoked—rather, it is a term which different speakers appropriate in different ways. . . .

Second, our examination of the concept suggests that it had a built-in, intrinsic understanding of the political as male territory. *Gemeiner Mann*, as the translation of the abstract group into a character, is only the most evident expression of this. Beneath the invocation of the *gemein* as a group which could act politically and according to recognized political forms—as in Augsburg in 1524—to impose its will, lay a notion of the collective as a group which would defend the city by force of arms, and which was bound together by the civic oath. Arms-bearing and oath-swearing were central to this notion of collective political belonging; and, of course, they were the areas from which women were excluded. . . .

But if the common man was imagined, in the early sixteenth-century commune, as the craftsman capable of bearing weapons, there was current another vision of the common man as the head of a house, a social father figure under whose governorship servants, wife, children, apprentices and journeymen lived. He could thus be seen as the representative of his house in the wider household of the commune. This was a role which was to be increasingly theorized in the literature of the Reformation and post-Reformation era. Yet, in the early sixteenth-century town, this was an obviously contradictory political theory: widows, who headed households, were not politically "common men"; and sons, servants and apprentices, who swore the communal oath, were not governors of households. Perhaps what the sixteenth century witnessed was a shift from a sense of political inclusion based on military capacity towards one centred on the notion of fatherhood, both biological and social.

All this, of course, is not to say that women were not political, or never took part in political actions. But if they did so, they had to act within a framework which constituted them as non-political. Female political action thus involved turning the world topsy-turvy; and often it remained chained to a mere inversion of the categories of male, political discourse.

Let me fly one final kite. In this paper, I have been concerned primarily with political senses of the word *Gemeinde*. But in German there is a strong ambiguity between political and religious *Gemeinde*, or congregation. The use of *Gemeinde* in its religious sense as a mobilizing principle of struggle was very common in the early years of the Reformation, particularly in the context of the campaign to subject the clergy to lay control. Thus, if an ideal of *Gemeinde* which drew much of its strength from a lay communitarian principle were applied to the organization of the church, perhaps it is not surprising that this vision, in mainstream Protestantism, allowed no sacral role for women.

One of the tasks of feminist history is to make women visible, to restore them to history. Yet we also need to discover where they are absent, and uncover the processes by which they are excluded. This is particularly true for the realm of political history, where we need to ask new questions in order to see how the public realm came to be constituted as male territory, in order to understand how women's exclusion from political power was connected to femininity itself. Reformation historiography has been dominated by a concept of community which has made it impossible to ask these questions. By simply taking over the contemporary term "common man" and, at worst, using it as if it were a sociological category, historians have been unable to see its sexual and social partiality. That the irony of the contrast between "common man" and "common woman" should pass unnoticed in a historical tradition which for the last twenty years has concentrated its efforts on subjects such as Reformation pamphlets, the commune and the Revolt of the Common Man, is a pointed illustration of this blindness.

But there is another sense in which historiography has remained faithful to the sixteenth-century texts by reproducing the vagueness of the terms "community," "common man" and "common good." The sixteenth-century texts—pamphlets, legal codes, guild records, chronicles and so forth—are determinedly ambiguous about the senses in which women are indeed members of the commune. This itself may suggest some interesting new directions for research. If the articulation of the different realms of men and women was itself unformed, what would this indicate about the flexibility of the distinctions between what historians of the nineteenth century might refer to as the public and the private? In a society where there was no clear division between workplace and living place, how might divisions between men and women be articulated; or might the female world turn out to be intrinsically indistinct? What might this indicate, too, about the terms in which we can discuss the possibility of what might be called a "female culture"? In this essay I have largely been analysing male political languages and rituals. We need now to try to locate women.

Gabriella Zarri

From Prophecy to Discipline, 1450–1650

[The Reformation of Martin Luther] ended up denying female sanctity just at the time when, toward the end of the fifteenth century, female saints had reached the apogee of their power and were recognized on both the historical and symbolic levels. . . . A position such as Luther's, long considered "progressive," in fact turned out to be the opposite: it powerfully inhibited women's power in both real and symbolic terms. There were, in fact, some moments in the fifteenth century that marked the high point in the Church's official recognition of women's power and knowledge. . . .

One such moment at the end of the fourteenth century was the University of Paris debate about whether or not to recognize the charismatic gifts of Bridget of Sweden. This was the first authoritative debate on female prophecy. On that occasion Jean Gerson, the university's chancellor, wrote his treatise on the *discretio spirituum*. Gerson there laid out the issues that for three centuries had given rise to attempts to rationalize, through subtle distinctions, the origin, nature, and effects of phenomena that could not be classified according to the theological and medical knowledge of the day—and indeed escaped the normal laws of sensory experience. . . . The attention, even obsession, with the discernment of

Gabriella Zarri, "From Prophecy to Discipline, 1450–1650," in *Women and Faith: Catholic Religious Life in Italy from Late Antiquity to the Present,* ed. Lucetta Scaraffia and Gabriella Zarri, translated by Keith Botsford (Cambridge, Mass. and London: Harvard University Press, 1999), 83–112. Excerpts reprinted by permission of the publisher. Copyright © 2001 by the President and Fellows of Harvard College.

spirits not only involved events ascribable to what was already institutionally sacred, such as prophecy, levitation, stigmata, or prolonged fasting,
but also inevitably involved phenomena of another nature, such as those
classed as demoniacal. . . .

The "scientific" attention Gerson gave Bridget's prophecies must
not have differed greatly from that which the inquisitors of Rouen gave
Joan of Arc's "voices," no more than the way the interests of the German
inquisitors James Sprenger and Heinrich Krämer in the witches they
observed differed from Gianfrancesco Pico della Mirandola's when faced
with Catherine of Racconigi's visions and struggles with the Devil.

Because they were linked with prophecy and affected the body,
charismatic religious experiences largely concerned women. As a result,
a considerable number of theologians and inquisitors followed and observed the behavior of women thought to be saintly, to evaluate the
orthodoxy of their devotions and revelations but primarily to gather and
circulate experiences and doctrines. Whence rose that male figure later
institutionalized under the name of "spiritual director." At this point, he
had a rather different role. He was witness and observer, rarely judge;
he was inclined to sudden shifts of position, to assuming the posture of
disciple, son, and guarantor of charismatic and prophetic gifts, which he
rarely questioned. . . .

A direct and immediate consequence of . . . cultural shifts [of the
sixteenth century] was the progressive eclipse of the "leadership" roles
achieved by women between the thirteenth and sixteenth centuries and
the establishment of a "male religion" characterized by the internalization and rationalization of religious phenomena—the direction of which
was officially recognized by the Church as resting on the authority of
Fathers, be these pastors, spiritual directors, inquisitors, or the male heads
of families. . . .

When in 1456 Caterina Vigri, a Poor Clare educated at the court of
Ferrara and fairly well known in her day for her culture and holy life, was
asked by her superiors in the order to found a new Strict Observance
Poor Clare convent in Bologna, Borso d'Este began diplomatic initiatives
at the court in Rome to keep the nun in his own city. These negotiations
failed and the prince wrote disdainfully to his agent, Ludovico Casella,
that it was a great setback to the city to lose "a saintly woman."

Caterina Vigri, the author of a book of devotions frequently reprinted
between the end of the fifteenth and the middle of the sixteenth centuries,
founded a convent in Bologna that drew support and protection from

the lordship of Bentivoglio. Throughout the modern era it was considered the most observant in the city. Caterina died in Bologna, performed miracles, and was the object of a considerable popular cult. Exceptional for the times, the city authorities set in motion the procedures for her canonization at the end of the sixteenth century, and finally, in 1712, she was proclaimed a saint.

Protected and sought after by princes, the founder of convents, the author of a book that revealed tendencies toward a "modern devotion" well beyond mystical excesses addressed to the men and women of her time, Vigri can be considered an exemplary figure of female sainthood in the fifteenth century. . . .

Between 1450 and 1520, in common with developments in the male religious orders, there was an unusual expansion of those monastic communities that drew their inspiration from the Observant movements. Reform of the older houses and the founding of new convents multiplied the number of convents in major rural centers and in the cities, in turn leading to the creation of new orders and various Observances. Among female orders, the Franciscan Observants led the way in reforming and founding convents, but the truly innovative element in the religious movements of the fifteenth century was the extension of the Third Orders and the rapid expansion of the *pinzochere* communities. These were unenclosed religious communities in which women could live either in their own homes with an ecclesiastically approved rule and habit or autonomously in little groups of three or four "sisters."

During the fifteenth century, alongside the expansion of the tertiaries and "open," uncloistered convents, there was—as is attested to by the discovery of many statutory charters or *modus vivendi*—a marked expansion in the numbers of *pinzochere* living in their own houses. . . .

The new institutional development here (it was to be followed a few decades later by the Ursulines and Angelics) was the affirmation and the approval of a form of religious . . . life without solemn vows, a foretaste of the congregations in simple vows that appeared in Italy at the end of the seventeenth century and reached their apogee in the nineteenth. . . .

The Third Orders were originally limited to married women, widows, or converts living at home; unmarried young women could not join, for their charity needed better protection. The foundation of secular tertiary institutes in the fifteenth century (such as Valentini's in Udine) or of regular ones (such as the Florentine Dominicans of Saint Catherine of Siena) was the work of widows and members of noble or rich families. Living in a community and offering their own means to support their less well-endowed fellow sisters, or girls unable to marry for want of a dowry, became an alternative for many widows who remained without protection and were often harassed, by either their own or their husbands' families seeking restitution and the use of their dotal property. To found a conventional institution or to manage a *bizzocaggio* of small dimensions was to give widows a way of continuing, as per custom, to handle their own money and determine their own way of life. . . .

After the recognition of the statutes of the regular Third Orders, new foundations marked time. The steady growth of the tertiaries and the *bizzoche* came to a halt. There were wars in Italy, the first news of rebellion in the Church drifted in from the empire, with it came preachers bearing a flood of new ideas. . . .

Political upheavals ensued in Italy as the first incursion of the French king Charles VIII and the usual scourges that follow war brought on a mood of collective fear, which was then accentuated in the first three decades of the century by an unbridled campaign of apocalyptic preaching. . . .

In the general cultural disorientation and social unease, with one drama after another, many new forms of action opened up for women. In the first three decades of the century, following in the footsteps of Catherine of Siena, mystics and prophets found a vast popular consensus in the world of the cities and courts. Women could balance out the apocalyptic fears stirred by itinerant street preachers; holy women did this by offering themselves up as sacrificial victims to God for the salvation of the people and the protection of their cities. Rich noblewomen or virgins could offer money and time healing the sick and protecting orphan girls. Cultivated princesses and ladies at court could breathe life into intellectual circles, and they tended to practice their religion in a way that was in part derived from Reformation doctrine. Between 1530 and 1560 charismatic women whose saintliness was widely recognized ventured into new forms of religious experience.

The reputation of sainthood that attached to one such noblewoman, Caterina Fieschi Adorno (d. 1510), Saint Catherine of Genoa, came from her care of lepers and syphilitics and the foundation of a large hospital for the incurable. . . . Her mystical gifts brought her recognition as a spiritual mother by a large number of priests and religious and lay persons; they gathered her revelations and doctrine in a *corpus* of her writings first printed in 1551. Catherine was particularly remembered as the creator of a movement that spread rapidly in the twenty years after her death. Her disciple, the notary Ettore Vernazza, founded the Oratory of Divine Love in Rome in 1517 and probably also the hospitals for incurables in Bologna and Savona (1513 and 1514). . . .

As part of the humanist debate on education in general, the idea that intellectual and cultural education for women could contribute to safeguarding virginity had a long and painful development in the first half of the sixteenth century, as the first schools for the education of the children of noble families were established. . . . The recognition that instruction, especially religious instruction, should be part of the education of girls, even if they were poor, was an original idea. It led to the formation of the most significant institute created in the first half of the sixteenth century, the Company of Saint Ursula, founded in Brescia by Angela Merici in 1535. This institution came about in response to the new religious and social demands of young women who, for want of a dowry, could not enter convents and dedicate themselves to the contemplative life or receive at least rudimentary instruction.

Powerfully innovative both in its internal organization and in its religious and social aims, the Company of Saint Ursula shows how original the feminine contribution to the renewal of religious life in the early sixteenth century was. Here, religious education was a priority in educating girls from the middle and lower classes. . . .

The prophetic tension that had aimed at Church reform had exhausted itself between 1530 and 1560 and given way to a consolidation of that welfare system—directed toward the recuperation and protection of women's honor—whose foundations had been laid by the Oratory of Divine Love. . . .

Events connected with the diffusion of Calvinistic and Anabaptist ideas in Italy—which gave rise among Sienese merchants or Venetian Anbaptists to the formation of *ecclesiae*, or churches, inspired by theological principles, moral practices, and organizational criteria now well defined—made it impossible to continue to ignore the problem of ecclesiastical authority. All the "spirituals" who for twenty years had been able to organize themselves into little groups in imitation of the apostolic life now had to choose whether to obey the authority of the pope or that of the charismatic leaders. . . .

By the time the Council of Trent solemnly pronounced its doctrine and reform on the cult of saints and holy images, the Church had already issued a number of cautions concerning the approval and diffusion of new cults. The Church's reservations on this score were effectively a sort of response to the criticisms of superstition raised by Erasmus and to the iconoclasm of some of the more radical exponents of reform. . . .

After the succession of triumphal canonizations and beatifications of the preachers of the Observance, and of mystical women engaged in Church reform in the late Middle Ages, the Roman calendar now showed a vast empty space. For over half a century, the pope and his consistory approved not a single canonization. . . .

The reorganization engendered by the Tridentine Church had an immediate effect on women's convents. It returned them to that regular discipline which had been the chief aim of the reform movements of the fifteenth and early sixteenth centuries. The process of extirpating abuses and rebuilding a connective tissue that would give women's collegial institutions at least a minimum of community life was a long one and not entirely successful. Effective efforts, however, were made to transform women's monasteries into places of protection, isolated from the external world with bars and bolts and made ever more agreeable in their interiors by enlarging the buildings and extending their courtyards and gardens. To compensate for the rigorous enclosure, the new amenities sought to create convents in which the monastic and urban imagination would find a counterpart on earth of the Garden of Eden or the heavenly Jerusalem. . . .

Even the more original female religious movements of the early 1500s were now subjected to reforms that strongly reduced their distinctive self-government. The Tridentine decree aimed at reforming nuns dusted off an old prohibition against women living in common without having made a solemn profession including enclosure. The regular Third Orders were thus compelled to become nuns of the Second Order, or their convents were suppressed. Congregations with a clearly religious mission . . . were transformed into monastic communities under one of the traditional rules. . . .

The normalization of monasteries, regular Third Orders, and female congregations greatly limited religious women's century-old freedom of association outside convents and the houses of their fathers. But the social and religious motives that had formerly inspired them gave no sign of flagging. . . .

The Tridentine decree may have intended to bring discipline back to the cloister by imposing enclosure, but it was unable to extinguish altogether women's desire for freedom and the lively movement that had, in the first half of the century, led to the creation of innovative religious groups such as the Ursulines and the Angelics. . . .

As they responded to the Tridentine injunction to clean up monastic discipline, the bishops neither could, nor sought, to eradicate the social problem of forced "vocations," but they did raise an obstacle to it by legitimizing female celibacy. By the last quarter of the century, it had become impossible, unlike a few decades earlier, for anyone to be scandalized that a young woman over twenty-five should choose to live at home with her mother rather than be consigned to marriage or the cloister. The same prelates who had fostered the rise of Ursuline institutions in various cities now convinced the fathers of families of the advantage of this new status for women. . . .

Being forced into a convent or being destined to look after their parents and nephews and nieces may have been an equally painful fate for individual women, but there is no doubt that the new option of female celibacy, heretofore frowned upon by society, opened up a legitimate role for such women, thus in the future permitting forms of cohabitation based on purely economic or social considerations. . . .

Tightening monastic discipline was not just a matter of putting up bars and walls, of imposing a rigorous enclosure; it also involved a slow and assiduous process of education and persuasion, a professionalization of nuns who, up to that time, had based their knowledge on the transmission of customary norms. . . .

The imposition of a uniform habit and the restoration of the monastic offices foreseen in the constitutions helped to reduce the power of the abbesses and prioresses and their vicars; likewise, they involved a greater number of women in sharing the responsibility for the welfare of the community. Discharging the tasks incumbent on the various monastic offices also required renewed efforts in the fundamental instruction of the nuns. It was no longer sufficient to know the breviary by heart; nuns actually had to be able to read and write. Monastic libraries were enriched with devout works and texts to be read in common. Reciting sacred dramas offered nuns archaic models of sanctity, while the comedies the nuns themselves sometimes produced reveal how professed nuns learned to convert love stories, such as Giovanni Boccacio's *Filocolo*, into spiritual terms.

Women's writing was refined and enriched by new literary genres at the end of the 1500s and in the following century: the requirement that the administration of the convent be accounted for led to an enlargement of the traditional book of Records and accounts of expenses; noting down the facts of daily life and contemporary events was accompanied by a desire to record the history of the institution in aulic terms. Reports on spiritual direction were transformed into written notations of thoughts, inspirations, and visions, which in turn gave rise to autobiographical forms of mystical writing.

The Renaissance involved the world of women; it enlarged their culture and their writing. While in the first half of the sixteenth century a few noblewomen in direct contact with humanists and intellectuals were able to join literary society as highly praised authors of poems, those women enclosed in convents read profane authors and cultivated writing for a long time thereafter, as a part of teaching. . . .

There were in fact two major specializations for monasteries: music, which added dignity to the liturgy and to the religious celebration of the patron saint's feast, and the education of young women of the nobility. Nuns were especially attracted to the former; they dedicated much of their time and energy, and internal conflicts, to questions of singing and the use of instruments. Music was a way of presenting themselves to the outside world as professionals in an art that was an integral part of the education of young ladies and one of the openings through which they could advance the prestige of their convent and the honor of the city. It was no different with education. They lavished care on their tasks and increased the numbers of their educational institutes, which now had to compete with the colleges in the education they gave.

In the latter part of the sixteenth century, the college was the experimental and innovative part of the system of instruction, which, though numerically it involved fewer students than male institutions, was vital to women. After the founding of Guastalla College, specialized institutions for the education of girls from the upper classes spread through the cities of northern and central Italy. As secular institutions, most of them were run by Ursuline or Dimesse communities whose professionalism focused on teaching.

Centered on teaching how to behave in a disciplined fashion with an eye to passing this knowledge on to future generations, women's educational institutions reflect a profound change in the models of perfection and sanctity. Women had played an active, historical role in their prophetic calls for reform of society and Church; now the exercise of charity and virtue became the high road for religious activity. The caution with which everything associated with saints and the veneration of living saints had been regarded from the 1530s onward turned into open suspicion. The fight against superstition intensified in the last two decades of the century, and the first two inquisitorial trials of women accused of feigning sanctity took place in the kingdom of Naples.

Distinctions between "true" and "false" sanctity—given the apparent similarities between the extraordinary events connected with extrasensorial phenomena, mostly among devout women—became increasingly difficult to make. The involvement of confessors and spiritual directors in episodes deemed to be expressions of sanctity fell under suspicion and were no longer tolerated. The hint of heresy was the foundation that permitted the Inquisition to move with broad powers in examining cases related not so much to doctrinal deviations as to matters of religious behavior. . . .

After all the doctrinal controversies over the cult of saints and the institutional crisis that overtook the religious orders, the ecclesiastical hierarchy's main efforts were devoted to reaffirming the value of sainthood and the constitution of a "new" hagiography that purged marvelous and magical elements from the lives of the saints. . . .

Between 1608 and 1610 the papacy gave a first clear indication of the image of perfection it proposed for the faithful. Church reform, charity, and virtue triumphed over mysticism and prophecy. The saints canonized (Francesca de' Ponziani and Carlo Borromeo) or beatified (Ignatius of Loyola, Isidore the Husbandman, Teresa of Avila, Philip Neri, and Francis Xavier), by Paul V, the latter confirmed as saints during the next pontificate, that of Gregory XV (1662), reveal the Church's desire to sacralize a broad spectrum of human conditions, characterized by type of conduct and status of life. Women were not left out. In her canonization bull, Francesca de' Ponziani (Saint Francesca of Rome), a noble Roman wife and mother, was singled out for her humility, her piety toward her fellow creatures, her renunciation of the prerogatives due her lofty status, and her work in founding religious communities. The Counter-Reformation may be said to have transformed her into a figure not unlike her humbled contemporaries. Teresa of Avila, whose fame was due above all to her contemplative life and her mysticism, was now exalted as a reformer of women's religious orders. . . . Women canonized in the succeeding centuries, with the exception of those nuns who followed Teresa's example and became reformers, mainly belong to the fertile, pre-Tridentine period. . . .

[A]bandoned in favor of a model of sanctity focused on behavior and virtue, mysticism in the early seventeenth century went through a sort of diffused and underground period. The generation after the Tridentine bishops studied it with interest, and mysticism was highly regarded in circles around Federico Borromeo in Milan and Alfonso Paleotti in Bologna, but it was also reduced to a more personal and intimate dimension and showed up mainly in private connections and writings, in the family or among adepts, seldom being institutionally recognized. . . .

Nonetheless, a massive unfolding of female devotion took place during the Baroque era. The home became a monastic cell. Growing privacy in the house allowed private spaces for middle-class women, and they had an ever greater opportunity to practice mental prayer and contemplation at home. Similarly, literacy spread beyond the confines of cloistered nuns. The Italian model of sanctity grew closer to the French idea of "devotion" and flowered in the second half of the seventeenth century. Baroque Italy and Spain seemed, in the first part of the century, to identify with the great Teresa of Avila, but nuns living at home and the Dimesse found their ideal in French religious practice.

In the mid 1600s there came from France the book that was to serve as a mirror for generations of devout Italian women, Paul de Barry's *Solitude of Philagia*. There they could read the following words:

> *Because you are alone in the tiny desert of your room, perhaps you will allow me some small praise of the solitary life . . . The time to go out into the desert is past, no one speaks of that sort of solitude any more. I want to make you enamored of an easy and agreeable solitude, that of your little Bedroom, your Cabinet or a Room in your House, to which you can withdraw on occasion and speak only to God and your good Guardian Angel.*

The severe ascetic practices of Baroque nuns in the seventeenth century and the domestic devotions of aristocratic matrons and *bizzoche* confirmed the success of the disciplining of religious behavior demanded by the post-Tridentine Church's reorganizations. But the triumph of the religion of the Fathers, based on rationality and the word, thus less open to specifically female values such as prophecy and images, failed to include in its fine chains that new status of celibate women legitimized by the Catholic pastors at the close of the sixteenth century.

Translated from the Italian by Keith Botsford

Sherrill Cohen

Asylums for Women in Counter-Reformation Italy

. . . To the extent that historians have examined the Counter Reformation's impact on women, they have largely illuminated its concern with
a particular segment of the female population: nuns and exceptionally
devout women in organized religious associations. The counter reformers
attempted to cleanse the convents of long-time abuses, turning them into
showplaces reflecting the respiritualized, reinvigorated Catholic church,
and they approved the formation of a small number of new religious
orders for women. . . . Yet the Catholic reformist movements, both those
of the early sixteenth century and the "official" Counter-Reformation
phase that postdated the Council of Trent, fostered certain policies that
in fact enlarged women's horizons. They sponsored alternative social
asylums for ex-prostitutes and unhappily married wives that offered wider
options to all women and were prototypes of important new social institutions for Western societies.

In the Catholic tradition women had long been treated as inferior
members of the Christian body social while they were permitted some
carefully delineated channels for rising to importance or power. Catholic
theology and ecclesiastical structure put a premium on virginity, with virgins of both sexes seeking to match this ideal through holy celibacy and
monasticism. But amid a religion and culture operating on the double
standard, the weight of living up to the ideal fell more heavily on women,
who had the Virgin Mary to look to as the shining exemplar of woman-
hood, than it did on men. The Church did not allow females to accede
to the foremost positions of ecclesiastical or spiritual authority, as priests
or preachers. Women did, however, play significant roles as heads of convents administering other women and as charismatic saints or holy figures
admired for their spirituality and approached for counsel in social affairs.

Sherrill Cohen, "Asylums for Women in Counter-Reformation Italy," in *Women in Reformation and Counter-Reformation Europe: Public and Private Worlds,* ed. Sherrin Marshall
(Bloomington and Indianapolis: Indiana University Press, 1989), 166–188. Copyright ©
1989 by Indiana University Press. Reprinted with permission.

Throughout the Middle Ages, women sought greater leeway to be active in religious and ecclesiastical life outside of the Church's specified prescriptions. . . . Generally speaking, the era of Catholic reform and the Counter Reformation ushered in more such attempts by women and by the Church to maneuver beneficially within the established structures. . . .

At the heart of the Catholic reform and Counter-Reformation movements lay a fervent philanthropic initiative. In place of the medieval Church's perceived corruptions and sanctioning of the purchase of divine grace through the sale of indulgences, the reformers wished to substitute a balance-scale of grace in exchange for true good works of mercy. By reaching out a helping hand to the poor and the distressed, they hoped to restore to Catholicism its integrity and humility. The needs of the poor glared forth in early sixteenth-century Italy, which had been devastated by years of war, famines, and an invading French army and the syphilis and other diseases thought to come in its wake. . . . In part through charity work the reformers carried out their apostolic drive to regenerate the religion, stave off defections to Protestantism, and guarantee the survival of Catholicism through the recruitment of the downtrodden, who were to be tutored in the faith. The sheltering and caretaking institutions founded by Catholic reformers did not simply mirror medieval charity donated to a passive "holy poor," but they embodied a new sort of transformative philanthropy that had the power to reinvigorate the Church and morally uplift the recipients of charity.

One flank of the innovative sheltering institutions founded by Catholic reformers consisted of settlements for ex-prostitutes. Asylums for ex-prostitutes sprang up or revived all across Italy: in Rome in 1520, in Venice in the 1520s, in Milan in the 1530s, in Vicenza in 1537, in Verona by the 1550s, in Padua in 1558, in Treviso in 1559, in Mantua in the 1570s, in Siena in 1575, in Florence in 1579, in Bergamo in 1596, in Pistoia in 1604, in Crema in 1608, and in Brescia in 1611. Their founders ranged from Verona's reforming bishop Gian Matteo Giberti to peripatetic Jesuits to many men and women of the laity. The notion of an asylum for women who wished to quit prostitution was not invented in the sixteenth century. Special religious orders and lay houses for penitent prostitutes had grown up sporadically throughout medieval Europe. But the nature and role of these asylums differed in the medieval and early modern periods, dependent on the changing social position of the prostitute and changing attitudes toward her in those epochs.

In the Middle Ages, spiritual and lay authorities held ambivalent views toward prostitution. Christian theologians abhorred all premarital and extramarital sexual intercourse as sinful fornication. Yet theology, canon law, and medieval mores operated on the double standard that more readily allowed men than women to indulge in the sin of fornication. So that nuns, wives, and daughters could remain as pure as possible, another group of devalued women had to exist to absorb the unlawful sexuality. To avoid the worse evil of having all females subject to illicit fornication, religious and lay authorities, relying on the example set by Saint Augustine in the fourth century, realized that they had to tolerate the lesser evil of prostitution. From the mid-fourteenth century in cities in France, Italy, Germany, and elsewhere in Europe, they went so far as to subsidize prostitution in municipal brothels to deter the rape of respectable women or other ignominies such as male sodomy.

At the end of the fifteenth and opening of the sixteenth centuries — times of crisis in public health, public order, and social relations — the tide of permissiveness toward prostitution turned. Legal regulations were harshened, subjecting prostitutes to tighter controls and often financial burdens in the form of taxes. This change in policy was accompanied by a revived campaign to convert harlots and, especially in Italy, an explosion of institutional asylums for the former prostitutes, who were known as *convertite*. . . . In addition to the multiple foundations of asylums for ex-prostitutes, there were also widespread measures in doctrinal and civil policy to encourage the reform of *convertite*. Saint Carlo Borromeo, on behalf of the archbishopric of Milan, and later the Sacred Congregation of Bishops and Regulars, made special provisions to smooth the way for *convertite* to enter orders and to profess monastic vows more readily than other entrants.

The Catholic reform movements of the sixteenth and seventeenth centuries also brought the proliferation of another set of important new institutions for women, establishments designed to prevent females from falling from virtue and turning to prostitution. Italian lay and clerical reformers, including such eminent figures as Ignatius Loyola, Carlo Borromeo, and Bishop Nicolò Sfondrati, sponsored an array of asylums willing to accept custody of females at risk. These included "refuges" (*rifugi*) for orphans, poor girls, widows, and for women with marital troubles, who were dubbed *malmaritate*. The establishments went under the names of Fanciulle Abbandonate (Abandoned Girls), Vergini Miserabili (Poor Virgins), Zitelle Periclitanti (Imperiled Single Females),

Casa di Soccorso (House of Assistance), Deposito (Depot), and Malmaritate. The custodial institutions existed in Venice (1539), Rome (1543), Bologna (mid-1500s), Modena, Trapani, Agrigento, Messina, Palermo (in the latter five settings, mid-1500s), Florence (late 1500s), Naples (1564), Cremona (1575), Milan (1570s), Brescia (late 1500s), Pistoia (1584), Vicenza (1600), Prato (1600s), and Turin (1684).

The *convertite* houses and the custodial asylums (which collectively will be referred to as the alternative institutions/asylums) often overlapped in intent, function, and populations. . . . The asylums ranged considerably in size, holding from under ten inhabitants to several hundred residents (the largest were bigger than most convents). Many females entered the alternative asylums on their own volition, and others arrived under coercion by their families or civil and religious officials. Although most inmates came from the working classes, the asylums occasionally sheltered females from the upper levels of society as well. In addition to their declared purposes both sets of institutions also served as dumping grounds for anomalous females, girls and women with whom authorities and families simply did not know what else to do. . . .

The three predominant life options open to medieval women—marriage, monasticism, and prostitution—became riddled with problems in sixteenth-century Italy. On the heels of the fifteenth-century demographic recovery from the catastrophic plague of 1348, marital ages and rates fell off. Dowry prices soared, and females could not marry as readily as before. Families frequently forced daughters to become unwilling nuns in monasteries, severely overburdening the resources of Italian urban convents. The many medieval cities, including Florence, that had subsidized civic brothels in order to deter sodomy or rape abruptly reevaluated these policies in the sixteenth century. As syphilis and other contagions infested Europe, frightened civic councilors adopted more stringent regulations designed to reduce the numbers of prostitutes.

At the same time, whether it was demographic pressure, urbanization, unemployment, inflation from New World silver, war, plagues, or famines that tipped the balance in a specific locale, poverty became highly visible and acutely troubling in this era. The emergence of the alternative institutions was related to women's limited options and to the economic difficulties of the period. The refuges seemed to offer a solution to problems prevalent in early modern Italian cities—unmarriageable women, overcrowded convents filled with surplus daughters, and the increasing stigmatization of prostitution. Furthermore, in the view of social authorities, the innumerable females in economic need merited institutional protection to preserve their virtue. . . .

Socio-cultural institutions and sheltering asylums in Italian municipalities set the tone for what women's role was to be . . . whether females were to take a public role in society's mainstream or were to be relegated to separate spheres. . . . Respectable women too were interested in developing avenues for life and action more satisfying than those their society had offered in the past. . . . Two core issues were at stake: the economic contingencies defining women's choices and the degree to which women could move away from the monastic ethos and its restrictions. . . .

The male and female civic activists who wished to ameliorate conditions for ex-prostitutes wrestled with the same questions. . . .

[W]e will explore the legacy of the early modern alternative institutions for females, drawing particularly on evidence from three Tuscan establishments: Florence's Monastery of the Convertite (1330s), the Florentine Malmaritate (1579), which specialized in married ex-prostitutes, and Pistoia's settlement for *convertite*, Santa Maria Maddalena (1604). . . .

The alternative asylums of the sixteenth and seventeenth centuries did not on the surface seem very different from convents. Although the degree of difference varied depending on whether administrators were lay or clerical, all of the alternative institutions persuaded their inmates to engage in certain religious observances, from participation in the sacraments of confession and communion to attendance at sermons to prayer. Like convents, the asylums all had sites where handwork, most likely sewing or weaving, was done. Some of the asylums built large facilities akin to monasteries with common spaces and multiple smaller chambers; other institutions occupied rented secular houses divided into a number of rooms. The alternative establishments generally had internal governments along conventual lines, with elected or appointed resident female supervisors and outside administrators who visited the premises. Life in the asylums seemed to be characterized by no more or less admixture of harmony and acrimony than in any monastery of the time. Yet, although in physical atmosphere and regimen the alternative asylums closely resembled traditional and reformed convents, I will argue that these early modern establishments were a distinctly new kind of institution. They advanced a new set of relationships concerning female control over property and women's autonomy. . . .

The early modern *convertite* houses and custodial institutions were tied to an emerging debate over women's relationship to property that would continue into subsequent centuries. At issue was the desirability of females having increased resources for their own economic support versus the threat of female economic and sexual independence unrestrained by the suasion of family or church or state. Church leaders like Archbishop Carlo Borromeo staked out one extreme position in the debate, as they pressed women to conform with the monastic ethos and submit to poverty, chastity, and cloister. At the other extreme were the lay bourgeois administrators of the Florentine Malmaritate house who prodded women to take greater financial responsibility for themselves by earning their upkeep and supporting themselves in the world.

The roots of Borromeo's position lay in the doctrinal conclave that launched the Counter Reformation, the Council of Trent (1545–63). Among other effects the decrees promulgated at Trent brought about wrenching changes in property relations at convents. Traditionally, income for the convent as a whole and for individual inmates derived from endowments, charity, and from the efforts of house members who labored at piecework and begged in the streets as alms-seekers (*cercatrici*). To fulfill their goal of respiritualizing the convents and eradicating the sexual license that had prevailed in some nunneries, the authorities at Trent produced regulations both to deter coerced monachation and to exact unblemished conduct from religious who had willingly professed vows. The churchmen set the age of consent for profession at sixteen, demanded that professed nuns and monks incorporate into the monastery any property and income, and called for strict cloister. . . .

Lay activists and some clerics took a starkly different view. They promoted a contrasting ethos of greater female access to property. This tendency found its fullest expression in Florence, the seedbed of European textile manufacturing and venture capitalism. The merchants who established the Malmaritate house in 1579 especially for married *convertite* believed that economic ills caused prostitution, and they proposed an economic cure. Aberrant married and single women who entered the Malmaritate were to be recycled to the world as trained laborers, capable of earning their upkeep and benefiting the body social. Although the administrators there did not wholly relinquish the idea that spouses, relatives, and benefactors ought to help sustain females, the twenty or so Malmaritate inmates were expected to assume the greater part of the burden for their own support. The founders demanded that financially solvent entrants contribute toward the reasonable institutional fees of three *scudi* per month, so that the ex-prostitute inmates would not "usurp charity."

Women too poor to do this at entrance would pay monthly taxes on the fruits of their labors at in-house cottage industries and retain the rest of their wages. Because the burgher administrators believed that possession of property stimulated the development of moral character, they encouraged the *convertite* to save their earnings and to safeguard their own goods. With all entrants listing their possessions in inventories and storing them in individual locked chests, the women could trust that when it came time to depart, they would be able to take away what they had brought and what they had earned. The Malmaritate regimen of training females for low-skilled jobs in the textile industry yielded society a cheap labor force. It profited the newly fledged workers as well. Although it did not thrust women out of the system of female subordination, it did offer them a step toward greater economic and social independence.

While both ecclesiastical and lay authorities saw value in a patriarchal system that took care of women, they expected women to contribute a certain amount, either a dowry or the fruits of labor, toward their own support. Yet the culture and social structures of early modern Europe put roadblocks in the way of women's true economic self-sufficiency. The same churchmen who wanted females to have ways of sustaining themselves other than prostitution ironically interfered with the nonsexual avenues of property accumulation that women found. In some cases, professed nuns may have found ways of getting around the Tridentine rules calling for an end to private property. Despite Trent's mandated inspections by ecclesiastical officials to monitor implementation of the reforms, at least at Florence's Monastery of the Convertite the streetwise ex-prostitute nuns managed in the decades after Trent to retain individual title to their property. At the monastery, whose population fluctuated between one hundred and two hundred women in these decades, the chief administrator assisted professed nuns in the rental of lands and buildings that they owned. The professed nuns at the Florentine Convertite also harvested personal savings from donations pledged to them and investments in the public debts, and they had the freedom to dispose of their property as they wished in their wills. They made loans, served as benefactors and guarantors for new entrants, and engaged in a wide variety of entrepreneurial schemes. . . .

A single impetus lay behind the Counter-Reformation church's directives concerning female institutional inmates and economic matters: the desire to bring all institutions, even those that were not convents, into closer conformity with the esteemed monastic ethos. Religious authorities knew that income-producing activities at the alternative institutions might interfere with spiritual exercises. The 150 residents at Milan's *convertite* house, Santa Valeria, had admitted to ecclesiastical inspectors that often they were too exhausted from spinning and housework to say their prayers. Counter-Reformation leaders attempted to spread their restrictive policies on property and labor to the new alternative institutions. They sought to limit the contact institutional inmates could have with the outside in arranging labors or soliciting charity. . . . As a general policy, the Church moved to replace an active means by which female inmates gleaned income with a more passive one. Rather than having inmates go to jobs outside or piecework within the asylums, the Church preferred to see female inmates adopt more of a religious function and await benefactions requiring the performance of religious rites in return. . . .

[A]ll male leaders whether of church or state shared one assumption. They felt that although women should produce labor and income to benefit themselves and society, females should not themselves control this process or its profits. Prostitution offended religious and lay authorities not only because women violated the virtue of female chastity many times over, but also because in exchange for sex the women acquired money in hand, a form of power. Female control over property went against the grain of early modern gender ideology and the legal strictures of early modern societies. . . .

The *convertite* houses and custodial establishments that emerged in the sixteenth and seventeenth centuries represented a transitional phase within the evolution of different types of social institutions for female populations. . . . Many medieval convents, third-order communities, and thirteenth-century orders and lay houses for penitent prostitutes were uncloistered and permitted some flow in and out, either official or de facto recidivism. Then, in the sixteenth century, the ecclesiastical authorities carrying out Tridentine policy tried to impose strict cloister on convents and on many other types of girls' and women's institutions too. Yet the *convertite* houses and custodial asylums that proliferated in that era offered a potent counter-image of more flexible social options for women. This tantalizing image became reality when the eighteenth-century schools and conservatories that evolved from the alternative institutions and from convents conceded to females fuller rights of autonomy concerning their fates.

Let us examine how the *convertite* and custodial establishments constituted a significant transition. We find that the Italian alternative institutions of the sixteenth and seventeenth centuries hewed to one of two models, the monastic model or the reinsertion model. The monastic model is exemplified by the post-Tridentine reformed monastery, in which the greater portion of the house's members—professed nuns—took vows to live a life of poverty, chastity, and obedience within the confines of cloister. . . . Many of the alternative establishments, on the other hand, were predicated on a contrasting institutional identity, what we will call the reinsertion model. This institutional definition assumed that inmates could return to the realm of private property and licit sexuality—return literally to society. . . .

The process of sorting out whether the new institutions were to resemble more closely one or the other of the two models provoked intense controversies among civil and ecclesiastical officials and institutional administrators, the latter coming from both lay and clerical ranks. The conflicts hinged on how much freedom of communication and mobility female inmates might have. Even in the alternative institutions that were not convents, inmates were subject to cloisterlike environments. Through supervision and locks on the outer doors, administrators limited residents' contact with the world in order to insure the sexual decorum of the inmates. . . .

The question of how to treat departures was a foremost policy issue. At times, women wound up decamping from an unhappy family situation by entering an institution only to then be unable to leave the institution when they wanted to. . . . One seventeenth-century Florentine institutional administrator aptly summed up the authorities' point of view when he spoke of "the dangers [unaffiliated females] court when they are at their liberty." . . . Many administrators, however, willingly discharged inmates when they felt some surety that the girls and women would lead decorous lives on the outside. They authorized inmates to transfer to other institutions, permitted women to go to relatives, and helped women to reunite with spouses or to find husbands and marry. At all of the alternative institutions an attitude of paternalistic guardianship prevailed. . . .

What did policies regarding departure and recidivism mean for the female inmates in these establishments? Some women welcomed restrictive institutional structures as an aid to self-discipline, like the Pistoian *convertite* in Santa Maria Maddalena who called for the house's transformation into a cloistered convent in 1621 and again in 1625. Some inmates detested the sense of confinement or actual claustration and fled from it, sometimes forfeiting substantial sums of money in order to do so.

Administrators duly recorded annotations such as this one from the early seventeenth-century casebooks of Florence's Monastery of the Convertite: "[Maddalena Martini] left . . . because she could not stand to be shut up so." Maddalena left to marry, and her earlier contemporaries in the Milanese *convertite* house Santa Valeria had likewise voiced their desire for husbands.

Other females found satisfaction in institutional life for finite periods of time. Women reacted positively to administrative policies that encouraged recidivism. The Florentine Malmaritate (1579) invited the return of former inmates who lost employment, and the government of Tuscany offered dowry subsidies to recidivist *convertite*. Occasionally strong-armed by the state into reentering but more often returning voluntarily, women made multiple essays at life in the alternative institutions. . . . The females who dwelled at the alternative asylums sought to come and go from institutions at their own self-determination. These women were not self-conscious participants in early modern feminism, the era's *querelle des femmes*. They did not articulate challenges to the ideology of female inferiority and subordination. But they did pit themselves against attempts to keep them enclosed against their will.

Experiments with the reinsertion model multiplied throughout the sixteenth and seventeenth centuries. Myriad shelters for females sprang up based on the premise that inmates would probably exit, and such institutions tolerated recidivism. . . . Archbishop Carlo Borromeo's Deposito and Soccorso in Milan (1570s) and Bologna's and Venice's *soccorso* houses (1589, 1590) intended to send their residents back into society. The average sojourn at the Bolognese institution lasted less than a year, and the administrators there allowed readmission of recidivists. . . .

Yet during these two centuries, reformers also sponsored new foundations of *convertite* houses that were from the start monasteries, and churchmen tried to turn existing establishments into enclosed convents. In the 1550s, the Venetian Cardinal Francesco Pisani, who supervised a Roman settlement of penitent women living by the Augustinian rule, together with Pope Julius III oversaw the transformation of the Convertite of Venice (1520s) into a cloistered Augustinian convent which held between two hundred and four hundred women over the course of the next century. . . . Everywhere in Catholic Europe, churchmen attempted to enforce claustration on often unwilling nuns and monastic vows on third-order communities.

Thus, the same two centuries saw both an ongoing experimental bent that accommodated women's desires for more freedom of action and a reluctance to break with the familiar approach of claustration. What did these contradictory trends mean? For every step toward more open institutions, clerical and some civil authorities grew frightened and took a step back toward the familiar. Certain innovative administrators were ready to promote a policy of reinsertion, but they wanted to keep the female inmates shut in and under guard while at the alternative institutions. Sixteenth- and seventeenth-century ecclesiastical and civil authorities, with the collaboration of some citizens and families, would not countenance the freedom for women to come and go from institutional communities as they pleased and to live at their own self-direction. . . . But the experimentation with the *convertite* and custodial institutions for females pointed precisely toward the solution of more open institutions for women in the future.

The *convertite* houses and custodial establishments mirror major changes in the history of social welfare institutions in European societies. Their surge in prominence coincides with what has been called the "great confinement" of the poor, criminals, and the mentally disturbed. Institutionalization of the marginal, whether to simply exclude them or to rehabilitate and reintegrate them, increased tremendously in the early modern era. . . .

The early modern alternative asylums were among the ancestors of later institutions for females that would serve both normative needs— schools—and problematic needs—prisons and halfway houses. Rehabilitative strategies that were first developed for the female inmates of alternative asylums gradually appeared as well in early modern and modern institutions for aberrant males or deviant segments of society. . . .

The longevity of the alternative asylums testifies to the valuable function they performed for women and society. . . . Alternative asylums . . . in Italy endured into the eighteenth and nineteenth centuries. . . .

An outpouring of charitable support from the public enabled the alternative asylums to thrive. These newly organized settlements matched and in some cases surpassed traditional religious and welfare institutions in garnering financial assistance from civil governments and from private benefactors. . . . The Italian public at large showed enormous enthusiasm for this quintessential Counter-Reformation philanthropic initiative of aiding moral reform and providing for social stabilization. Bourgeois females became involved in establishing and financing the institutions out of a mixture of motives. Gentlewomen could derive a sense of their own virtue and well-being from helping aberrant or endangered women. At the same time, they knew that they, too, might conceivably pass a sojourn at the asylums temporarily or permanently. They had a stake in making such institutions as livable as possible.

The influence of the alternative institutions stemmed not so much from the numbers of female inmates housed—a handful in one city, a few hundred in another—as from their structural and symbolic importance. Distinctly different from the ad hoc measures taken in the Middle Ages to shelter needy females, the early modern asylums were, rather, formal societal institutions recognized as existing for this purpose. The asylums had long-term significance: they spawned new sorts of secular residential communities for females in the form of schools and conservatories, and the *malmaritate* houses represented a novel way of criticizing and side-stepping marriages. . . . For several centuries, until secular divorce won acceptance in most Catholic societies, the *malmaritate* houses with their institutionalization of marital grievance served as the Catholic alternative to divorce. . . .

Jeffrey R. Watt

The Impact of the Reformation and Counter-Reformation

. . . Protestants introduced a number of changes that seem at first glance to have been positive for women. Luther, Calvin, Zwingli, and other reformers preached the spiritual equality of men and women. Moreover, the exaltation of marriage, the rejection of celibacy as the ideal state, the introduction of divorce and remarriage, the rejection (at least in theory) of a sexual double standard, all appear on the surface as progressive for women. . . .

Jeffrey R. Watt, "The Reformation, Women, and the Control of Marriage," "The Impact of the Reformation and Counter-Reformation," in *The History of the European Family*, ed. David I. Kertzer and Mario Barbagli. Vol. 1: *Family Life in Early Modern Times 1500–1789* (New Haven and London: Yale University Press, 2001), 130–139, 150–152. Copyright © 2001 Yale University Press. Reprinted by permission of the publisher, Yale University Press.

In other respects, however, Protestant reformers did little to change medieval Catholic attitudes toward women. They accepted without question the view, embraced by medieval scholastic thinkers who had drawn inspiration from Aristotle, that women were by nature inferior. Citing the apostle Paul, Protestant reformers believed that women were supposed to be silent in church. On this issue, Calvin stood out from other reformers by noting that this stemmed from tradition rather than from divine commandment. Although he thought women might eventually be allowed to preach, he certainly made no effort to effect change in this area.

All . . . reformers[, Protestant and Catholic,] continued to believe that women should be subject to . . . their husbands and fathers. Luther clearly believed that a woman's place was in the home and that her role as breeder was fundamental: "Women are created for no other purpose than to serve men and be their helpers. If women grow weary or even die while bearing children, that doesn't harm anything. Let them bear children to death; they are created for that." He further preached that God intended wives to be subject to their husbands because of their inherent inferiority: "The female body is not strong—it cannot bear arms, etc.—and the spirit is even weaker; according to the normal course of events, it follows [that] . . . woman is half-child. Let everyone who takes a wife know that he is the guardian of a child. . . . She is thus a wild animal; you recognize her weakness of mind." Calvin too stressed female inferiority and, citing Paul, insisted that a wife is to the husband as the body is to the head.

In the later sixteenth century, Lutheran Germany witnessed the publication of numerous pamphlets that described the proper relationships between husbands and wives. These works were part of a new literary genre, "household literature," which included various pedagogical publications, most notably sermons, that dealt with marriage and the family. Since Protestants viewed marriage as the normal state, they presumed that women were destined for the roles of wife and mother and were less tolerant than Catholics had been of women who were not under the authority of a male. With many references to Scripture, Protestant literature displayed a strong abhorrence of such "masterless" women. Moreover, some misogynist Protestant literature offered instructions on wife-beating, ridiculed henpecked husbands, and condemned domineering wives as a violation of nature. By and large, Protestant and Catholic writers of the Reformation era agreed that wives were supposed to be obedient, pious, and silent.

Protestants eliminated many avenues of religious expression that had been important to women in pre-Reformation Europe, most notably the nunnery. Although this had been an option only for the well-to-do, Protestantism provided no opportunity for women to hold any church office or to live so independently of men. While some nuns welcomed the opportunity to leave convents and get married, others strongly resisted and expressed resentment that practitioners of the new faith placed no value on the religious life. In Germany, some nunneries managed to survive long after the territory in which they were situated had rejected Catholicism, a testimony to the tenacious persistence of the sisters. Protestants also disbanded lay confraternities, including those solely for women, which oversaw charitable acts, provided for members in need, and offered a useful outlet for lay piety. They did not replace these institutions with any other all-female groups. Finally, the elimination of the veneration of the Virgin Mary and the saints meant that one could no longer pray to a female figure or celebrate holidays in honor of special women. Clearly prayers to the Virgin Mary and the female saints had been a particularly important part of popular piety for women; women comprised the overwhelming majority of those convoked by Geneva's Consistory for adoration of the Virgin. . . .

[Historians have paid special attention to the control of marriage in Catholic and Protestant areas, analyzing (among other things) the impact of Protestants' acceptance of divorce, as opposed to annulment or separation, and subsequent remarriage.] All of the main Protestant reformers recognized the possibility of divorce and subsequent remarriage under certain circumstances. . . . A general theme among reformers was that divorce was possible only in cases of matrimonial fault—that is, one of the spouses had to be the guilty party, the other the victim. Divorce was not considered a remedy for marital breakdown *per se* but as "a punishment for a matrimonial crime and as a relief for the victim of the crime (the innocent spouse)." Protestants held that the Catholic . . . separation [, which did not allow remarriage,] was a travesty of marriage. Since the married state was appropriate for most people, it was deemed immoral to subject individuals to indefinite separations which forbade remarriage. . . . Under certain circumstances, Protestants therefore viewed divorce as an appropriate solution to marital dysfunction.

Most prominent among the grounds for which one could file for divorce was adultery, the only ground found in all divorce doctrines and legislation among continental Protestants. Protestant reformers gave far more importance to adultery as a ground for divorce than had Catholics as a reason for separation. For Catholics, adultery was simply one of a number of possible reasons. The increased significance accorded it by Protestant was a result of their emphasis on the Bible as sole authority. Adultery was the only ground for divorce clearly and unequivocally mentioned in the Bible: "I tell you, then, that any man who divorces his wife for any cause other than her unfaithfulness, commits adultery if he marries some other woman" (Matthew 19: 9). . . .

While they universally recognized adultery as a legitimate reason for divorce, many Protestant reformers and matrimonial courts recognized other grounds, most prominently desertion. The principal justification for divorce for desertion or prolonged absence was that after a certain period of time, one could assume that the absent spouse was dead. In many ways, divorce in these cases resembled a "substitute death certificate" for the absent spouse. Significantly, this manner of dissolving a marriage had not been unknown before the Protestant Reformation. . . .

If the laws passed in Protestant areas in Reformation Europe set an important precedent in allowing divorce and subsequent remarriage, they did not lead to widespread instability in sixteenth-century households. Throughout the Protestant world, divorces remained rare in the sixteenth and seventeenth centuries, despite contemporary moralists' claims to the contrary. According to archival documentation of matrimonial litigation, no European state experienced an annual divorce rate that even reached one per 1,000 residents. (By comparison, the US rate in 1980 was 5.2 per 1,000 people.) In Zurich, for example, the *Ehegericht* [Marriage Court] awarded 28 divorces for the years 1525–1531, which represents 0.74 divorces per 1,000 people per year. In Reformation Basel (1525–1592), 374 people received divorces, equivalent to a divorce rate of 0.57 per 1,000 residents. Research on marital litigation in states such as Augsburg, Württemberg, Neuchâtel, Zweibrüken, and Geneva reveals that divorce was considerably less frequent than even these meager rates.

The large majority of divorces awarded by Protestant courts in Reformation Europe were based on the grounds of adultery or desertion. Although a person who received a divorce for reason of absence resembled a widow or widower, Protestant tribunals referred to this procedure as a divorce, not a declaration of widowhood. Moreover, although Roman Catholic canon lawyers had recognized the possibility of dissolving a marriage after a spouse's extended absence on the presumption of death, Catholics had not developed a coherent policy with respect to the abandoned spouse, and ecclesiastical courts were generally reluctant to permit remarriage without proof of the absent spouse's death. Nevertheless, because of precedents in canon law, some sixteenth-century Protestants who obtained divorces for abandonment might have received permission to remarry even if they had remained Catholic, a further indication that the Protestants' introduction of divorce did not cause a revolution in the institution of marriage.

People seeking divorce on the ground of desertion generally had to wait a long time before filing suit. Whether it be the malicious desertion of the household or the absence of a husband who left the country on business, tribunals ordinarily would not hear a case unless the spouse had already been absent for several years, usually seven, the term set by canon law. In the absence of evidence of the spouse's death, courts strictly observed this long waiting period before granting divorces for desertion, generally requiring the same delay both for male and for female petitioners. (The large majority who filed suit on this ground were women, since men were much more apt to travel long distances as merchants or mercenaries.) Neuchâtel's matrimonial court was even known to require spouses of banished criminals to wait seven years before awarding divorces. Such a case began in 1597 when Isabelle Gallandre asked to be divorced from Jean Bedaux, who had abandoned her and fled the country in September 1596 after having severely beaten his mother and left her for dead. Although she produced affidavits of the sentence of banishment rendered against Bedaux, Gallandre was required to wait the full seven years since his departure, the divorce being granted only in October 1603.

In light of the Protestant reformers' diatribes against the celibate life—they asserted that the majority of humans were incapable of such rigorous abstinence—it seems cruel and inconsistent to force someone to live chastely for years and wait patiently to see if the absent spouse will return. This is particularly so in cases such as Gallandre's inasmuch as her husband's crime seems to the modern observer to be reason enough for a divorce. Rarely, however, did the courts make exceptions to the usual waiting period.

Those who filed for divorce because of adultery received divorces more quickly. In dealing with divorce cases based on adultery, members of Protestant tribunals almost invariably exhorted the innocent party to forgive the adulterous spouse and preserve their married life. If the evidence of adultery was beyond question and the plaintiff persisted, however, he or she was almost guaranteed success. Among those suits that were rejected were those of people who were guilty of complicity by allowing their spouses to carry on extra-marital affairs or who had unwittingly forgiven their spouses' infidelity: borrowing a notion from canon law, the courts held that if a person had sexual relations with his or her spouse despite knowing that he or she had committed adultery, the coitus was viewed as a sign of forgiveness and the innocent party no longer had grounds for divorce. [Apart from such rare cases, however, if there was ample proof that a person had committed adultery and the innocent spouse refused to forgive this infidelity, the latter almost surely could have a divorce.]

For a combination of reasons, adultery was more often cited against wayward wives than unfaithful husbands in divorce cases. One factor was the nature of the proof of adultery. If the concrete products of adulterous affairs were illegitimate children, then a woman whose husband was absent for a lengthy period would have a difficult time concealing a pregnancy. If, on the other hand, an unfaithful husband did not actually get caught in the act of coitus, he ran the risk of being discovered only if his partner revealed his name. Moreover, women generally had more economic deterrents to divorce than men; women who lived without the support of their husbands encountered more financial difficulties than did men who lived without the support of their wives. Social mores also played a role. Prior to the Reformation, adultery in Germany was defined as the sexual union of a married woman with any man other than her husband; a married man who had an affair with a single woman was not subject to prosecution. By contrast, in the sixteenth century married men comprised the majority of those convicted of adultery in some German Protestant and Catholic states, but adultery nonetheless was more often used against women in divorce litigation. In Reformation Europe, men undoubtedly continued to view their spouses' adultery as a greater affront to their honor than did most women. In Zurich from 1525 to 1531 men initiated nearly 60 percent of divorce cases based on adultery, and more than twice as many men as women were plaintiffs to such suits in Augsburg during the period 1537–1547. In Reformation Neuchâtel, among plaintiffs who sought divorces for reasons of adultery, males outnumbered females by two to one. During the time of Calvin, twenty men, but only six women, received divorces in Geneva from adulterous spouses.

Few divorces were awarded on grounds other than a adultery or desertion. Throughout Europe only the Reformed courts of Neuchâtel and Basel regularly granted divorces on other grounds. Even in these states the absence or adultery of a spouse was the basis for over three-quarters of the divorces awarded. Other complaints occasionally alleged as grounds for divorce were illness and sexual dysfunction. Terminating a marriage because of impotence was nothing new. Since canon lawyers put so much emphasis on procreation and the sexual aspect of marriage, they understandably denied the right to marry to those incapable of having sexual relations. Consequently, Pope Gregory IX (1227–1241) declared impotence an impediment to marriage, and any marriage that an impotent person contracted would be null. Rarely, however, was impotence cited in divorce cases in Reformation Europe, and plaintiffs to divorce cases based on sexual dysfunction enjoyed far less chance of success than those grounded on the infidelity or prolonged absence of spouses. Divorce for sexual dysfunction generally involved marriages that had not been consummated after several years of cohabitation, unions which might have been annulled in pre-Reformation Roman Catholic courts. Significantly, sexual dysfunction ceased to be a ground for divorce once the marriage had been consummated. In addition to cases of impotence, a few other divorces were initiated for medical reasons. Here again, the courts clearly hesitated before granting divorces because of illness. For example, in 1552 a man in Valangin, a semi-independent seigneury within the Principality of Neuchâtel, sought a divorce from his leprous wife. Despite the fact that she had been sick seven years and showed no hope of recovery, the judges declared that the man was "still to live for a while abstaining from marriage, judging that he must not receive a marriage separation until God calls his wife to him." For this couple, marriage was to endure in sickness and in health till death did them part. Simply put, neither impotence nor illness was a significant basis for ending a marriage in Reformation Europe.

Conspicuously absent among recognized grounds for divorce was cruelty. Like Catholic authorities before them, Protestant magistrates deplored excessive domestic violence and sought to minimize it. Tribunals not infrequently convoked couples for domestic discord, urging them to mend their ways. Protestant judicial authorities, however, virtually never awarded divorces for cruelty alone. That cruelty did not constitute grounds for divorce is aptly demonstrated by a case heard by Geneva's Consistory. In August 1542, Calvin and the other members of the Consistory convoked a lumberjack who had beaten his wife so severely that he put out one of her eyes. . . . The Consistory admonished the man to be more gentle with his wife but also ordered the woman to obey and live peacefully with her husband and not to provoke him. At no point was divorce even mentioned as a possible solution. While such police actions against domestic violence were not uncommon, only rarely did courts in any state allow divorce suits based [only] on cruelty to be heard. The marriage court in Reformation Augsburg did hear five divorce cases based on cruelty, but none of the requests was granted.

Throughout Europe, both Protestant and Catholic couples who could not tolerate each other might simply separate without receiving judicial permission to do so. Although such separations were illegal both before and after the Reformation, communities and magistrates often preferred to turn a blind eye to such separations rather than force unhappy couples to live together. Moreover, although reformers had criticized judicial separations, some Protestant courts did allow couples to separate in cases of extreme cruelty. Notwithstanding his overall opposition to [judicial separations] . . . Luther favored separation rather than divorce in such cases. By contrast, Calvin went so far as to say that a Protestant wife must not leave her physically abusive husband unless her life was actually in danger. Since putting out an eye was not reason enough, the degree of abuse that merited a separation was obviously extreme. Indeed, only once during Calvin's time did Geneva's Consistory award even a temporary separation for cruelty or abuse. In 1553 the Consistory convoked Bertin Beney and his wife Loyse Leffort because they were illegally separated. Testimony revealed that Loyse left Bertin after he had repeatedly beaten and threatened to kill her. Bertin's own father, himself a member of the Small Council, [Geneva's chief governing body that also served as a criminal court,] testified that he saw Bertin draw his sword and threaten to stab Loyse. For his misbehavior, the Small Council sentenced Bertin to a week in prison and allowed Loyse to live with her mother until he learned to behave. They remained legally separated until 1555, when Loyse obtained a divorce because Bertin had committed adultery.

This temporary separation, however, was the exception that proved the rule. In tightly knit Reformed areas, such as Geneva and Neuchâtel, authorities had the means and the will to force married couples to live together. For Protestants, divorce was supposed to replace the judicial separation. Barring the very limited grounds for divorce—basically adultery and desertion—married couples had to live together till death did them part. In short, although Protestant reformers and magistrates deplored domestic violence, they believed that cruelty, unlike adultery, did not affect the principal ends of marriage which they still identified to a considerable extent with sexuality—that is, with procreation and the quenching of the sexual impulse through monogamous intercourse. Simply put, the introduction of divorce did not cause disruption in European families as divorce remained quite rare throughout the Reformation period. Although its introduction in Protestant areas set an important precedent, centuries would pass before divorce became common anywhere in Europe. . . .

In both Protestant and Catholic areas, on both the continent and in England, matrimonial courts in Reformation Europe generally heard more suits pertaining to the formation rather than the dissolution of marriages. Suits to enforce marriage contracts tended to be the most common form of litigation. In handling cases of disputed contracts, Protestant judicial authorities consistently recognized as valid only those marriage promises that had been contracted in the presence of witnesses and, in the case of minors, with parental permission. Although they rejected the tenet of canon law that consent was the sufficient condition for contracting a marriage, Protestants certainly viewed freely given consent to marry as a necessary prerequisite for contracting binding promises, requiring the presence of witnesses merely to ensure that consent had been given. The majority of litigants who tried to enforce disputed marriage contracts failed in their suits, primarily because they did not provide sufficient evidence that binding promises had been made. [Significantly, most studies of court records further reveal that men actually comprised the majority of plaintiffs to enforce marriage contracts.]

Judicial authorities in Reformation Europe took the betrothal very seriously. If both parties were legally capable of contracting promises and had freely agreed to marry in the presence of others, they were generally expected to execute their engagements. In the [English] diocese of Ely in the sixteenth century, breach-of-promise cases were more often initiated by the church courts than by one of the parties themselves; couples in Ely could not simply dissolve a marriage contract at their own volition. In Reformation Neuchâtel, there were cases in which neither party wanted to honor an engagement but were obliged to do so. . . . [since judges viewed] marriage vows as indissoluble. . . . [Protestant judicial authorities] began showing greater flexibility in the seventeenth century, yet tended to follow canon law tradition, deeming marriage contracts binding from the moment of consent, not from the consecration of marriage in church.

In determining the validity of disputed marriage contracts, courts showed a certain flexibility, at times deviating from the letter of the law. In a few cases, courts in Protestant and Catholic areas ruled in favor of pregnant female plaintiffs to contract disputes even though there were no witnesses to the alleged marriage promises. In these cases, the male defendants typically acknowledged having had sexual relations with their accusers but emphatically denied that they had made marriage promises.

In a legal tradition that goes back to Roman law, a couple might be judged married simply by the way they acted in public and interacted in their daily lives. If a couple spent much time together and the man treated the woman as a man behaves toward his wife, courts in exceptional cases might recognize them as married even if they had not celebrated a wedding or betrothal in the presence of witnesses. Courts made such decisions, however, only when the women in question enjoyed an impeccable reputation and were of comparable social status to the men they accused. . . . [I]n early modern Holland, women had very good chances of winning suits involving men of comparable status. By contrast, female servants who were debauched by their masters might be able to secure a dowry from their seducers but had virtually no chance of convincing the courts to order a marriage between persons of such disparate backgrounds. This effort to ensure that spouses were of comparable status was certainly not initiated by the Reformation. It was the continuation of a long tradition, the roots of which can be found in Roman law.

All told, Protestant tribunals did not mark a radical break with Roman Catholic traditions with regard to the control of marriage. Evidence from matrimonial litigation reveals more continuity than change in the formation and dissolution of marriages. . . . [Moreover, in light of these findings, it is very difficult to sustain the view that the Protestant Reformation enhanced the position of women through the control of marraige. The rejection of cruelty as a ground for divorce and the preponderance of male plaintiffs in marriage contract litigation and in divorce suits based on adultery indicate that there were limits to the degree of support that women could expect from Protestant matriominal courts.]

Bosse, "The Blessing." (© *Bridgeman Art Library/Giraudon*) A Protestant family prays before a meal, an example of family devotions that were promoted by Luther, Calvin, and other reformers. On the wall directly above the head of the patriarch is a painting reproducing the words from Exodus 20, "You shall have no other gods before me."

PART

The "Success" of the Reformation

Since the 1970s, a topic of considerable debate has been whether the Protestant and Catholic Reformations were successful. Gerald Strauss deserves credit for initiating this most stimulating discussion with his path-breaking 1975 article, excerpted here, "Success and Failure in the German Reformation," the arguments of which he later reinforced and expanded in *Luther's House of Learning: Indoctrination of the Young in the German Reformation* (Baltimore: Johns Hopkins University Press, 1978). According to Strauss, in the early Reformation, Luther and other religious leaders were confident that through education, rank-and-file parishioners would assimilate and enthusiastically embrace "proper" Christian beliefs and practices. In the sixteenth century, catechisms were written for the various Christian confessions, outlining clearly and succinctly the principal beliefs of each major religious group. Strauss consulted a rich and abundant form of primary source: visitation reports, written up annually by officials who were sent out to take account of the state of affairs in rural Lutheran parishes. According to Strauss, these records reveal that throughout the sixteenth century, even decades after territories converted to Protestantism, the rural population demonstrated a remarkable ignorance of and hostility toward Lutheranism. Nor was

201

the German peasantry deeply imbued with Roman Catholic piety—like Delumeau, Strauss finds that the popular piety among rural folk was heavily laden with magic and had little to do with the formal doctrines of Christianity. The issue of the success of a religious movement depends of course on one's perspective. The "success" of pastors and authorities in implementing reform might run contrary to the strong wishes of German peasants. Strauss is specifically studying whether the Reformation realized the goals that Luther and other reformers strove for. Claiming that we must measure the reformers' success by the standards they set for themselves, Strauss asserts that the evidence from the visitation records leaves no doubt that the Reformation was a failure.

Strauss's essay has stimulated much debate, as seen in the other essays reproduced here. In his work on Reformation Germany, C. Scott Dixon finds much evidence that lends support to Strauss's thesis of failure but nonetheless sees some significant changes taking place in peasant mentality. On the basis of records for rural Brandenburg-Ansbach-Kulmbach, Dixon observes that attendance at schools was poor and that pastors were consistently disappointed in the results of catechetical instruction and in the impact their sermons had on parishioners. Local rural elites viewed Lutheran pastors as a threat to their own power, and in spite of the clergy's efforts, rural folk continued throughout the sixteenth century to maintain certain Catholic and "popular" beliefs and practices, including popular magic. Nonetheless, Dixon does find certain important changes in mentality, as rural parishioners eventually assimilated some beliefs, heretofore alien to them, which were promoted by the Lutheran clergy. This is aptly seen in changing popular attitudes toward witchcraft; peasants began to associate witchcraft with the worship of the devil, a view that entered their minds through the persistent preaching and prodding of the educated clergy.

In his broad essay on the success and failure of the Reformation, Geoffrey Parker looks at the evidence for the Protestant and Catholic Reformations throughout Europe. Parker notes that some have criticized Strauss's use of visitation records, asserting that by their very nature they are skewed toward noncompliance—the visitors were much more likely to mention in their reports those who were not attending church, could not recite their creeds, or dabbled in magical practices than those who faithfully conformed to the pastors' wishes in word, deed, and thought. Parker, however, defends the visitation registers that show, he claims, that the visitors themselves did not have unrealistic expectations about the religious knowledge rural parishioners and clergymen should have. Like Strauss and others, Parker notes that the Protestant reformers themselves were certainly dissatisfied with the fruits of their labors, believing that the Reformation was basically a failure. Although they too were often disappointed, Catholic reformers may have come closer to realizing their goals than their Protestant counterparts for a variety of reasons, including a greater willingness to compromise when faced with well-entrenched popular traditions. Catholic leaders tried, when possible, to sanctify rather than eliminate certain popular beliefs and practices and sought to simplify as much as possible religious instruction. Parker also notes that the Reformation was an unqualified success in Lutheran Sweden, a country that in the sixteenth and seventeenth centuries was spared both foreign invasions and divisions within Protestantism and whose religious and political leaders were in lock-step agreement on the religious education of the young. Although its population was overwhelmingly rural, by the late 1600s Sweden could boast extremely high literacy rates for both males and females, who showed an impressive understanding of the basic tenets of their faith. Sweden, however, was exceptional. Most generally, Parker finds that by 1650 the Reformations had indeed enjoyed some success—the clergy of 1650 was better educated than ever before, liturgical changes were firmly in place, and the moral behavior of the laity had been modified through the oversight of ecclesiastical and political authorities. The changes had been slow to take hold, however, and definitely fell short of what both Catholic and Protestant reformers had sought.

In his very impressive overview of the history of Reformed Christianity, Philip Benedict acknowledges that the "success" of the Reformation fell short of the goals set by Calvin and other reformers. Noting that the results differed considerably from place to place, Benedict maintains that Reformed Christians tended to be more effective in imposing social discipline than their Catholic or Lutheran counterparts. More important, gently criticizing the confessionalization paradigm for blurring significant differences in the piety of various religious groups, Benedict concludes that the Reformed faith brought about some important changes in mentality within a few decades of its establishment. If parishioners' knowledge of the cate-chism did not meet the expectations of the clergy, evidence nonethe-less shows that they rather quickly assimilated Reformed teachings against "idolatrous" practices. They accepted, for example, that babies who died without baptism were not necessarily damned, that certain periods of the year did not require fasting or preclude the celebration of weddings, and that prayers for the deceased could not influence the fate of the dearly departed. Violent behavior and sexual misconduct also apparently declined in Reformed areas, sug-gesting that church discipline enjoyed some success in inculcating new moral sensibilities.

As these various works indicate, many leading early reformers, both Protestant and Catholic, no doubt were quite dismayed to find varying degrees of popular resistance to some of their reform-ing efforts or to see them altered or appropriated by common folk in a way that violated the wishes of the reformers, as aptly seen in Luther's aggressive condemnation of the German peasant revolts in the 1520s. Moreover, Protestant and Catholic reformers surely would have been somewhat disappointed if they could have wit-nessed the state of their churches in the mid-seventeenth century. Still, the issue of failure and the evidence for it are problematic. Even if reformers' lofty goals of changing the hearts and habits of common folk were never realized entirely, one may still question whether the entire movement of reform should be labeled a failure. Although religious change, be it inspired by Protestant or Catholic reformers, undoubtedly was achieved more readily in the more lit-erate urban areas than in the countryside, even rural parishioners would eventually identify strongly with the Lutheran, Calvinist, Catholic, or Anglican churches in which they were raised, even if their knowledge of Christian doctrines did not measure up to the standards set by earlier reformers.

Gerald Strauss

Success and Failure in the German Reformation

A hundred and thirty years ago the Catholic historian and church politician Ignaz von Döllinger scored a polemical point by using the Protestant reformers' own words to prove his contention that the evangelical movement in Germany had failed in its objectives. The first of Döllinger's three volumes on the Lutheran Reformation consists almost entirely of quotations from eighteen reformers, led by Luther and Melanchthon, who speak of their defeat in explicit terms and vivid language. No change for the better had occurred in the hearts and minds of men. On the contrary, they said, all was worse now than it had been under Rome. Melanchthon's deep pessimism became evident as early as 1525. A decade or so later Luther began to vent his despair in increasingly gloomy outpourings of his bitter disappointment over public indifference to the Gospel and the absence of any visible effects of his work on the thoughts and lives of his fellow Germans. Assembled in Döllinger's book these utterances make a powerful argument for his case against the Reformation. . . .

I shall beg for the moment the question of what constitutes "success" in the Reformation. Let us first recognize it as a fact that most of the leading participants in the Lutheran movement during its first half century or so came to believe that they had been defeated. . . . Luther himself foresaw the demise of the evangelical movement, and his loyal followers did not fail to point to his prediction as the legitimation of their own disillusionment. . . .

It will be useful to remind ourselves at this point that speculations of a cosmic nature must have coloured this pessimistic assessment of the course of the Reformation. Men who had read Daniel and Revelation, who studied the stars and contemplated the senility of nature as they anticipated the approaching end of the world knew what to expect from

Gerald Strauss, "Success and Failure in the German Reformation," *Past and Present* 67 (1975): 30–63. Reprinted with permission of Oxford University Press and Gerald Strauss.

their own time. Nonetheless the many expressions of discontent make a poignant contrast to the assertive optimism of the movement's early years when Luther could write exultantly of the reformation he had inaugurated: "I declare, I have made a reformation which will make the popes' ears ring and hearts burst"; and of "the substantial benefit, peace and virtue it has brought to those who have accepted it." . . .

It has not usually been noticed that much of the reformers' early optimism rested on their conviction that they had found a way to implant evangelical Christianity in the minds of their fellow men, particularly in the minds of the young, who represented the movement's best hope of survival. Religious instruction would root the principles of the faith in the impressionable minds and malleable characters of children and adolescents, with beneficial results inevitably to follow when the new generation came to adulthood. . . . Luther's own catechisms, in preparation since 1523, were ready in 1529. Proving almost at once their merit as instruments for training pastors and for instructing the young and the ignorant, they generated countless emulations. . . .

A vast literature on the education of children, dating back to pagan and Christian antiquity and tended as a living tradition by pedagogical writers throughout the centuries, supplied reformers with a body of theoretical evidence to show that all but a very few were capable of learning and that the learning process—providing it began early in the child's life, was pursued methodically, limited its aims to individual talents, and employed appropriate methods—was bound to produce lasting results. That the older generations were too far gone in ignorance and corruption was a matter of general agreement among reformers. . . .

In 1524, the date of his tract *To the Councillors of all the Cities in Germany,* Luther abandoned for all practical purposes his earlier notion that fundamental Christian concepts of religion and citizenship could be taught in the home. As late as 1523 he had recommended as a model (*eyn gemeyn exempel*) the constitution of the town of Leisnig, according to which each householder was obliged to teach the Bible to his children and domestic servants. But results of this procedure were disappointing. By the later 1520s everybody knew that parents were not doing the job of giving a Christian upbringing to their children. . . .

The upshot of such painful reflections was that reformers willingly collaborated with political authorities in drafting school ordinances setting up educational systems in cities and territories wherever Lutheranism had become the established religion. As is well known, these school ordinances, which are nearly always integral parts of comprehensive ecclesiastical constitutions, laid down detailed and explicit regulations covering teaching, curriculum and conduct. . . . Municipal and territorial school authorities, composed of secular and ecclesiastical officials working jointly, wrote curricula, selected books, drew up lesson plans, appointed teachers, and controlled the enterprise by means of inspections and examinations. Apart from taking leading rôles in the drafting of school ordinances, reformers gave their formal blessing to the dominant rôle of the state in educational (and of course ecclesiastical) matters. . . . [R]ulers and magistrates were addressed as "fathers of our youth" and granted the sweeping regulatory powers implied in this description of the nature and scope of their authority.

By far the most promising instrument for religious and moral instruction was the catechism. Lutherans took justified pride in their development of the catechism as a means of teaching the elements of the faith to the young and simple, claiming its reintroduction into Christian practice as a distinctly Protestant contribution. . . . Its aims were clearly stated in a memorandum prepared in 1531 by a group of Nuremberg theologians while that city's council was considering the establishment of public catechism lessons as a matter of policy:

> *Catechism is Christian instruction for children. By this we do not mean only that such instruction should be given to children alone, but that all Christians must from the age of childhood learn and understand the catechism. "Catechism" comes from the word "echo," which means reflected sound, for in catechism lessons we teach by saying aloud a sentence or two which the learner then repeats in the manner of the reverberation of the human voice in a great hall or in a forest. And this speaking out loud and repetition is to be kept up until the children can recite the entire catechism word for word without missing a syllable.*

The question-and-answer form adopted by Luther for his Shorter Catechism of 1529 proved ideal for purposes of rudimentary indoctrination and was never seriously challenged. For the sake of simplicity and orthodoxy authorities also stressed the need to keep always to the same text, to make no additions and attempt no innovations in content or wording. This, too, goes back to Luther's warning that young minds are easily confused by diversity. . . . In actual fact, however, there existed . . . a bewildering profusion of different catechisms in Lutheran Germany. . . .

It was a long time before control through territorial visitations reduced this profusion to something like the desired uniformity. In the meantime, however, catechism teaching was taking root, at least to the extent of making instruction mandatory in parish schools and churches as an obligation imposed by ecclesiastical constitutions. . . . In rural areas, that is to say for the preponderance of the population, the sexton—called *Küster* in the north and *Messner* in the south, normally a rural artisan by trade—was responsible for catechism teaching. His emphasis was on plainness of instruction. Little was expected of common folk in the way of comprehension. But in cities, and in the hands of able preachers, cate-chisms could offer substantial food for thought. Some played rather heavy-handedly on the consciousness of inherited sin, evidently attempt-ing to use induced sensations of shame and guilt as a means of exerting social control; others made light of this. Some catechisms confined themselves to basic religious instruction. Many others tried also to in-culcate civic virtues and discipline. . . . Some catechisms were intended for use in the class-room, others for instruction in church. A few were turned into primers. Luther's Shorter Catechism usually served as the source for these.

If all this failed to produce results, it was not for lack of conviction, nor of methodical effort on the part of the reformers and their school-masters. . . . The generally accepted model of the mind described the learning process as an essentially mechanical activity in which facts were stored in the memory for later recall, much as a scholar used the infor-mation, tags and sentences he had entered under appropriate categories in his commonplace book. . . . [N]early every human being was believed able to absorb and retain enough knowledge to allow him to be a useful member of church and society. To make him learn what he needed to know, pedagogues concentrated on practice and discipline (*exercitatio*) as the means of implanting knowledge, habits and values. . . . Education was mainly training, and every child could be coached in right ideas, sound purposes and good habits, assuming only that the intellectual and moral conditioning process was begun in infancy and was maintained throughout childhood and adolescence as a methodical and relentless programme of habituation.

No other word turns up as frequently in the school ordinances and visitation articles of the Reformation as "habituation" (*Gewöhnung, consuetudo, usus*). . . . Formed early in life, habits are fixed in maturity and become second nature. . . . This implicit reliance on the powers of habituation to effect a permanent conditioning of thoughts, values and habits goes a long way toward explaining the universal trust placed in catechism drill with its repetition of memorized questions and answers and its incessant, often life-long reiteration. . . .

Let us sum up. As we see the educational ideas and practices of early Lutheranism from the vantage point of institutions, curricula, instructional materials and methods, we can understand the original trust placed by the reformers in the promise of their movement. Where so much legislation had generated so many schools, where able pedagogues and theologians had written so many useful teaching books, where such general agreement existed on the right techniques for imparting knowledge, and where political and ecclesiastical authorities were so eager to demonstrate their interest in the whole enterprise, it would appear that learning was bound to take place and that evangelical principles could not fail to come to permeate personal and social life.

This confidence, and the enterprises on which it rested, suggest, it seems to me, a fair criterion for judging the success of the reformers' labours. Did their pedagogical effort bring about the anticipated results? Were men improved in some way as a consequence of the new education? Was society made better by the edifying instruction pressed upon the young? Had the adult population in Lutheran territories acquired some basic religious knowledge by the end of the sixteenth century? Had anything changed in the consciences and minds of men as a result of the Reformation?

I think that we do have in this point a means of assaying the success of the Reformation, using—it should be emphasized—as our touchstone the reformers' own criteria, which were of course not political but religious and moral. . . .

Fortunately we have in our grasp a suitable instrument for studying these results, for measuring them, and for judging their relation to the reformers' original purposes. Our instrument is the church visitation and the written record surviving in visitation protocols. Great quantities of these documents are extant; most still repose unprinted in the archives although some have been published. . . .

As is well known, the Lutheran reformers revived what they considered an ancient apostolic practice of periodic inspections of Christian life and manners in parish congregations. The political circumstances under which the Reformation was established strengthened the already firmly rooted medieval custom of associating secular and ecclesiastical authorities in the planning and execution of visitations. Luther's appeal in 1525 to Elector John to inaugurate such a visitation in Electoral Saxony, and

Melanchthon's *Instruction of Visitors to the Pastors* of 1528 (with a vigorous preface by Luther) provided the programme for all subsequent territorial and municipal visitations. Their purposes were, at the beginning, to discover conditions which the introduction of the Reformation was intended to correct; subsequently to investigate the population and its ecclesiastical and secular leaders in order to determine how firmly the—by now officially defined and established—Reformation was taking root. . . .

It is easy to see why the visitation scheme appealed to governments strongly committed to bureaucratic procedures: it offered excellent opportunities for supervision and control. Visitors themselves were given little freedom of action. . . . Interrogation formularies were drawn up, very long ones in some cases, with explicit, probing questions entering deeply into all areas of public and private life. . . . The deep-seated distrust of human nature which was then the hallmark of the governing mentality prompted authorities to oblige visitors to press parishioners for information critical of their clergymen and other officials, as well as of their neighbours. . . . All respondents were urged to tell on each other. In Saxony every cleric was asked: "Can you report anything suspicious about the teachings of your colleagues?" . . . Recorded answers to such questions were often explicit enough to allow us to satisfy our curiosity about popular life at the village, hamlet and town level.

Armed with their questionnaire, visitors appeared at pre-announced places to which the official visitation mandate had summoned local worthies and citizens. Respondents were examined one at a time and their replies written down on makeshift pads. . . . The requisite number of individuals having been interrogated, the visitors moved on to the next place. Their tour completed, they retired to make clean copies of the collected information. One clean copy was despatched to the consistory, or whatever the central office of the territorial church organization was called; another went to the secretariat of the territorial ruler. The latter copy was confirmed by receiving the ruler's seal and became the official protocol of the visitation. Normally it is these protocols that survive in the archives. In making use of them the historian must, of course, remember that visitors may occasionally have altered data in accordance with what they wished their superiors to know, or with what they thought the latter might prefer to hear. It is not clear, however, whether visitors would have wanted to make local conditions appear to be better than they found them, or worse. An argument might be made for either of these temptations. My guess is that attempts on the part of visitors to aggravate or gloss over the largely unpleasant information they had gathered tend to cancel each other out, and that the visitation protocols cast an accurate reflection of conditions as they were.

Ecclesiastical and political authorities took the information received with the utmost seriousness. Protocols were closely examined and discussed in the synods and consistories charged with supervision of religious life. . . .

General reform was clearly the overriding purpose of these visitations. . . . In order to discover how broadly and deeply God's Word was in fact being planted among the population, every visitation instruction contained questions intended to test the religious knowledge and moral conduct of parishioners old and young. Most questions were taken directly from the territorial catechism, and respondents' replies allowed authorities to determine how well and how soundly people were being instructed. Thorough visitations—and by no means all visitations were thorough; they varied considerably from time to time and place to place—began by testing the local pastor on his religious knowledge and on his effectiveness as a preacher. . . . Other questions related to preparation of sermons and the response of auditors, to the number of parishioners regularly attending communion and catechism instruction, and to suspected reasons for the deplorable moral standards found to prevail in the population. . . .

Following the examination of pastors, visitors turned to the general public. The Visitation Mandates ordered them to examine "the common people" in their knowledge of the catechism, but this did not always prove possible if time was short. In . . . Saxony in 1578 it was therefore decided to concentrate the questioning on children. In each parish a certain number of children were put through their paces. Where poor performance pointed to the failure of parents to compel their children's attendance at catechism lessons, the former's "insubordination" was reported to ducal authorities. . . .

Such examinations took place at regular intervals in nearly all German territories, Protestant and Catholic, secular and spiritual. There can be no doubt that they produced comprehensive and elaborately detailed evidence on which to base considered judgements concerning the effectiveness of religious edicts, ecclesiastical constitutions, school ordinances, and previous visitations. . . .

It should be said at this point that our evidence is somewhat deficient in one important respect: it offers us little solid information on the state of religious knowledge in the larger cities. Visitations were not very well received in urban parishes. Territorial dignitaries found clergy and parishioners resentful of interference from above, and unco-operative to the point of sullenness. The general result of this was that authorities abandoned attempts to inspect cities through parish visitations. . . .

Let us now look at the evidence gathered by territorial visitations from the 1530s to the end of the sixteenth century. . . . When the Electoral Saxon visitors informed Duke John Frederick in 1535 that the common people, following the bad example of nobles and burghers, "hold in many places of your realm the servants of God's Word in contempt," the duke might well have reflected that seven years—the period since the first territorial visitation in Saxony—had not been enough time for the Gospel to be firmly implanted or for a new generation of effective pastors to be trained. Unfortunately the visitations of 1574 and 1577 showed that conditions had not changed forty years later. As before, pastors and sextons everywhere complained of poor church attendance and poorer attendance still of catechism sermons. . . . No wonder that blasphemy, fornication, adultery, drunkenness and gambling abounded. Admonitions and threats are useless, the pastors note. We warn them, reports one, "but they answer 'why pray? The Turk and the Pope are not after us!' " . . . Children perform poorly in catechism exams. . . . Several reasons are suggested for this disgraceful state of affairs: the obtuseness of the population, addiction to drink and fornication so deep-seated that no preacher can hope to change it, the peasant's habitual tight-fistedness (when a child is sent to parish school his parents usually remove him before the end of the quarter to avoid having to pay the fee), above all a deplorable lack of concern with religion, indeed with the state of their own souls.

Territorial rulers tried to counteract this lack of interest, but they could think only of using instruments which had already failed them: stricter mandates, longer sets of instructions to visitors, more systematic methods of inspection, a six-stage method of dealing with offenders, from "fatherly admonitions in private" to the full ban proclaimed by the synod. But these steps did not help. Visitations in Electoral Saxony continued to prove that even late in the seventeenth century no change had taken place. . . .

Visitations in the duchy of Brandenburg told the same story. . . .

It was possible, of course to find in regional and local circumstances the explanations for such behaviour. In some places Catholicism and Lutheranism had succeeded each other for a while with every change of ruler. The innumerable religious controversies dividing and inflaming Protestants against each other are likely to have contributed to the common man's religious confusion. Wars, natural catastrophes, epidemic diseases took their toll. Relics of feudal obligations imposed labour service on some groups of peasants even on Sundays. Chaotic social conditions in some regions made people reluctant to leave their homes on Sunday for fear of robbery. The authorities knew all this, and no doubt considered it in their policies. . . .

Even where the church was organizationally and financially in good shape the religious attitudes among the public were often deplorable. In the duchy of Lauenburg, for example, visitors described a sound and smoothly functioning ecclesiastical apparatus. But the reports on moral conditions and the admonitions contained in the visitation recesses reveal outright disrespect for the church among the population. In Gronau in 1581 "the congregation behaved shockingly, refusing to answer a single question so that the examiner had to break off the visitation." An attempt to explain such insolence by the presence of "Anabaptists" in the community carries little conviction when one reads of the universal drinking, whoring and other abominations detailed in the protocols. Conditions in this duchy show how little even the most determined governments could do against lack of religious interest. . . .

It needs to be stressed that the scenes depicted here are not the whole picture. Well endowed and expertly staffed Latin schools in towns and cities turned out soundly trained pupils. Visiting such institutions evidently gave officials much pleasure. Village schools, too, were found on occasion to be functioning effectively. As might be expected, the situation varied enormously from region to region. The point is, however, that while élite institutions produced able ministers, and while children and youngsters acquired in an occasional local school the rudiments of a religious education, very little of this transferred itself to the general adult population on whose everyday lives and thoughts the formal religion, Catholic or Protestant, seems to have made little impact. . . .

The evidence of the visitations speaks for itself; no comments are needed. Lutheranism had not succeeded in making an impact on the population at large. Early hopes for a renewal of religious and moral life in society were not fulfilled. Experiments in mass indoctrination were stillborn or turned out not to work. The Gospel had not been implanted in the hearts and minds of men. An attitude of utter indifference prevailed toward the established religion, its teachings, its sacraments and its ministers.

To say this is not to argue that there were among Lutherans in Germany no men and women of serious, sincere and informed piety. Our evidence is inconclusive for the larger cities where we would expect to find such people. We ought surely to suppose that things stood brighter there for religion than in the hamlets and villages of the countryside. . . . Cities had abler pastors, more and better schools, and more effective means of control over conduct. But . . . [t]he documents contain enough complaints from theologians and preachers to suggest that city people were no paragons of piety. . . .

A fully coherent explanation of the phenomena described in this article would require more space than is available here. A few factors may however be suggested. It should first be noted again that the reporting procedures of sixteenth-century visitations differed among themselves. . . . Generally speaking . . . the more exhaustive the questions, the more disheartening the information brought to light. It also stands to reason that geographic and economic factors must have operated in the obvious way: isolated and poor parishes were more likely to persist in ignorance than well-to-do places in touch with urban culture. Still, as I have tried to show, the evidence does not suggest that religion was taken more seriously by the comfortable than by the poor. Occasionally an effective pastor or school-teacher could overcome the general laxness, but the protocols, which are not self-serving in this respect, make it clear that the absence of tangible Christianity among the people was not usually due to lack of pastoral effort. The interminable theological polemics of the time must have had a deadening effect on people's religious interest. On the other hand there is also a strong possibility that visitation protocols occasionally confound religious indifference with confessional opposition to politically enforced creeds: Catholic to Protestant and vice versa, Zwinglian to Lutheran, and so on. One gets the impression that the most knowledgeable, serious and courageous Lutherans were to be found in hostile environments such as northern Bavaria under the rigorously Catholic régimes of Albrecht V and Wilhelm V. In this as in so many other instances, strength of conviction seemed born of adversity. Where people had learned to adjust to the routine of officially sanctioned orthodoxy, on the other hand, their religious interest seems to have diminished. . . .

One other point seems worth making here. The evidence of the visitation protocols supports the view—much emphasized in recent years—that the operative religion of country folk, and perhaps of many city-dwellers as well, had much less to do with the doctrines of established Christianity than with the spells, chants, signs and paraphernalia of ancient magic lore and wizardry, the cult of which flourished unaffected by the imposition of new or old denominational creeds. To call the persistence of these magic practices a "counter culture" to the official culture of Christianity is perhaps an overreaction to our belated discovery of this fact of popular life. But there can be little doubt that magic cults held the trust and engaged the interest of the majority of the populace at a time when the official religion as preached from pulpits and taught in catechisms became increasingly abstract, dogmatic and detached from the concerns of ordinary life. . . .

Magic was pervasive and deep-seated in popular culture. . . . Hostile religious authorities showed themselves unbendingly intolerant of deeply ingrained folkways. The persistence of occult practices in popular life is therefore certainly a cause, as well as a symptom, of the failure of Lutheranism to accomplish the general elevation of moral life on which the most fervent hopes of the early reformers had been set.

C. Scott Dixon

The Reformation and Rural Society: The Parishes of Brandenburg-Ansbach-Kulmbach, 1528–1603

. . . Educational reform was not a real possibility until mid-century. The church and education were inseparable developments; they worked on each other in a mutual field of influence. The mid-century reform of the Ansbach church under Georg Friedrich also ushered in a period of educational innovation. The synodal ordinance of 1556 ordered that, in addition to the monastery schools, many of which should be resurrected along the lines of the Saxon model, reform should reach to the parishes: "not only in the cities, but rather in the larger villages schools should be established and . . . properly maintained." Where there was no schoolmaster, the sexton, chaplain, or (in the last resort) the pastor should instruct the children in his stead. . . .

[T]he majority of the schools to be dealt with in this study were smaller, village schools—German schools—which taught only the basics of language and the catechism. . . .

A competent schoolmaster in every parish was of course a paramount goal of the reformers. This was a noble ideal, but suitable instruction could only be effective if the children went to school, and the evidence exposes truancy as a common offence. In the summer months in particular, during the harvest season, the children worked in the fields. . . . Poor attendance and missed classes remained a problem for the reformers throughout the century. Parish children would go to school in the winter months, in the absence of a harvest, in search of a warm hearth, and wait for the thaw. Came the spring, the schools were nearly empty. . . .

And yet despite the picture painted by these poor reports, the Reformation did make some inroads in the quality of higher education on offer. During the reorganisation of the external church under Georg Friedrich the educational superstructure was constitutionally altered for the better. The Latin schools were reformed, the number of scholarships increased, and the system was centralised, so that each schoolmaster (in theory) had to answer to the consistory. . . .

Educational reform in Brandenburgh-Ansbach-Kulmbach was nascent; the educational improvements envisioned by the reformers did not reach fruition during the sixteenth century. The reformers did not have the concrete educational system at their disposal capable of endowing the rural populace with a lasting knowledge of the Lutheran faith. Village schools were few and inadequate; educators were untutored, underfed, helpless when earnest, unchecked when careless. The schooling system in the villages at the end of the sixteenth century was little better than it had been in the late-medieval period. Granted, some progress had been made. By 1633, the consistory was mounting a serious effort to standardise the quality of the village schoolmasters. But given the spirit that saw the birth of the 1533 church ordinance and the scale of reform it envisioned, many clergymen may have viewed this 1633 ruling as one hundred years too late. . . .

Appended to the 1533 church ordinance was a lengthy treatise written by Andreas Osiander which served as a summary of the faith—the catechism. . . . The catechism, in its standardised format of question and answer, its terse, central tenets of the faith unfolding in rhythmic sequence, was the ideal mnemonic tool. Lutheran thinkers soon realised the value of these disposable booklets. A catechism, observed Johannes Brenz, is "a short synopsis of all of Scripture, containing for us everything necessary for true and eternal salvation . . . so that the catechism can really be termed "a small Bible." In most Lutheran regions, elementary religious education was communicated through the catechism. In Württemberg the Bible itself was not used by the students until (the equivalent of) the fifth or sixth form. Up to that stage the children learned of the faith through the catechisms.

The clergy of Brandenburg-Ansbach-Kulmbach were among the first in Germany to publish catechisms. Andreas Althamer (aided to some extent by Johann Rurer) published a catechism in 1528, which was reprinted in 1529. That same year Kaspar Löner drew up a catechism for the children in Hof, and it was soon used in the other parishes of Kulmbach. Once Luther's larger and smaller catechisms appeared, they quickly became the standard texts in the principality. But other works circulated as well. . . .

Without a doubt the most common complaints to emerge from the visitation returns related to the poor performance of the catechumens. The visitors of Konradsreuth (to select a representative example) lamented: "among all of the children . . . we have not found one who knew the catechism and its short interpretation." Most of the children refused to go to the session, so it is no surprise they learned so little. The pastor of Unterlaimbach estimated that of the 150 children in his parish, perhaps twenty attended catechism sessions. Nor could the pastor expect the older parishioners to enforce attendance; the adults were regularly cited as the worst culprits. When admonished to attend, older villagers, such as Linhardt Böchner of Wernsbach, dismissed the catechism as playing no practical role in their lives; work was more important than the catechism. . . .

The response to the catechetical experiment was poor. The reality of the endeavour to impart the principles of the Lutheran faith through the catechism was much less than the ideal, and the early aspirations remained a ghostly rhetoric of reform which never took shape. In this matter, more than any other, a clear voice is sounded in the textual remains: it is a voice of sadness, frustration, and despair. "Oh, that I had water enough in my head, and my eyes were springs, that I might mourn, day and night, for the great sins of the people." . . .

The Word was fundamental to the spread of the Lutheran faith, and it follows that the frequency of sermons remained a primary concern throughout the sixteenth century. Each of the visitation commissions was instructed to inquire into the quality of the preaching, as well as the number of services given in the course of a week. . . .

It is doubtful whether the quality of the pastor's sermons was a major concern for the parishioners. Although the focus of the early evangelical movement was Scripture and the salvation-inducing pure Word of God, disrespect for the parish sermon continued throughout the century. As early as 1531 Georg the Pious was issuing mandates to stop the "contempt, derision, ridicule [*belachen*], blasphemy, and abuse" poured on the Word and the servants of the church. Poor church attendance was an oft-cited offence in the visitation returns; it was referred to as the "common complaint" of the clergymen. And it remained a common complaint "everywhere" until 1611 and beyond. . . . In the face of such lassitude (or perhaps resistance) many towns must have opted for a precaution similar to Kulmbach's 1572 effort: the council ordered the gates closed during the sermons. Unless they had special dispensation (*sundere ehaft*), no one was allowed in or out of the city.

Nor did the Sabbath command greater reverence. When there was work in the fields, few parishioners attended the weekend service. . . . In Hof the visitors noted how the failure to honour the Sabbath was no longer considered a sin. The parishioners would go about their business on Sundays and Holy Days without a thought about the church. . . .

Lutheranism was not going to convert the peasantry with words, at least not during the first century of reform. This was not due to a lack of effort on the part of the pastors. The parishioners had no excuse at their disposal, so claimed the clergymen of Schwabach and Roth: if they wished to learn of the faith, the opportunities were myriad. . . . If Lutheranism were to make inroads, it had to force itself upon the parishioners; it had to be the only alternative in the field of religious action. And if it could not effect this through the spoken word of God, or through the written word of God, then it would have to set itself up as the sole champion of God, the sole custodian of his grace and favour, and the lone tributary of his power. It would have to limit access to the divine; it would have to discredit its rivals; it would have to erase the medieval Catholic church from the popular memory. . . .

Confession was central to the medieval cycle of worship. The Christian believer viewed the sacrament as a spiritual pilgrimage from grace to sin, sin to confession, absolution, and satisfaction (penance), and then back to grace. Confession enabled the individual Christian to receive the grace of God while at the same time it restored the wayward sinner to the communal fold. . . .

The Lutheran assault on the Catholic practice of confession must be understood within the context of Luther's theology. . . . Luther did not believe that the sinfulness of man could ever be fully revealed; man was both sinner and saved, absolution could not wash the sins away. Only Christ could infuse man with grace, regardless of the amount of remorse or contrition on the part of the sinner. Luther thus presented the medieval notion of penance with two fundamental objections: first, absolution is unconditional, and requires nothing for its validity beyond Christ's sacrifice; and second, absolution cannot be "achieved": it only works if the sinner has true belief. . . . [O]n the eve of the Reformation most parishioners viewed the process of confession, absolution and penance as an "automatic" means of acquiring God's grace. . . . The Lutheran notion of confession deprived the act of its "magical" potency; instead of automatically received grace, the Protestant confessor could do no more than reveal to God his or her remorse—the rest was in God's hands. The parishioners were expected to realise the gravity of their sins in the confession and the reasons why they should fear God. Confession became a forum for soul-searching with no guaranteed or immediate reward. It was no longer a perfunctory or automatic rite.

In Brandenburg-Ansbach-Kulmbach the confessional, as a result, assumed a new significance. Confession became a form of private counsel (*ratforschung*) with the clergyman. It was left to the individual to come to terms with his own sin. . . . And yet, although the Lutherans shifted the focus of confession from the automatic efficacy of absolution to the private state of contribution and penance, it was still very much regulated and facilitated by the clergyman. . . . The pastor could demand that each communicant confess before the reception of the sacrament. Lutheran pastors thus had the power to use the confessional as a means of controlling their flocks. . . .

The Lutherans thus desacralised the act of penance and instituted a practice of confession whose efficacy was reliant upon the faith of the penitent. To ensure that the parishioners understood the importance of confession, it was made a prerequisite for the reception of the Lord's Supper (a practice not too far removed from the "forced confession" of its Catholic predecessors). . . . Is it possible to determine whether the average parishioner complied with the demands of the Lutheran form of penance? . . .

The few references relating to confession would suggest that it had failed to become the forum of soul-searching the reformers envisioned. People were reluctant to discuss their sins in detail with the confessor. To a large extent confession remained a token obligation infused with sacramental significance. The parishioners felt uneasy whenever they were denied access to confession in times of urgency. One of the charges brought against pastor Peter Hochmuter in 1596 related to his refusal to grant absolution to a peasant woman near the throes of childbirth. The peasants still sought the protective agencies of the rite of absolution. . . .

The sacrament of baptism, on the other hand, enjoyed an ambiguous status. The Lutherans preserved baptism as a sacrament instituted by God; it was a sign of his promise. Unlike the Catholic idea of the efficacy of baptism, however, which temporarily set the Christian free from original sin, Luther believed that baptism, like the Word, conveyed the promise of salvation through the grace of God. . . . The Lutheran reformers tried to deemphasise the popular notion of baptism erasing sin, expelling demons from the wailing child, and "purifying" and protecting the soul of the infant. As might be expected, this notion was slow to take hold. . . .

Of primary importance for the Lutheran authorities was the task of disenchanting the powers attributed to the baptismal sacramentals: the water, the salt, the oil. This crusade was mounted in vain. Parishioners continued to believe in the charged and unique qualities of baptismal water. . . .

[I]n theory the distinction between a spell and a prayer is that the former claims an automatic efficacy and the latter relies upon the will of God; this division was blurred in practice. . . . Sixteenth-century charms regularly called upon the power of Christ, God, or the Trinity to help those in need. Not only was Christ called upon, but He played an active role in the fulfilment of the wish. Equally, the peasantry frequently entreated Christ and Mary in spells and verses to overcome illness, to protect the crops or the animals, and to secure the welfare of the parish. There is no doubt that spells and incantations were thought to possess a power of themselves, especially core verses rhymed in succession. . . . Throughout the sixteenth century the parishioners of Ansbach and Kulmbach believed that an appeal to Christ, to Mary, to the Father, or indeed to the godhead, would elicit a response. The church was tapped for its sacral protection, as it had been for centuries.

The popular belief in the powers of the divine—that they could be harnessed for earthly ends—ran counter to the Protestant insistence on man's impotency and his inability to do anything to tempt God's favour.

. . . People like Friedrich Fischer of Baudenbach, a man who nailed INRI on his threshold in the hope that it might help his bodily pains, were brought before the visitors and admonished to put away these relics of medieval belief. . . .

The Lutheran reform did not desacralise or "disenchant" the church during the course of the sixteenth century. . . .

The Reformation did not cleanse Ansbach and Kulmbach of popular magic and its practitioners, despite the fact that it was a conscious goal of the movement and its leaders. . . . Such popular beliefs, and the "superstitions" attendant upon them, were the manifestations of a parish mentality which remained unchanged throughout the first century of reform. . . .

For the religious authorities, magic was a crime against the faith[, but] . . . the parishioners did not order the world in such systematic terms. Fundamental to all forms of popular beliefs was the notion that a power could be conjured, harnessed, and then applied to specific tasks. . . . The distinction between magic and religion, so clear to educated men like Johann Weyer, was blurred in the parish mind. . . .

Thus it was left to the Lutheran authorities to mark the boundaries between popular magic and religion, and in doing so, the reformers not only drafted a catalogue of forbidden beliefs, unprecedented in its intimacy, they also asked the parishioners to betray their deepest convictions. . . .

Protestant demonology placed greater weight on the theological implications of recourse to magic. To use magic was to submit to the temptations of the Devil. . . . The parishioners grew wary of recourse to magic, but not because the "reform of popular culture" convinced the peasantry it was wrong in principle; rather, they soon began to recognise that the forbidden practice of magic (*Zauberei*)—now strongly equated with the Devil—might elicit the attention of the authorities. . . .

[I]t is neither feasible nor presumed that, in a study situated in a single century in a single land, one can assess the impact of the Reformation on the popular mind with any real authority. All that can be said with certainty is that in Brandenburg-Ansbach-Kulmbach the Reformation did not purge the parishes of popular magic. . . . Nevertheless, by using materials which amplify the conflict between traditional parish culture and the church, it is possible to illustrate aspects of the initial impact of the reform movement on the parishioner's expressed beliefs. . . .

Unlike the reform of morality, which relied upon the imposition of restraint and the displays of power, the Lutheran campaign against popular beliefs found its forum in the parish mind. . . . [T]he Reformation did not eradicate recourse to magic; but with the threat of punishment ever present, the parishioners gradually integrated the ideas of the church and began to consider their own beliefs in relation to the ideas of the "elite." Rather than consider their tradition of thought as at odds with the church, the parishioners first assimilated the idea of demonic intervention to explain away their reasons for recourse to popular magic. It was only later, when popular magic could not avoid the brush of diabolism, when each rite or gesture had a corresponding tie with the Devil, that magic and religion could no longer be held in separation. Popular beliefs were slowly invested with a changing set of values as the parish mind was drawn into a more systematic context of thought. This is not the erasure of one tradition of beliefs by another, but its gradual distortion. . . . [I]t is likely that over the course of time select practices were signally discredited or considered suspect, and so the parishioners were then forced to view certain forms of magic in relation to others. Gradually a template of order emerged—from the forbidden to the allowable—and the worlds of magic and religion were given firm boundaries. . . .

Out of the reforming passions unleashed by the evangelical movement in the 1520s the margraves eventually created a Lutheran church. In the first decade of reform, the secular authorities, acting on the orders of the margraves, monitored events in the parishes. . . . The church itself grew into a more efficient institution: Marriage courts were established, a consistory was created, synodal articles were issued, visitation commissions patrolled the parishes in the autumn of each year and sent their reports back to Ansbach. The process was slow, and it suffered its share of setbacks, but by the end of the century the margrave was at the head of an ecclesiastical institution completely under his charge. With its network of officials and its sophisticated administrative reach there could be little doubt that the villager would ultimately have to come to terms with the intrusion.

The intrusion of the Lutheran clergyman, if less systematic, was a more intimate and immediate style of trespass. In many ways the Lutheran pastor was *the* innovation of the Reformation; the men themselves were frequently different in kind from their Catholic predecessors. The clergy became better educated and more willing and able to fulfil the tasks expected of them, whether that meant the preaching of the Gospel, the dispatch of their sacerdotal duties, the policing of moral transgressions, or the education of the young. . . . In the eyes of the villagers, however, the Lutheran pastor made an impact at another level. The clergy were not prized for their theological acuity, nor admired as proselytisers, but rather resented as disturbers of the peace. . . .

Although the Reformation movement was as much concerned with how the parishioners acted as what they believed, the Lutheran authorities in Brandenburg-Ansbach-Kulmbach failed to implement the strict moral code they preached. Confessionalisation, social disciplining, "the reform of popular culture"—these are useful labels to describe a programme of rule, a rhetoric or policy of control which emerged with a vigour in tandem with sixteenth-century religious change. There is little doubt that the parishioner became an object of unprecedented scrutiny; customs, morals, and local diversions occupied the attentions of the authorities as never before. But there is also little doubt that village life in Ansbach and Kulmbach was not markedly altered, in spite of this increased surveillance. . . . The traditional monopoly of rule enjoyed by the local elite remained an obstacle to the pastor's efforts to introduce stricter disciplinary measures. What is more, once they recognised what a threat the Lutheran pastor was to their local liberties, the ruling elite began to look for ways to discredit the clergyman and weaken his status in the parish. . . .

Above all, the Reformation might be seen as a massive campaign of indoctrination, an unyielding drive to purge the parishes of the residues of Catholicism and the delusions of popular beliefs. Brandenburg-Ansbach-Kulmbach was a Lutheran principality, and, like other Protestant states, placed its trust in the strengths of education and the sober appeal of the church sermon. But the reform of schooling, while it was improved under the auspices of the Lutheran margraves, remained for the most part an urban event. . . . [T]he Reformation's drive to erase the Catholic church from the parish memory was not successful: The local church remained a receptacle of the sacred, the sacraments were worked as reservoirs of automatic sacrality, the sacramentals manipulated as conduits of divine power. The belief system of the rural parishioner, in short, was not disenchanted in answer to Lutheran demands. Nor were the parishes purged of popular beliefs, such as magic, soothsaying, charming, or astrology—these and similar practices remained staples of daily life. . . . And yet, in so far as it can be perceived at this distance, there was a change in the way people perceived the powers inherent in the natural world. With the attack against magic in full swing, and the threat of prosecution ever present in the parish mind, there is reason to suspect that the parishioners began to view the world in the terms created by the Lutheran church. Like Katherina Hoser, guided by a foreign logic and pressed by a very real risk of correction, the villager began to invest traditional practices with alien values. . . .

[T]he Reformation in the countryside, from its very outset, was less compromising than the type of reform movement common to the cities. The margrave dictated the course of reform without paying heed to the wishes of his subjects; mandates and ordinances poured off the presses defining the parameters of godly thought and behaviour; the margrave's higher officials, secular and spiritual alike, worked to enforce the will of the territorial church. But in all of this the parishioners were not passive participants in a massive reforming campaign. The Reformation in the countryside was not just a stand-off between two opposing world-views, a static acculturation. In the realm of ideas, a gradual syncretism took place; in the realm of church and parish relations, there was a gradual transformation in the exercise and understanding of power. The Reformation did work its way into the rural culture of Ansbach and Kulmbach, but not in the form its supporters envisioned and not with the effects they had hoped for. . . .

Geoffrey Parker

Success and Failure During the First Century of the Reformation

. . . Before entering the debate on how [Gerald] Strauss's evidence should be interpreted, it is important to note that a very similar canvas has been painted for other Protestant areas in the first century after the Reformation. Visitation returns have also been used (together with other sources) to suggest that standards were little better in some Calvinist areas of Germany and in the Dutch Republic, as well as in much of rural

Geoffrey Parker, "Success and Failure During the First Century of the Reformation," *Past and Present* 136 (1992): 43–82. Reprinted with permission of Oxford University Press and Geoffrey Parker. A revised version of this article appeared in Geoffrey Parker, *Success is never final: empire war and faith in early modern Europe* (New York: Basic Books, 2002) 226–252.

England, Scotland and Ireland. There is thus no shortage of complementary material to support Strauss's verdict on Lutheran Germany:
that, at least in the eyes of its own leading practitioners, Protestantism had
largely failed to arouse a "widespread, meaningful and lasting response to
its message" for one, perhaps two, and in some areas even three generations after the Reformation."

However, despite the apparent consensus concerning so many of the
principal Protestant areas of early modern Europe, the evidence presented by Strauss and others has been subjected to heavy criticism. To
begin with, it is generally recognized that the criteria adopted for measuring "success" and "failure" were, to say the least, narrow. They were
certainly not those of (for example) contemporary Catholics, few of whom
doubted that the Reformation had been a roaring success. The testimony of leaders like Ignatius Loyola, who believed that only the strongest
counter-measures would halt the triumphant advance of Protestantism,
is reinforced by the reports of the Catholic clergy charged with extirpating Protestantism in countries won back to Rome concerning the
Reformation's evident success at grass-roots level. Thus the foreign
priests who arrived in England in 1554 to eradicate all traces of heresy
were appalled to find vernacular Bibles chained up in almost every parish
church, "which we removed because of the great damage they were
doing in that kingdom."

So why was this impression of Protestant "success" not reflected in
the visitation records? Three separate explanations may be offered.
First, the visitors frequently neglected the cities, where other sources
often reveal a learned and diligent clergy serving an enthusiastic and
well-informed congregation. . . . Secondly, the visitors were neither im-
partial enumerators patiently compiling a statistical profile of religious
awareness, nor yet market researchers testing consumer preferences for
competing products. Instead they were collecting data for their local
authorities, either to justify their own labours or (more often) to back
appeals for better state funding for the performance of God's work: they
might thus be tempted to dwell upon any deficiencies encountered in
order to persuade their governors of the need for remedial action. . . .
Thirdly, and in spite of all this, James Kittelson has pointed out that some
of the rural areas covered by visitation returns in fact recorded remarkable successes. His "report from Strasbourg," covering fourteen country
parishes between 1555 and 1580, shows an enviably pious population
who knew their catechism satisfactorily, attended church frequently,

and partook of the Lord's Supper regularly. Likewise, . . . in Scotland, the church leaders of St. Andrews in Fife noted in 1600 that "the peopill convenis sua [= so] frequentlie to preaching that the kirk may nocht convenientlie containe thame" and an overflow chapel had to be opened.

These contradictions have led some scholars to discount the evidence drawn from the visitation records. Some . . . believe that . . . analysis of visitation returns would remain suspect because of the nature of the source itself; for, at first sight, both the methods and the questions of the visitors appear unreasonable. We may feel pity for the ministers of Brunswick-Calenberg who were asked, in 1584, "Can Man exercise his free will in spiritual things?," because even those well enough versed in the language of theology to know that the correct Lutheran answer should be "no" were then told to justify their response from Scripture. And apparently "difficult" questions were also put to the laity, such as "What [does] each man owe to Caesar and the government, and what must he give to God?" . . .

But this objection cannot be sustained. The ignorance revealed by the visitation returns was not due solely to "difficult questions" and "unfamiliar language" because, on the one hand, visitations were frequent enough in some areas that the pastors (at least) should have known what to expect while, on the other, both the questions and the correct answers were normally available in advance. . . . It is hard to disagree with the verdict of Scott H. Hendrix that the visitors in the sixteenth and seventeenth centuries—and therefore Strauss in the twentieth—"graded Luther where Luther himself would have chosen to be tested."

So where should historians stand now? Kittelson is surely right that, if we seek a definitive answer to the question of success and failure, all the available relevant records must be given systematic study. This is particularly true of the visitation returns, since they offer a uniquely detailed range of information on the spiritual life of both ordinary clergy and lay fold. It is true that their proper interpretation presents some methodological difficulties; but so do the other "serial" sources generated by the Christian churches, such as parish registers, inquisition records and church court minutes—and yet, in time, members of the historical profession have managed to find ways of using all of them. . . .

[E]ven the sample of Protestant visitation returns already available has undermined for ever the triumphalist claims of confessional apologists and some clerical historians that the Reformation enjoyed either uniform success or (a few areas apart) deep popular support in the sixteenth century. On the contrary, the surviving evidence indicates a widespread inability on the part of the reformers—not just in one, but in several different countries—to create an acceptably pious laity within the first century of the Reformation. The evidence of "failure" is certainly not universal, but it was enough to depress the reformers, and it is also enough to require some tentative explanations from historians. . . .

The precise "impediments" which the reformers encountered . . . might be grouped under two headings: *production* and *consumption*. To begin with the former: there was a major problem inherent in the Protestant message itself, for Christian theology is neither simple nor self-evident. To understand the central doctrines—the Trinity, the Incarnation, the Resurrection and the New Covenant—requires instruction, reflection and (often) correction. In general the pre-Reformation church had not insisted on the need for either priests or laity to master theology, for it regarded as its first task the provision of the "mysteries" (the sacraments) which enabled men to gain salvation. In many areas it was therefore considered enough for the clergy to be able to recite the Lord's Prayer and the Creed; to know what the seven sacraments were; and to be sufficiently familiar with Latin to read the mass. . . . [T]he reformers changed the entire thrust of the Christian message. What had passed for piety in the fifteenth century—pilgrimages, processions, veneration of relics—was now normally execrated as superstition; instead familiarity with the Bible and Christian theology were seen as crucial, because faith alone could save. In Patrick Collinson's terse phrase, "The successful practice of the Protestant religion required literate skills."

Now such a transformation clearly could not be achieved overnight, for there are only a limited number of religious virtuosi in the world at any one time, and it takes time to win ordinary people over to new ideas. . . . Nevertheless the early reformers made a heroic effort to explain their message. Their preferred medium was the printing press, and they began with the Bible and catechism, translated into the vernacular and published in vast numbers. Luther's German New Testament went through 253 editions between 1522 and 1546; 100,000 copies of his *Shorter Catechism* of 1529 were printed before 1563, and 500,000 copies of his German Bible between 1534 and 1574. In England over six hundred separate question-and-answer catechisms were produced between 1540 and 1740. The output of polemics and devotional works was likewise phenomenal. . . .

But the effectiveness of this immense effort hinged upon a critical question: just how many people in early modern Europe could read? . . .

To insist . . . that man needed a sound knowledge of Christian doctrine in order to be "saved" presupposed the existence and maintenance
of a numerous, educated and conscientious parish clergy. But that was
rarely the case during the first century after the Reformation. . . .

[After the conversion to Protestantism, many areas, including regions
in Germany and England, witnessed a dramatic decrease in the number
of clergymen who were ordained. One reason for this is that] ordinands
were now expected to possess detailed theological knowledge, vocational
dedication and verbal dexterity to an unprecedented degree. . . . Not
surprisingly, amid the uncertainty prevailing immediately after the Reformation, such men became very hard to find. Many of the universities,
where the best ordinands were trained, went through a period of acute
contraction after the Reformation. . . . [F]inally, once sound theological
education got underway . . . attention was lavished in many areas upon
the training of court preachers and professional theologians rather than
of humble parsons who would devote their lives to catechism classes
and simple sermons. . . .

[I]n the early decades, the various Protestant creeds were reluctantly
forced to depend heavily upon the services of those clerics already in
office, even if their theological commitment to the new orthodoxy was
more flexible — or more superficial — than some thought proper. Thus in
Saxony at least a third of the clergy in office in 1530 were (like Luther
himself) former priests or monks. . . . In Scotland about one-half of the
reformed ministry in the 1560s had formerly been Catholic priests or
monks (and five ministers had been bishops). . . . Clearly the assimila-
tion of such large blocs of conservative (not to say unsympathetic) opinion reduced the level of detailed Christian knowledge dispensed in the
parishes affected, and served as a considerable brake on the spread of
reformed views.

In time, it is true, a clergy that was both quantitatively and qualita-
tively acceptable became available in most Protestant countries. . . .
But, unfortunately for the progress of the Reformation, the serious disruption caused by a change of creed was seldom something that happened only once. On the contrary, several Protestant areas switched
their religion repeatedly. Thus the official creed of the Rhine Palatine
altered at the accession of each new ruler: Lutheran in 1546, Calvinist in
1560, Lutheran again in 1576, Calvinist again in 1583. Each change was
marked by the expulsion of all incumbents who would not conform,

leaving numerous parishes vacant, so that the pastorate was continually below full strength between 1576 and 1590. . . .

The impact of war on religious practice could be even more disruptive. Thus in the first phase of the Dutch Revolt, the clergy of each side were prime military targets: the Army of Flanders hanged any Calvinist ministers and elders that they encountered, while the "Sea Beggars" frequently executed priests, monks and nuns. . . .

Such were the impediments to the early progress of Protestantism on the "supply side." And yet, even had all of them been miraculously overcome, and a full complement of dedicated pastors somehow installed permanently in every parish, there were still considerable obstacles to effective evangelism on the "demand side." For, after the printing press, the principal means of disseminating the Protestant message was preaching, and here the reformers ran into a further barrier posed by the extraordinary linguistic fragmentation of early modern Europe. . . . In Holland, despite the desperate shortage of ministers in the early years, when the church at Rotterdam asked their brethren abroad to send a new preacher in 1575 it was specified that he should be a local man because "the ministers from Friesland or the eastern Netherlands will not be understood here by the local people [because of their accent]." The situation on the Celtic fringe of Britain was even worse because a large part of the population understood no English at all. . . .

However, even where the basic Protestant texts were translated relatively swiftly into the vernacular, and the language of minister and congregation was the same, orally spreading the Protestant gospel to ordinary people still presented problems. . . . Many . . . mid-seventeenth-century Protestant leaders, from almost all countries, execrated in similar terms the "incorrigible profanity of the multitude" who seemed totally, almost congenitally, incapable of learning and remembering Christian doctrine. . . .

The Protestant leaders seem to have convinced themselves that their religion could—and should—only be comprehended through words. . . . But . . . in early modern Europe the written word and the literal exposition were neither "plain and direct" nor "everyday." And therefore to abolish all media of diffusion except the Word was not a simplification, but rather a complication. . . .

There was thus a clear evolution in the use made of the various media by the Protestant evangelists which helps to explain both the movement's initial "success" and its later "failure." In the early days, when they were desperate for popular support and anxious to demonstrate their distinctness from Catholicism, the reformers made full use of all available channels of communication—print, sermon, music, art, satire and drama. . . . But once converts were made and a loyal, learned congregation established, these attitudes and practices changed. Now it was no longer enough just to criticize and ridicule the opposition; there was a whole new theology to explain. Furthermore, once the small learned groups became the élite of an established church, with the power to coerce all their fellows to attend services, every preacher faced a new dilemma: should he address himself to the familiar, enthusiastic and reassuring faces of the committed, or to the sullen, somnolent or blank stares of the rest? The answer was obvious. Although some ministers struggled to cater for both, . . . most pitched their teachings primarily at the true believers. . . .

Believing that theatres provoked indecency, serious (and sometimes successful) efforts were made in many countries to legislate them out of Christian life. It was the same with festivals (which, it was claimed, led to vice), games (which were said to cause violence), recreation (which produced idleness) and dancing (which allegedly aroused lust). All were proscribed. Instead of trying to identify Protestantism with local values and practices, as Luther and his contemporaries had done, subsequent generations of reformers sought to suppress everything that was not rooted in Scripture. And yet in early modern times such things were too deeply ingrained to be extirpated. . . . It needed . . . more than sermons to fill the gap left by the rituals and religious demonstrations which were now disparaged and discouraged as vain superstition. . . .

The argument above receives indirect confirmation from the experience of the Roman Catholic church during the age of the Reformation. There is plenty of evidence to suggest that, when they relied primarily on the written and spoken word, the Catholics ran into precisely the same problems as their rivals: lamentable ignorance among the clergy and "incorrigible profanity" among the masses, particularly in rural areas. . . .

[T]he visitation records from the Catholic heartlands in the later sixteenth century often make as dismal reading as those of the Protestant areas. . . . The pastoral reforms decreed by the third session of the Council of Trent (1562–3) have rightly been seen as crucial: a seminary and synod in each diocese, a Sunday school and confraternities in each parish, and so on. But the speed with which the decrees were enforced

has not always been noted. Many bishops held a diocesan synod immediately after their return from Trent, publishing the Council decrees as
a sort of preface to the synodal acts. Next they made haste to organize a
seminary in their diocesan capital. . . . The number of ordained clergy
now rose swiftly, after a short but sharp fall during the Reformation crisis,
and their quality also improved thanks to the introduction of regular
visitations which many Catholic leaders saw (just like their Protestant
counterparts) as critical for improving pastoral standards. For Archbishops
Carlo and Federigo Borromeo of Milan, visitations became almost an
obsession: the former scarcely wrote a letter to a fellow bishop without
mentioning them, while the latter organized his visitations like a military
operation, with his staff preparing detailed maps and plans of every parish
to be inspected. In marked contrast to the contemporary investigations
of the Protestants analysed by Strauss, those pursued by the Borromeos
found little cause for complaint: a diligent and well-informed priesthood
served a laity which, in both social and sacramental terms, was highly
satisfactory. Even in areas where the results of the first post-Tridentine
visitations were appalling—such as the archdiocese of Cologne, where, in
1569, 30 per cent of the clergy were found to have concubines, 15 per cent
illegitimate offspring and 35 per cent (including almost every member
of the chapter) Protestant leanings—subsequent episcopal tours revealed
a dramatic improvement. By 1620 concubinage, illegitimate children
and religious deviance among the clergy had all been more or less eradi-
cated from the area.

Simultaneously education improved religious awareness among the
laity. All over the Catholic world schools were opened and reformed in
order to teach sound doctrine to the young. To take a striking example,
in 1536 Castellino da Castello opened a "School of Christian Doctrine"
to teach the elements of faith to the children of the city of Milan; but by
1564 there were twenty-eight such schools in the city, instructing some
two thousand children, and by 1599 over 120 schools teaching approx-
imately seven thousand boys and six thousand girls. . . . There was also
keen attention, as in Protestant lands, to teaching the catechism to the
literate and illiterate alike. In Spain, for example, the records of the Inquisition reveal a steady improvement in religious knowledge even
among those brought in for questioning about their orthodoxy: thus the
proportion who could recite their catechism perfectly to the Toledo tri-
bunal increased from 40 per cent in 1555 to 80 per cent in 1575, while
the proportion who could recite their prayers correctly to the Inquisitors

of Cuenca rose from 37 per cent in 1540–63 to 64 per cent in 1564–80, and to 80 per cent in 1581–1600.

This remarkable picture of lay piety, so different from that painted for many Protestant areas, may be ascribed in large part to three factors. First, the Catholics were prepared to compromise with traditional religious customs, and strove to salvage and sanctify many of the traditional practices that the Protestants denounced as either idolatry or vanity — veneration of relics, exorcism, processions and pilgrimage. Moreover, where the Catholic church did suppress, it tried to fill the gap with some new interstitial religious rituals — "Calvaries," new saints' days, miracles and confraternities. Secondly, they made full use of all the media available to them: pictures, prints, plays and songs as well as catechisms, schools, sermons and visitations. Thus a vast output of Catholic devotional literature, often printed in large letters on small pages and accompanied by explanatory illustrations, was produced "for the sake of simple folk"; while in the "dark corners" of the Catholic world specially trained preachers (often drawn from the new religious orders) went on carefully co-ordinated "missions" armed with a set of portable religious pictures, showing the Christian as a pilgrim in the world with the different paths to salvation and perdition, to be used when words alone seemed to puzzle a congregation.

Thirdly, and perhaps most important, the Counter-Reformation church went out of its way to simplify the Christian faith for the benefit of its congregations. In 1578 the *Instructions* issued to the clergy of the archdiocese of Lyon advised parish priests to make only elementary sermons — "probably nothing more than recitations of prayers and the Ten Commandments together with a brief lecture on the catechism." . . . In the south Netherlands, ravaged by decades of bitter religious war, the Catholic clergy in the seventeenth century likewise concentrated on providing "an uncomplicated faith" for their charges. . . .

And yet, amid all this apparent "success," some devout Catholics could still perceive a measure of failure. Thus in the south Netherlands, whereas spectacular results were recorded in the *ad limina* returns of the bishops to Rome during the first half of the seventeenth century, the reports of the rural deans to their bishops were far more pessimistic. It was not a question of insufficient numbers of clergy, for by the 1640s almost every parish had its priest, . . . nor was the problem infrequent preaching, for the deans usually found that church services and catechism classes were held with due regularity. It was the unwillingness of the laity to attend either that undermined the clerical effort. Government legislation was required before traditional religious practices were abandoned and the people forced reluctantly into the churches. . . .

There was, by 1700, only one large Protestant state which had achieved all the aims of both reformers and counter-reformers, and where a pessimistic sense of "failure" was apparently absent: Lutheran Sweden, a rambling rural kingdom of about 2,500 parishes. Although a Swedish Bible and a Protestant church order were introduced under Lutheran guidance during the 1520s, there were several schisms and deprivations between 1531 and 1611; and not until the 1620s (and the foundation of *gymnasia*) was a proper education offered for ordinands. Thus far, the Swedish experience differed little from that of other Protestant lands. Thereafter both the quantity and the quality of the clergy improved dramatically, until by 1700 most parishes had two highly trained ministers—one for religious instruction and the other for teaching in the school. But Christian education in Sweden was not confined to church and classroom. All heads of household were required by law to teach young children to memorize their catechism at home; then, either at the growing number of parish schools or at the houses of pastors or church elders, the children learned to read and comprehend what they already knew by heart, and both abilities were examined annually by the minister. After the 1620s the results of these yearly tests were recorded parish by parish, and six grades from "cannot read" to "reads acceptably" were awarded; later the examination registers were scrutinized and verified by the rural dean. By the mid-seventeenth century the high standards found elsewhere (if at all) only in great cities like Amsterdam were being achieved on a national scale in the Swedish countryside, and before long they were surpassed. For by the end of the seventeenth century the registers revealed reading literacy rates of 90 per cent for both males and females in the central dioceses (Uppsala and Västerås) with only slightly lower rates in the southern parts. Comprehension of the scriptural set texts was almost equally high. . . .

But why did this remarkable Protestant success remain unique? It was not that the Swedish church had different aims from its fellows, for it did not; rather it enjoyed three practical advantages. First, there was total continuity of effort: no foreign invasion or civil war interrupted the patient labours of the ministers, elders and rural deans after the early seventeenth century. Secondly, and no less important, there was a total identification of aims between church and state, of which their co-operation in the task of "indoctrinating the young" was but one example. And finally, and perhaps most important of all, there was no schism within the Swedish Protestant establishment. Not only did the kingdom escape those damaging changes of creed that left parishes deprived for years of any minister: the clergy was also largely free of the need to engage in polemical exchanges with its rivals and enemies.

Elsewhere things were very different. In Germany the Lutherans were divided for at least a generation after the master's death into Philippists and Gnesio-Lutherans; in the Netherlands Calvinist Gomarists attacked their fellow-Calvinist Remonstrants; in Scotland Episcopalians fought against Presbyterians; in England Puritans vied with Arminians. And everywhere much time was spent in trying to discredit the Catholics. . . .

Such, then, were the roots of the despondency among the leaders of the Reformation. They seem to have become obsessed with a particular set of religious values that left no place for any alternatives, and little space for any sense of satisfaction. By the mid-seventeenth century, it is true, Protestantism had become firmly established in large parts of Europe. It had created not one, but several distinct Christian creeds; it had produced a clergy whose morals, education, religious knowledge and preaching skills were, in general, far higher than ever before. . . . A casual traveller to any Protestant church from Saxony to Scotland or from Stockholm to Zurich would have recognized instantly that it was not Catholic: the structure might date from pre-Reformation times, but the liturgy, the music, the layout and the interior decoration had all been transformed. And if the same traveller had surveyed the actual behaviour of Protestant congregations—that is to say, noting what they did, as well as what they did not do—then once again the Reformation would have been seen to have clearly made its mark. . . . [P]arishioners . . . showed some enthusiasm for the new liturgy—the Book of Common Prayer in England, the Book of Common Order in Scotland, and so on—and vigorously opposed attempts to tamper with it.

But it had been a long, slow process, and by 1650 it was still far from over. At the end of the first century of the Reformation, Protestantism remained in many areas largely what it had been at the start: "an urban event." . . . For historians, as for many reformers, the considerable successes of the first hundred years of Protestantism will no doubt continue to be viewed within a broader framework of failure.

Philip Benedict

New Calvinist Men
and Women?

The *Longman Dictionary of Contemporary English* offers as one definition of *Calvinist*, "Having severe moral standards and tending to disapprove of pleasure." . . . [T]he view that would identify Calvinism as the most austere of the major post-Reformation confessional families and the one most focused on promoting disciplined moral behavior no longer commands agreement among Reformation historians. For upward of a generation, historians of Catholicism have emphasized that the devotional practices of the Catholic Reformation encouraged laypeople to pursue a disciplined life of piety whose features shared many elements with those promoted by the English apostles of practical divinity. More recently, prominent German historians have advanced the view that "social disciplining" was an offshoot of the "confessionalization process" and a common concern of all three major post-Reformation confessional families. . . .

    The recent emphasis on the similarities among the various post-Reformation confessions has been a salutary corrective to the denominational self-absorption and self-congratulation that long marked so much of the historical literature about early modern religion, but it may be wondered if the impulse to see the various confessions as all brothers under the skin has not been carried too far. Those who have championed the new theory of confessionalization have generally been content to indicate the analogous features within the various confessional traditions, rather than comparing their prevalence and impact. Furthermore, much of the theorizing about confessionalization ignores the nuances of the precise belief systems in question and consequently fails to explore the possible implications of these belief systems for the psyches of those raised within them. . . . This . . . [study] explores how thoroughly the founding of Reformed churches changed the manners, morals, and

Philip Benedict, "New Calvinist Men and Women?" in *Christ's Churches Purely Reformed: A Social History of Calvinism* (New Haven and London: Yale University Press, 2002), 429–431, 482–489, 518, 526–530, 544. Copyright © 2002 by Yale University Press. Reprinted with permission.

beliefs of those raised within them, and how distinctive the Reformed tradition might have been in doing so. . . .

[T]he triumph of a Reformed reformation was followed time and again by harsher civil laws against certain violations of the divine commandments. Once in place, Reformed consistories and synods often appealed to the secular authorities for further measures against vices that they perceived to be on the increase, worked in tandem with the magistrates in certain instances to suppress such vices, and referred certain kinds of crimes to the secular authorities for punishment rather than handling them inside the church. But the Lutheran and Catholic Reformations were also often accompanied by harsher legislation against different forms of sin, notably sexual misbehavior, blasphemy, the size and lavishness of wedding celebrations, and gambling. Furthermore, within certain other confessional traditions, most notably the Lutheran, state campaigns to punish vice more severely constituted the core of the process of "social disciplining" in the wake of the Reformation. Both the relative extent of the intensification of penalties against various sorts of misdeeds in Catholics, Lutheran, and Reformed countries, and the relative thoroughness of the laws' enforcement, are thus relevant for assessing Reformed reformations comparatively.

Unfortunately, there have been few comparisons of the severity of the relevant laws across territories of divergent confessional affiliations. . . . Until more research has been carried out, discussion of this topic must remain highly speculative. But consider a working hypothesis: prior to the Reformation preoccupation with ensuring community purity through legislation against adultery, blasphemy, and luxury was more intense in some regions of Europe than others, Switzerland and south Germany being among the centers of such focus. With the Reformation, the issue intensified and spread across the Continent in areas affiliated with all three major confessions, but this trend was most marked in Reformed territories.

The legal penalties decreed for adultery seem to support these hypotheses. This was a crime about which the Old Testament offered clear guidance, for according to Leviticus 21:10 adultery merits death. A broader campaign against sexuality outside of marriage was already under way in parts of Europe as the fifteenth century gave way to the sixteenth, as is illustrated by the closing of public brothels across much of Germany and France. Within this context, the Carolina, Charles V's new law code of 1532 intended as a model for the individual territories of the empire, included tougher penalties for many sexual offenses, including the death penalty for adultery. Local law revisions that followed in Catholic and Lutheran as well as Reformed portions of the empire repeated this last provision, demonstrating that the institution of the death penalty for adultery was hardly confession-specific. But the roll call of Reformed territories in which the death penalty was instituted for adultery in the wake of the Reformation was especially long and widely dispersed. At a minimum, it encompassed . . . Basel, Scotland, Geneva, Béarn, the Palatinate, Friesland (from 1586 to 1602 only), Zweibrücken, Bern, Virginia, Transylvania, Massachusetts, and England (from 1650 to 1660 only). . . . Leading Reformed ministers argued strongly for such a policy, and its institution in most areas was linked to the cause's ascendancy.

Because the execution of an adulterer was sufficiently unusual to be noted by contemporaries, researchers have some idea of whether or not the laws were applied. In the Geneva of the period 1555–75 they certainly were. . . . Beza noted with some pride that a prominent couple met death for the crime in Orléans when that city was under Huguenot domination in 1563, while in the Palatinate in 1571 a man was decapitated for impregnating his serving woman. But these instances appear to testify primarily to the exceptional climate that prevailed in these places in these years, for death sentences appear never to have been handed down for adultery in either Basel or Massachusetts. . . . In Scotland, the most common penalty for adultery appears to have been the repeated Sunday appearances in the stool of repentance in the front of the church decreed by the kirk sessions. There was often a gap between the letter of the law and the reality of judicial practice. . . .

Another indication that in an era when laws were being stiffened across Europe they were even stiffer in Reformed territories comes from a comparative study of the police measures enacted by the local communities of the religiously divided Grisons during the sixteenth century. Here, local measures against dancing, drunkenness, and sexual offenses multiplied in Catholic as well as Reformed communities in the generations after 1520. Nevertheless, the volume and scope of legislation on economic and sexual behavior enacted in the Reformed communities exceeded that in the Catholic communities. . . .

The limited information currently available still suggests that the Reformed may have earned their reputation for severe moral standards and hostility to pleasure, even if there was a gap between the letter of the laws passed and the manner in which they were enforced. . . .

Great hopes of moral renewal accompanied the spread of the Reformed cause, and consistorial systems of discipline were the essential agencies of attempted renewal wherever they were established, but the ultimate question is, Were the Reformed truly reformed in any meaningful way? . . .

The most illuminating studies of church discipline have been those that have supplemented the statistical investigation of the activity of the church boards with close reading of the details of the cases they handled or with complementary evidence from other sources. . . . In Emden, the endless crusade against drunkenness waged by the city's presbyterium seemingly cannot be credited with any significant long-term impact on alcohol use because not only did such cases remain numerous, but the details of the cases of inebriation changed little over time and contemporary observers at the end of the period still saw drunkenness as the "tribal vice" of the East Frisians. On the other hand, a new sensitivity toward violence does appear to have developed by the end of the seventeenth century: a number of those convoked before the presbyterium in the 1690s admitted their actions had violated principles of "Christian gentleness," whereas no spontaneous mention of such principles appears in the evidence from the earlier time periods studied. In Amsterdam, too, the details of the cases of insults and brawling that came before the kerkeraad imply that less crudely violent forms of behavior came to characterize the city's residents as the seventeenth century advanced. Likewise in Scotland a student of aristocratic life has demonstrated the decline of the blood feud in the years between 1570 and 1625. The new church presbyteries cannot claim all the credit for this transformation, for the clergy preached strenuously against taking an eye for an eye, and the crown used its legal and patronage powers to combat the practice. Still, the domain of interpersonal violence and impulse control does appear to have been one in which the pressure of the church tribunals made a difference.

Sexual behavior appears to have been another such area. The numerical frequency of cases of sexual misconduct rarely declined over time, but it will be recalled that in the Netherlands people began to be regularly summoned and reprimanded for casual instances of fornication in the later seventeenth century; previously such cases were exceptional. . . . A broad study of Scottish illegitimacy rates finds a fall from a national average of 5.3 percent in the 1660s to 3 percent in the 1720s. The evidence does not permit the calculation of trustworthy rates before that time, but other forms of data suggest that standards of sexual propriety were laxer yet in early sixteenth-century Scotland, children born out of wedlock being accepted with relatively little stigma. In the wake of the Reformation, Scottish aristocrats reduced the frequency of their sexual adventures outside marriage or at least carried them on more discreetly. Not only does the surveillance of sexual misconduct appear to have intensified; it also appears to have gradually inculcated among the populace at large a more explicit recognition of the church's ethical norms, even among those who violated them. Several studies also credit the consistories and chorgerichten with reinforcing the importance of the nuclear family and encouraging a new tenor of marital relations.

Thanks to the existence of an entire academic discipline devoted to studying the production and consumption of works of art, how fully church members obeyed the churches' injunctions against making and possessing objects associated with Catholic idolatry can be assessed particularly well. . . . It appears the great majority of Reformed artists were willing to defy the disciplinary code of their church rather than to pass up lucrative commissions. On the other hand, the artistic objects displayed in Reformed homes differed strikingly from those owned by their Catholic neighbors in religiously divided Metz in the middle of the seventeenth century. The Huguenots scrupulously avoided crucifixes and paintings of crucifixion scenes. Only a few owned the sorts of paintings of the Virgin, the saints, and the Magdalen found by the dozens in the city's Catholic households. If this was more broadly typical, virtually all church members had internalized their confession's abhorrence of owning potentially idolatrous images, even if most artists and artisans in their ranks refused to accept the economic and professional scarifice entailed in ceasing to produce such objects for Catholic use.

Assessing Reformed discipline comparatively is an even more delicate matter. . . . Comparing the Reformed to the other two major post-Reformation church families, . . . it would appear that the Reformed churches had the most vigorous disciplinary systems, even when the disciplinary mechanisms that existed within the other confessional traditions are duly recognized. Reformed consistories or Ehegerichten existed in many more regions that did the comparable systems found in some Catholic or Lutheran territories. They exercised a more continuous oversight of church members' behavior than did the visitation systems of most Lutheran and Catholic churches—or the church courts of England, for that matter. . . . If much still remains to be learned about the operations of the various forms of church and state discipline in Lutheran and Catholic territories, the conclusion is likely to be that they were generally a less continuous presence in community life than the Reformed consistories or Ehegerichten. They also did not play the role in reconciling private disputes and intervening in family disputes that these institutions did. . . .

The belief that the reforming of the church would effect a dramatic moral transformation of the wider community regularly accompanied the initial surge of the Protestant cause across Europe; the dream of a reformation of manners continued to fire the imagination of church members throughout subsequent generations; but the realities of the behaviors changes attempted and achieved through the creation of new systems of church discipline fell far short of the highest hopes. . . . [I]n certain times and places, a Calvin, a Melville, a Voetius, or even a more anonymous local reformer of morals like an Isaac Sylvius of Layrac might inspire a vigorous plan to promote these habits by identifying and summoning before the consistory a large number of those who strayed. These instances, however, were more the exception than the norm. Most church disciplinary bodies contented themselves with dealing with the most notorious sinners or a more restricted range of sins. In the early years of France's Reformed churches, its consistories went on a relatively wide-ranging moralizing offensive, but once the fear of losing members to the Catholic majority became overriding and the minority status and political vulnerability of the church became inescapable, its disciplinary ambitions shriveled. In Scotland, the new church courts had to tread cautiously from the start, and while they grew more confident and more assertive in time, they rarely extended their reforming to the full orbit of sins that their counterparts in other countries endeavored to attack. Only in such regions as Emden and canton Bern do the church tribunals appear to have been able to exercise steady pressure across the generations to effect a broad moral transfiguration among the population at large. Even there, they often made little headway in eradicating customs deeply rooted in local folkways and everyday patterns of sociability. Hearty drinking bouts remained the despair of church elders throughout Germanic lands. . . .

Still, the ample capacity of human beings to resist efforts to reform them is not the whole story, and ministerial proclamations of failure should not be taken at face value. . . . [T]he disciplinary actions of the various Reformed churches did effect detectable changes in many areas of behavior, above all where they were abetted by such contemporaneous developments as the strengthening of the state's control over the exercise of permissible violence. Feuding, interpersonal violence, and sexual misconduct apparently declined. The importance of the nuclear family may have been strengthened and a new tenor of marital relations encouraged. The evidence of church members in the late seventeenth century expressing sorrow for their un-Christian anger or spontaneously confessing sexual misconduct to the consistory testifies that the pressure of church discipline helped to inculcate a new moral sensibility. . . . Above all else, the presence of consistories and chorgerichten in so many Reformed churches would have made the experience of belonging to one of these churches that of living under a constant measure of surveillance by the church's elders. In those areas in which the ideals animating these institutions remained alive and were successfully conveyed to the congregation, they would have made the experience one of participating in a community of believers who felt a measure of responsibility for each other's behavior. In these ways, discipline truly was the sinews of the church. . . .

[As for religious education, t]he strong emphasis on catechesis and family Bible reading within the Reformed churches . . . produced only mixed results insofar as mastery of the catechism was involved. While the marks handed out by ecclesiastical visitors rose as the generations passed, many rural church members still had a shaky knowledge of these texts at the end of the seventeenth century. Literacy skills and especially the ability to read, however, had become quite widespread by this period in most Reformed communities, and a large segment of the population would have owned a Bible or other devotional book. It's impossible to know whether in any particular family this would have served as the basis for regular family devotions, for irregular reading and prayer in church, or simply as a talisman used to protect the family against harm, as folklorists have shown the Bible to have been used across the German-speaking world in the eighteenth century. Many humble church members nonetheless did acquire acquaintance with Scripture, and that the Reformed reformation promoted a new relation with the printed word characterized by the intensive reading and rereading of the Bible and devotional classics is plausible. In this domain, the Reformed differed from their Catholic neighbors, even if they were not more likely to have attained writing skills useful for their occupations. . . . Reformed Protestantism was indeed a religion of the book, and one that brought religious books into many humble households by the end of the seventeenth century. . . .

[How much enthusiasm or hostility did people show toward Reformed piety?] In the first years of the Reformation in those regions in which the

Reformed church established itself in defiance of the authorities, part of the population ardently embraced the central elements of the Reformed message, often at high risk to its safety and prosperity. . . .

Wherever the Reformation was imposed from above by an act of state, many more new church members were initially apathetic or hostile, and a far smaller percentage of church members eagerly embraced their new identity, especially in agricultural villages. . . . In these territories, the creation of a new Reformed identity and new patterns of religious life required a longer process of indoctrination and acculturation. Movement in this direction was generally visible within a generation, but it was decidedly uneven. All that can be observed in the domain of catechetical mastery is a modest increase in the percentage of those accounted to have learned the catechism well and a corresponding decline in the percentage of those judged to have learned it poorly. On the other hand, when allowance is made for reading aloud in family groups, a sizable fraction of the rural population of many areas would have gained access to the Bible and books of piety by the late seventeenth century, and some villagers undoubtedly began to make the singing of psalms and the reading of Scripture part of their regular domestic routine. Numbers of communicants remained highly variable: in the Pays de Vaud, most church members participated each time the ritual was celebrated, but in the Palatinate and England, many declined to do so except at Easter. . . . The most rapid and consistent change seems to have been the eradication of Catholic survivals and the enforcement of conformity to the new ritual and liturgical order. Church members grew more comfortable with waiting to baptize their children and began to marry during Lent, whereas they had previously hesitated to do so. The celebration of abolished holy days withered. This change appears to have been completed in most areas between 1600 and 1650.

In a world in which many simply conformed to the established church, the ultimately accepted transformation of the ordinary practices of worship must be accounted one of the major religious changes wrought by the establishment of the Reformed churches. The narrative of events showed time and again that both those strongly committed to the cause of the Reformation and those deeply attached to Catholic practices were activist minorities; but this does not mean the mere conformism of the remaining majority lacked personal meaning to those who simply accepted whatever rituals the authorities decreed. Even for mere conformists, the words of the established liturgy became the phrases that

235-243 photocopy

scan / -pdf.

43-0569

JF195
2004-44798 CIP

Altinay, Ayse Gül. **The myth of the military nation: militarism, gender, and education in Turkey.** Palgrave, 2004. 206p bibl index ISBN 140396281X, $59.95

This title suggests that the myth of the "military nation" in Turkey was not and is no longer the myth that legitimizes the discourse of Turkish nationalism—it is. Rather, Altinay (anthropology, Sabanci Univ., Turkey) argues that in the 1990s, for the first time in the republican history of Turkey, the reigning discourse of Turkish ethnonationalism was being challenged by war resistance movements and conscientious objectors to the Turkish government's war against the Kurdistan Workers Party (PKK.) The author explains how the ideologies of Turkish ethnonationalism used Sabiha Gökçen, the adopted daughter of Kemal Atatürk and Turkey's first woman combat pilot, to incorporate women more strongly into the largely male-led Turkish nationalist movement. The fact that Gökçen bombed rebelling Kurds in 1937 ironically contributed to the strong resurgence of Kurdish nationalism in the 1980s and 1990s which, in turn, contributed to the increasing resistance to Turkey's military nation-state. The nascent resistance to the concept of the military nation, however, led Turkish nationalist ideologies to adapt their narrowly focused military-nation discourse to a more comprehensive ideological-political discourse. This new tactic has led to a further securitization of the state, not unlike what has occurred in the US as a result of the 9/11 attacks. **Summing Up:** Highly recommended. General readers, and undergraduate and graduate collections and large urban libraries.—R. W. Olson, University of Kentucky were remembered in times of trial to comfort, inspire, or make sense of events. The patterns of the fixed rituals shaped the patterns of people's lives. Familiarity eventually bred attachment . . . [and] the visceral reaction against the many forms of Catholic devotion now branded as superstitious, together with the sense of personal superiority to such benighted stupidity, that, as journals and travel accounts testify, many Reformed Protestants felt when they observed Catholic rituals. . . . [T]he claim that Reformed Reformations promoted a certain disenchantment of the world is difficult to deny. A Reformed pattern of worship also gave time a more regular shape. It . . . downplayed the final deathbed struggle to die a good death and emphasized instead the obligation of living a life of faith. These important changes followed from mere conformity. . . .

[T]he great shortcoming of the recent emphasis on the parallel consequences of the Lutheran, Reformed, and Catholic Reformations is that it downplays each faith's distinctiveness *within* the domain of culture and religious life. For all of the undoubted similarities between the various confessions and for all of the porosity of confessional boundaries to the motifs and practices of the new devotion of the late sixteenth and seventeenth centuries, it made a difference in people's life experience whether they were raised as Lutherans, Reformed, or Catholics. It made a difference as well where and when within each tradition they were raised, for none were monolithic or static. Each confession had its own set of styles of devotion. Each had its own doctrinal and psychological points of friction.

Even for those church members who did little more than observe the basic obligations of their faith, the confession they professed molded elements of their sensibility, subjected them to specific forms to ecclesiastical and communal oversight, and became a vital component of their social identity. Ordinary Reformed believers experienced a very different relation to the Bible and to other complex written texts than did their Catholic counterparts. They came to hold a deeply rooted antipathy to the use of images in worship and to certain forms of relations to holy places and holy objects that bred a visceral reaction against these practices when they saw them among Catholics. They were inclined to believe they were uniquely liberated from superstition and hence especially enlightened. . . . For the most thoroughly committed and pious Reformed believers, the fact of belonging to the tradition shaped their religious experience, psychology, and pattern of social relations more profoundly yet. . . .

Suggestions for
Further Reading

This brief bibliography is intended to serve as an introduction to some important secondary literature available in English. It does not include the works that are excerpted in this volume.

General Overviews

Hsia, R. Po-chia, editor. *A Companion to the Reformation World*. Oxford: Blackwell, 2003.

Jensen, De Lamar. *Reformation Europe: Age of Reform and Revolution*. Second edition. Boston: Houghton Mifflin, 1992.

Lindberg, Carter. *The European Reformations*. Oxford: Blackwell, 1996.

Pettegree, Andrew, editor. *The Reformation World*. London: Routledge, 2000.

The Theory of Confessionalization
and Social Discipline

Benedict, Philip. "Confessionalization in France? Critical Reflections and New Evidence." In *Society and Culture in the Huguenot World, 1559–1685*, ed. Raymond A. Mentzer and Andrew Spicer, 44–61. Cambridge: Cambridge University Press, 2002.

Boer, Wietse de. "Social Discipline in Italy: Peregrinations of a Historical Paradigm." *Archiv für Reformationsgeschichte* 94 (2003): 294–307.

Bossy, John. *Christianity in the West 1400–1700*. Oxford: Oxford University Press, 1985.

Hanlon, Gregory. *Confession and Community in Seventeenth-Century France: Catholic and Protestant Coexistance in Aquitaine*. Philadelphia: University of Pennsylvania Press, 1993.

Harrington, Joel F. and Helmut Walser Smith. "Confessionalization, Community, and State-building in Germany, 1555–1870." *Journal of Modern History* 69 (1997): 77–101.

Hsia, R. Po-chia. *Social Discipline in the Reformation*. London: Routledge, 1989.

Mentzer, Raymond A, editor. *Sin and the Calvinists: Morals Control and the Consistory in Reformed Tradition*. Kirksville: Truman State University Press, 1994.

Monter, William. *Judging the French Reformation: Heresy Trials by Sixteenth-Century Parlements*. Cambridge, Mass.: Harvard University Press, 1999.

Nischan, Bodo. *Prince, People, and Confession: The Second Reformation in Brandenburg*. Philadelphia: University of Pennsylvania Press, 1994.

O'Malley, John W. *Trent and All That: Renaming Catholicism in the Early Modern Era*. Cambridge, Mass.: Harvard University Press, 2000.

Poska, Allyson M. "Confessionalization and Social Discipline in the Iberian World." *Archiv für Reformationsgeschichte* 94 (2003): 308–319.

Schilling, Heinz. "Confessional Europe." In *Handbook of European History, 1400–1600*, ed. Thomas A. Brady, Heiko Oberman, and James D. Tracy. Vol. 2: 641–670. Leiden: Brill, 1995.

Popular Religion

Burke, Peter. *Popular Culture in Early Modern Europe*. New York: Harper and Row, 1978.

Christian, William A., Jr. *Local Religion in Sixteenth-Century Spain*. Princeton: Princeton University Press, 1981.

Davis, Natalie Zemon. "From 'Popular Religion' to Religious Cultures." In *Reformation Europe: A Guide to Research*, ed. Steven Ozment, 321–341. St. Louis: Center for Reformation Research, 1982.

Ginzburg, Carlo. *The Cheese and the Worms: The Cosmos of a Sixteenth-Century Miller*. Trans. John and Anne Tedeschi. Baltimore: Johns Hopkins University Press, 1980.

———. *The Night Battles: Witchcraft and Agrarian Cults in the Sixteenth and Seventeenth Centuries*. Trans. John and Anne Tedeschi. London: Routledge and Kegan Paul, 1983.

Ruggiero, Guido. *Binding Passions: Tales of Magic, Marriage, and Power at the End of the Renaissance*. Oxford: Oxford University Press, 1993.

Scribner, Robert W. *Religion and Culture in Germany (1400–1800)*. Ed. Lyndal Roper. Leiden: Brill, 2001.

Tentler, Thomas N. *Sin and Confession on the Eve of the Reformation*. Princeton: Princeton University Press, 1977.

Thomas, Keith. *Religion and the Decline of Magic: Studies in Popular Beliefs in Sixteenth and Seventeenth Century England*. Oxford: Oxford University Press, 1971.

The Reformation of Rituals

Davis, Natalie Zemon. "The Sacred and the Body Social in Sixteenth-Century Lyon." *Past and Present* 90 (1981): 40–70.

Diefendorf, Barbara B. *Beneath the Cross: Catholics and Huguenots in Sixteenth-Century Paris*. Oxford: Oxford University Press, 1991.

Eire, Carlos M. N. *War Against the Idols: The Reformation of Worship from Erasmus to Calvin*. Cambridge: Cambridge University Press, 1986.

Flynn, Maureen. "Mimesis of the Last Judgment: The Spanish *Auto de fe.*" *Sixteenth Century Journal* 22 (1991): 281–297.

Forster, Robert and Orest Ranum, eds. *Ritual, Religion, and the Sacred: Selections from the "Annales: Economies, Société, Civilisations"*. Trans. Elborg Forster and Patricia M. Ranum. Baltimore: Johns Hopkins University Press, 1982.

Gregory, Brad S. *Salvation at Stake: Christian Martyrdom in Early Modern Europe*. Cambridge, Mass.: Harvard University Press, 1999.

Koslofsky, Craig M. *The Reformation of the Dead: Death and Ritual in Early Modern Germany, 1450–1700*. London: Macmillan; and New York: St. Martin's, 2000.

Myers, W. David. *"Poor Sinning Folk": Confession and Conscience in Counter-Reformation Germany*. Ithaca: Cornell University Press, 1996.

Scribner, Robert W. *Popular Culture and Popular Movements in Reformation Germany*. London: Hambledon Press, 1987.

Spierling, Karen E. *Infant Baptism in Reformation Geneva: The Shaping of a Community, 1536–1564*. Aldershot and Burlington: Ashgate, 2005.

The Reformation and Gender

Davis, Natalie Zemon. *Society and Culture in Early Modern France*. Stanford: Stanford University Press, 1975.

Diefendorf, Barbara B. *From Penitence to Charity: Pious Women and the Catholic Reformation in Paris*. Oxford: Oxford University Press, 2004.

Giles, Mary E., editor. *Women in the Inquisition: Spain and the New World.* Baltimore: Johns Hopkins University Press, 1999.

Harrington, Joel F. *Reordering Marriage and Society in Reformation Germany.* Cambridge: Cambridge University Press, 1995.

Kingdon, Robert M. *Adultery and Divorce in Calvin's Geneva.* Cambridge, Mass.: Harvard University Press, 1995.

Ozment, Steven. *Ancestors: The Loving Family in Old Europe.* Cambridge, Mass. and London: Harvard University Press, 2001.

———. *When Fathers Ruled: Family Life in Reformation Europe.* Cambridge, Mass.: Harvard University Press, 1983.

Rapley, Elizabeth. *The Dévotes: Women and Church in Seventeenth-Century France.* Montreal: McGill-Queen's University Press, 1990.

Roper, Lyndal. *The Holy Household: Women and Morals in Reformation Augsburg.* Oxford: Clarendon Press, 1989.

Schutte, Anne Jacobson. *Aspiring Saints: Pretense of Holiness, Inquisition, and Gender in the Republic of Venice, 1618–1750.* Baltimore: Johns Hopkins University Press, 2001.

Watt, Jeffrey R. *The Making of Modern Marriage: Matrimonial Control and the Rise of Sentiment in Neuchâtel, 1550–1800.* Ithaca, N.Y.: Cornell University Press, 1992.

Wiesner-Hanks, Merry. *Women and Gender in Early Modern Europe.* Second edition. Cambridge: Cambridge University Press, 2000.

———. "Women, Gender, and Church History." *Church History* 71 (2002): 600–620.

Wunder, Heide. *He is the Sun, She is the Moon: Women in Early Modern Germany.* Trans. Thomas Dunlap. Cambridge, Mass.: Harvard University Press, 1998.

The "Success" of the Reformation

Graham, Michael F. *The Uses of Reform: "Godly Discipline" and Popular Behavior in Scotland and Beyond, 1560–1610.* Leiden: E. J. Brill, 1996.

Haigh, Christopher, editor. *The English Reformation Revised.* Cambridge: Cambridge University Press, 1987.

Hsia, R. Po-Chia Hsia. *The World of Catholic Renewal 1540–1770.* Cambridge: Cambridge University Press, 1998.

Kittelson, James. "Successes and Failures in the German Reformation: The Report from Strasbourg," *Archiv für Reformationsgeschichte* 73 (1982): 153–174.

Mentzer, Raymond A. "The Persistence of Superstition and Idolatry among Rural French Calvinists." *Church History* 65 (1996): 220–233.

Pettegree, Andrew, editor. *The Reformation of the Parishes: The Ministry and the Reformation in Town and Country.* Manchester: University of Manchester University Press, 1993.

Strauss, Gerald. *Luther's House of Learning: Indoctrination of the Young in the German Reformation.* Baltimore: Johns Hopkins University Press, 1978.

Watt, Jeffrey R. "The Reception of the Reformation in Valangin, Switzerland, 1547–1588." *Sixteenth Century Journal* 20 (1989): 89–104.

Whiting, Robert. *The Blind Devotion of the People: Popular Religion and the English Reformation.* Cambridge: Cambridge University Press, 1989.